Around the World in Seven Years

Salisbury, Julie
[Seven year journey around the world]
    Around the world in seven years : one woman's life-changing journey
/ Julie Salisbury.

Previous edition published under title: A seven year journey around the
    world.
Issued in print and electronic formats.
ISBN 978-1-77141-120-2 (pbk.).--ISBN 978-1-77141-121-9 (html)

    1. Salisbury, Julie--Travel. 2. Voyages around the world. 3. Self-
actualization (Psychology). I. Title.

G465.S242 2015   910.4'1   C2015-900392-X
                                             C2015-900393-8

Around the World
in Seven Years

A Life-Changing Journey

Claud

*A sneak preview of
what makes me shine*

Julie Salisbury

Julie Salisbury

Author Photo: Greg Salisbury
Editor: Nina Shoroplova
Production Editor: Jennifer Kaleta
Cover Design: Marla Thomas

To my dear sister Tina
Who never faltered in her support and love
for the crazy things I did;

To my mum who was mostly confused about my life decisions,
but still stuck by me;

To Greg, my dear husband,
who always gives me unconditional love.

In memory of Bea who made me promise to write her letters
every two weeks, and then returned the letters to me four years
later and told me to write a book. I'm sorry she did not get
to see it.

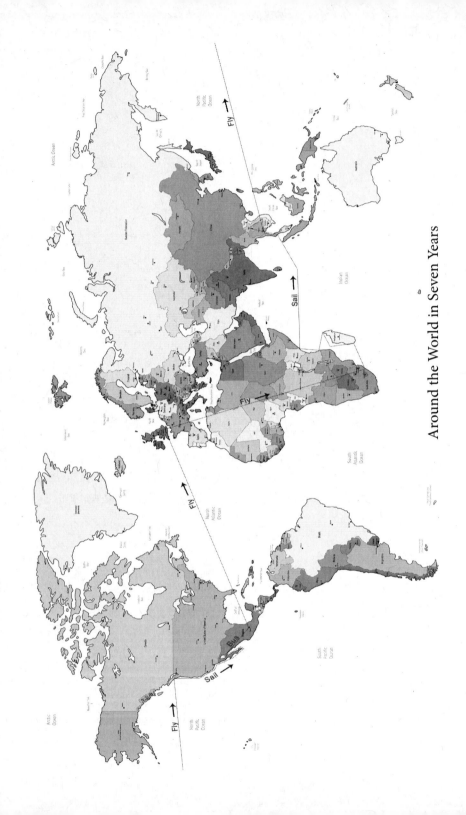

Around the World in Seven Years

Acknowledgements

I first started this book when I lived with CJ for five days on the River Mekong in Vientiane, Lao. Several years later, CJ, an English teacher, was the first person to read my full manuscript, edit it, and add her comments by email from Lao. She then proofread the second edition when she visited Victoria in the summer of 2008.

Big thanks to my soul sister Leanne Robinson who juggled editing my book and cofounding a non-profit with me to help the village of Dey Krahom, in Cambodia, subject to an illegal land grab. Seven years later, she now lives in Cambodia full time, helping many through LICADHO Canada. Lee, you have the biggest heart I know, and I admire you for dedicating your life to helping others.

Thanks to my wonderful team at Influence Publishing and my authors, without whom I would not have a purpose. Every day I am reminded about the journey of writing your story and the difference this makes in your life when you take the time to reflect. Every day I have conversations with Influence authors who experience closure as they heal from their past and celebrate with gratitude the life they now live. Every day my staff learn from the many stories that they are often the first to hear. I am forever grateful for all the authors who have the courage to authentically share their stories with the world so that other people can learn from their experiences. I am honoured that I have been given the purpose in life to help them share those stories.

Thank you Joan and Dan Christensen in Colorado, USA for all the time you spent helping me. Keep sailing! Thanks also to Henri and Natasha van Bentum for introducing me to the Circumnavigators Club and bringing to my attention the fact I had actually circumnavigated the globe (by accident!).

Thank you, Greg, the love of my life and my dear husband, for supporting and loving me, and for believing in me when it seemed just a dream to start a publishing company. Thank you for stepping into the role of technical director, typesetter, bookkeeper, production director, photographer, and graphic designer (and any other task you can help with).

Posthumous thanks to my dear neighbour Gail Burr-Tilley, who said she stayed up all night reading my manuscript, because she couldn't put it down! So sorry she did not see it in print.

Finally, I want to thank all those people who are willing to share their stories to help others. Do not leave it too long, it will change your life.

Contents

"Stuff your eyes with wonder ... live as if you'd drop dead in ten seconds. See the world. It's more fantastic than any dream .... Ask no guarantees, ask for no security, there never was such an animal. And if there were, it would be related to the great sloth which hangs upside down in a tree, all day, every day, sleeping its life away."
Ray Bradbury, *Fahrenheit 451*

Introduction

Seven years. Seven years travelling around the world (1998-2004) and seven years since I first told my story in 2008. It seemed appropriate that I should revisit what finding purpose really means to me, seven years after I first published my book. I wanted to reflect how travelling around the world changed my life. How did burning my bridges to the UK affect my decisions going forward? Did I know I was searching for purpose, or did I just think I was chasing the dream of love? Haven't I just returned back where I started, working twelve-hour days but for way less pay? I know I am a very different person to the one who left the UK in 1998 with a backpack and a dream, but how did this experience make me the person I am now?

It happened slowly, mostly unconsciously. I was an observer of different cultures, different values and beliefs, different environments, different people, different countries. My former self was slowly being woken up by all that I saw around me. I saw love, real love, real community—mostly in less-developed countries that only had love to fall back on.

When I lived in the UK, I didn't think love was real. I had convinced myself it was the elusive feeling that advertising told me I could only achieve by smelling the right way, wearing the right clothes, living in the right house, and being successful in the right career. I saw it rarely, so it must only exist if you succeeded in all those things. Then you could have it all and sail off into the sunset on a shiny white yacht with a handsome smiling husband by your side.

I was sailing off into the sunset, but my yacht was steel and painted blue with rust marks, and my handsome husband was a penniless backpacker with bad teeth and a balding head, who said this was a "win–win—you've got the cash; I'm a skipper."

Did I know what I was getting myself into? I knew nothing

about sailing, living on a boat, offshore cruising, survival, or how I would feel at sea a thousand miles from the nearest land with no refrigeration, no fresh water, no shower, and no decent food. What kind of dream did I think I would be living? Did I really think this would turn out to be the true love I was searching for? A life of adventure, the "easy life" like I saw on the posters in the bank—the happy smiling couple anchored off a powder-white sand beach in turquoise waters framed by jumping dolphins and palm trees?

I was only thirty-two and I was about to set off for my "retirement." I did not hesitate to burn all my bridges; this was the chance of a lifetime and I had no plans to go back.

Finding my purpose would not have been possible without writing this book—without journals and letters that allowed me to retrace the steps, find the clues to purpose, and consciously figure out how I arrived where I am today. The understanding that we don't figure out this thing called life until we make the decision to examine it, does not start until you write. When you write, the clues appear before you as your life unfolds one page at a time. You start to understand which event led to the next event, how your feelings changed through these experiences, and how life became "more."

The book gave birth to a new me: one with more clarity and focus about what led me to the place I am at now, a conscious choice to follow my heart, trust my intuition and live authentically. At the time, I had no idea that it was the book that changed my life, rather than the travelling around the world. Which came first to finding purpose in my life—the subject of the book or the book itself? I felt like I had suddenly come alive. It was the book that was giving me my direction.

When you live a life on purpose, the whole world suddenly lights up because it's not just about you anymore. Is that what opens up the world of love? You hear so much about "being of service," but are we designed as humans to only function as part of the whole if you actually ARE part of the whole?

Is that what I witnessed in those less-developed countries? Is the reason those people smile so much and give so much love (when they don't even have the basic human rights of food, water, and shelter) because they are acting as a community, in service to one another? Is that what I witnessed in Chagos when I lived on a desert island for three months in the company of other boats? People who needed to be of service to one another to survive?

Is being of service in community the basic human condition, whereas money, materialism, and consumerism have made it all about the individual person?

If I had found this purpose during my travels, would the colours have been brighter, the memories clearer, the feelings deeper, the experiences richer? Would I have remembered any of what happened in those seven years without photos, journals, and letters? Why did I have such a weak vision of those experiences? Why does it feel I am reading about someone else when I read my journals, and now seven years later, when I re-read my book? Did this really happen to me? Am I the only person to circumnavigate the world and not remember very much about it because I wasn't actually "awake" the whole time?

So, this book is not really about the travel stories, although I am sure you will enjoy reading about them (I did, since it gave me the chance to relive them). I sometimes feel that I journaled about the first four years of my travel like a naive observer of the many cultures and countries I visited.

If love had entered earlier in this story, the reflections would have been easier to capture, but that was not meant to be. I could only keep the experiences intact and vulnerable by sharing my journal notes and letters about how I felt in that moment.

This book—my book—is really about the journey of waking up through the process of writing a book about my journey. Writing a book about your journey will bring you to life, wake you up, allow you to retrace your steps and the clues of your life, and open up your heart (if you are willing to be vulnerable). It is a journey that will lead to colours being brighter, memories more vivid, and your heart being open to letting love in.

Only when your heart opens to the possibilities will you allow love in. This is the most beautiful thing in the world: opening to love that was always there while you were just not awake enough to see it.

My purpose is to help the world wake up and welcome in love by suggesting you revisit your life and follow the clues to find your purpose through writing your story. It will be a hard journey, but as you become the observer in your life, the clues will lead to your purpose. I often wonder how these experiences of travelling around the world would have been different with my eyes wide open.

This second edition of *Around the World in Seven Years* retains my journal entries and diary excerpts of my world travels by sea from 1998 to 2004, plus my original writing from 2008, when I first wrote my book. I've added in Year 2015 reflections on my journey—a journey that began physically and became purposeful through mental, emotional, and spiritual reflection.

✿ Chapter One ✿

Enlightenment

*"Enlightenment: A Philosophic movement of the 18th Century
marked by questioning of traditional doctrines and values, a
tendency towards human individualism, and an emphasis on
the idea of universal human progress, the empirical method in
science, and the free use of reason."*
Oxford English Dictionary

I am the happiest I have ever been in my whole life. I am a true
nomad. I spend the summers in beautiful British Columbia
(BC), living in my RV, and the winters in Mexico, on my
sailboat. I do not own a house and I live on a tight budget with
very few belongings. I am living my passion of helping others
to write their books, which I discovered to be my purpose. It
is 2008.

Ten years ago I was living in England in a beautiful three-
bedroom Victorian house overlooking the golf course,
earning $90,000 a year, and driving a Mercedes-Benz. I had an
extraordinary career, which involved travelling Business Class
around the world, and I was married to the "perfect" husband.

Yet, I felt deeply discontented with life and felt something
really important was missing—I just didn't know what.

It all started in 1998. I was thirty-two and I didn't want for
anything. I spent my days rising at 7:00 a.m., driving for an
hour to the office in my Mercedes, working for ten hours a day,
and dashing home in time for *Coronation Street* on the TV
and a microwave dinner. Repeat until Saturday. Saturday: go
shopping and spend as much money as I wanted on whatever
took my fancy. Sunday: visit the golf club with my husband and
friends.

This seemed to be the life everyone was living, so I really didn't understand why I was so unhappy and bored. After all, I had a great job with a great salary and perks. I thought it was maybe a mid-life crisis, but surely I was too young for that?

Graeme, my best friend of twelve years, had just returned from travelling for the last two, and I knew as soon as we got together that I could really open up to him and try and explain how I was feeling. I was really looking forward to seeing him; we always had great, honest conversations, and his absence made me realize how much I had missed him.

"So, you got married while I was away? Sorry I missed the wedding." Out came all the photos, followed by some real truths that I realized I'd never discussed with anyone before.

"The thing is, Graeme, I know John isn't exciting, but he's 80 percent of what any woman would want from a good husband. He is caring, we talk non-stop, and help each other constantly by off-loading all our problems with work. He isn't the greatest love and I always feel I come fourth in line to his work, his golf, and his child from his previous marriage, but it's a lot more than most people are lucky enough to find."

I wondered who I was trying to convince.

"So what is it, Julie? Time to change jobs again?" asked Graeme.

"Well, yes, but I need to do something completely different; a new challenge. I need some excitement in my life."

"Well, I know what you mean; I know exactly what I want from my life now that I've been travelling. I've come back to the UK to save enough money, and then I'm going to buy a yacht and sail around the world."

"A pipe dream, Graeme?" I said with a smile on my face. He was always a dreamer. "But, what the heck, sounds like a good plan. Can I come with you?"

I remember that conversation so well, because it was ironic. That was the kind of spontaneous thing I wanted to do with my life.

People often say, "I don't know what I want, but I know what I don't want." Well, I knew, but I had far too much responsibility to have Graeme's freedom. He had no ties, no wife, no house, and no career or need to fit into society. He was a free agent and at the end of the day, he was my best friend and I'd only just got married.

Despite all the odds against it, it all happened very fast following that first reunion. I wanted to see more of Graeme, but he had to find work, so I suggested he redecorate my kitchen for a generous fee. John knew Graeme was my best friend, so he had no problem with him staying at our house for a couple of weeks.

I'm sure he now regrets that decision, because in the time that Graeme was staying at our house, I started to have fun again and I fell in love with my best friend. By the time I'd realized what had happened, Graeme told me that he'd always loved me, but would never do anything to influence my feelings toward him. The feelings I had for him were completely overwhelming, and I was being the ultimate bitch to my husband, but I simply couldn't help myself. To deny how I felt would be selling my soul, but to leave everything? I didn't think twice about it. I just knew it was the right thing to do.

I suddenly had a whole new perspective on life, but I knew John, my family, and my friends would not understand why I had to throw away my "perfect" marriage, house, job, and possessions to run away with a "long-haired hippy" with no prospects.

John took it very badly. I tried to keep Graeme a secret because I thought it would make it worse, but in the end, it was the only way I could get him to understand what I was doing. How could he understand otherwise how I had changed so suddenly? He tried everything to win me back, and boy, did that hurt, but I needed to go through that pain myself to test my own beliefs in my new way of life. I never looked back, and once Graeme and I decided that we were going to live our dream, life changed very quickly. All the things that were once so important—expensive clothes, make-up, possessions, eating out—suddenly meant nothing to me.

For six months, Graeme and I did nothing except work and save money. We moved into a tiny bedsit above a butcher's shop, which had a miniature two-ring camper stove, an old settee, a double bed, and a view of the public car park. Graeme made bread, and I took peanut butter sandwiches to work every day to save on the cost of pub meals or takeouts. We didn't have a television and we didn't go out.

For the first time in my life, I worked for one reason only: to make money. And I hated every moment of it. Now I had nothing in common with the other "high-fliers" I worked with. I couldn't talk about films or television programs. I'd sold all my designer clothes, so I obviously didn't discuss the latest fashion or my spending sprees at Kookaï. I sold all my gold jewellery, and once the Estée Lauder ran out, that was the end of that. Shunning normal society and protocol, I didn't fit in anymore. The only reason I stuck at it was the date I was clinging onto when we would fly to South Africa to look for our yacht and sail into the sunset with no expectations or accomplishments to comply to. One month after my devastating decision to leave my husband, beautiful home, and great job to travel around the world, I looked back at my diary and read my own words, which actually sounded quite sane.

Diary Excerpt: April 14th, 1998

Nearly a month later, it feels clearer already. I've been conditioned from birth, through childhood and adulthood, for an "expected" way of life. Parents endeavour to give their children "the best" so, in turn, we can also give our children "the best." Whatever the definition of "best" is, it tends to mean material belongings. When you "achieve" this, what do you do then?

I did achieve everything expected of me but I made the mistake of thinking I was doing it for myself.

Suddenly I feel wise now that I've had the big responsible job, which comes with the immense car, big salary, and foreign travel and, of course, reverence and recognition. Now that I've lived in the large house with the nice garden, had the "social" friends of the same status and, to top it all, had the big white wedding, I'm wise. I've suddenly realized I've achieved what Mum, Dad, relatives, and "friends" told me I was supposed to achieve.

I suppose I felt special because I had "overachieved" until suddenly I realized I wasn't doing this for myself. I was habituated to this way of life; I didn't even consider there was an alternative.

My friend Tanya is someone I've always admired. She made the decision to look for another life travelling, and she's still doing it four years on. I still admire her but somewhere, I think, she may have gotten lost again. We always managed to meet, as she backpacked around the world and I travelled for business. The first time I hadn't seen her for twelve months and I wrote to say I was due in Hong Kong in three weeks, we made a joke of it and said, "Let's do lunch in Hong Kong," and we did. I will never forget the way she really appreciated staying the night in a business hotel and hopped off with the mini soaps and shampoo, and most of my wardrobe.

After that, we always tried to meet up when I did my trips to the Far East. We always had such a giggle shocking everyone in the bar with her backpacker clothes and hair. But then, when she left Hong Kong and I was due to go out again for the third year, I thought, "Shit! Why do I want to sit on a plane for twelve hours, eat terrible food, live in a rabbit cage for three weeks, and visit hot slave-labour factories in China?"

I realized I didn't actually enjoy it that much but I thought it was cool to meet my best friend "for lunch" and "brag" or tell people, "Oh, I'm leaving for Hong Kong on Friday" or "Did I tell you the time ... blah, blah?" As soon as I didn't have Tanya to meet there, it completely lost all its appeal.

So I left the job (usually, after two and half years I get bored and look for a new challenge), and consciously went for one that meant I didn't have to go to New York or Detroit or Frankfurt or Amsterdam. Most importantly, I wouldn't have to visit the Far East for two weeks at a time. My next round of trips was going to start again, and I had to get out before that.

I traded that job for one that didn't require international travel and paid an even bigger salary. It seems most people consider international business travel a perk before they have to do it regularly. But, of course, that didn't help. I'd just traded in one type of travel for another; to sit on the M1 or M25 motorways, sit on trains and tubes, and stay in different slightly larger concrete cells they fondly call "hotels."

I was at a loss. How could I stop this sadistic cycle? I had no idea what the alternatives were.

Well, if you take down the shutters of "convention" and expectations, you'd be very surprised. There's a whole world out there to be enjoyed; not to live to work, but to work to live, experience, and enjoy. I always made excuses why I couldn't go travelling, like I was "too small/not strong enough/couldn't cope without the luxuries in life/needed to work in order to have a challenge and achieve." Anyway, how could you find someone you're so comfortable with that could share it with you, rather than go alone?

I've also realized, perhaps without fully realizing it, that I am a woman (strange as that sounds) with the needs of a woman. Man was historically a cave man, to hunt, protect, and provide for the woman. A woman has a different set of skills from a man, like multitasking and nurturing, whereas men tend to focus on one task at a time (like hunting and protecting). Despite being the "independent" woman, I've realized I need a man I can share this with. The reason I now say things are clearer is that I've found that man. The fact is I actually found him twelve years ago. I'm just a bit slow and I guess I needed to go through the process of accomplishment to understand that you really do have other choices in life.

So now I work for a different reason, to earn money. To save so I can now choose an unconventional way of life. This does mean that the motorway travelling, selling, and staying in concrete hotel rooms are even harder to bear. The difference is now it's for a reason and I'm clinging onto a date six months down the line when we can cruise into the sunset.

When I read that later, I think, "Wow, girl, you were brave." But I also remember the incredible pain I caused my family and friends at the time. Seven years later, I realize that I had been raised like a magician who observes and analyzes, then remembers things so that I could be graded. We all are. We then work hard and put in the time to "prove" our knowledge, but mostly we forget that our true purpose in life comes down to our relationships. We're too busy adapting our energy to fit into our traditional tribe, which in the first world mostly ignores the importance of community. Maybe it was my experience of learning the less-developed world's tribal ways that broke that vicious cycle. When I discovered this, only then could I start to consider what would make my life more complete.

Diary Excerpt: April 20th, 1998

Of course, to eschew traditional society means you will unavoidably cause a lot of hurt to those close to you who understand nothing other than this way. Family will not understand, but I hope mine will eventually. Close friends do understand, but they are the easy ones. Why would a person who has succeeded within society, suddenly, in three weeks, want to throw it all away?

Parents who are from a different generation that lived their whole lives conservatively (and clearly remember the ration-

ing that war caused) find it the hardest. They expect you to
live up to their image of success, and don't really want to
encourage you to grow as an individual; they want you to be
what they couldn't be. I remember telling my parents I was
going to the Far East on a business trip and was astonished
by the reaction. I expected them to be "delighted," not worried, because I thought I was living up to their expectations
of success. Of course, once I came back in one piece without
any deadly diseases, it was easier for them to accept my departure the second year. By the third year, they were able to
ask me in casual conversation when my next trip was due, as
though, now, it was a "normal" way of life (and because their
peers were impressed that their daughter was going on such
exotic business trips).

Leaving my husband was not so easy. Within the way of life
I was leading, John was the perfect husband. He loved me, he
cared about my work, and we talked and helped each other
with our careers, socialised with our work friends, and lived
in a wonderful dream house with a dream garden. Everyone
now says, "You lucky girl. Why throw all that away?" I can
simply answer that he was perfect for that way of life. Once
careers, houses, possessions, colleagues to impress, and cozy
living were not important to me anymore, he was no longer
perfect. The fact that our first wedding anniversary was only
three weeks after I made the decision, made the pain even
more difficult.

I was determined to make a new life work, and it seemed
that my new attitude to life was already causing dislike of the
material world.

Diary Excerpt: June 17th, 1998

I'm now getting very intolerant and really despise work. It's
getting progressively more difficult to cope with the driving
(my back has started to play up again), and the politics are

insufferable. Graeme keeps saying, "Only ten weeks to go."
And I know I really need to stick at it to make the last of the
money we need. It would be so easy to avoid the "horrible
bit," but it really is the quickest way to make money. I now
carry a picture of a Roberts 45 sailing yacht with me, and
every time I'm tempted to tell them to "stuff it," I look at
the picture of the boat and remember why I'm still working.
It really isn't that much longer. It's a shorter timescale than
when I first started this diary.

We're really moving up a gear in the preparation. I now
know the phonetic alphabet, which is used for radio trans-
missions to avoid misunderstandings. It's actually fun spell-
ing out my name that way—Juliet, Uniform, Lima, India,
Echo—and I try and use it whenever I can—even on the
telephone at work when someone needs something spelled
out. Graeme did his Yachtmaster theory exam last week and
hopes to do the practical before we leave. I've become really confident about Aromatherapy and believe I can trade
with it. I've made quite a few blends and treat all our own
ailments with oils now, and they work. I'm sure you need a
natural feel for it and I really enjoy doing it. I'd like to get a
professional diploma for practising, but the ones available
seem very superficial and expensive. For now, I might wait
until we get to South Africa and see if I can get a correspon-
dence course to study.

I really can't wait for our new way of life, and so I don't
want to wait for a divorce and a settlement. I'll probably end
up having to leave behind the problems of my old life, like
the house, marriage affairs, etc., unfinished. I might regret
it, but the only compromise from John's point of view is to
simply sign everything over to his name, because I chose to
leave. I don't like leaving business unfinished, because Mum
and Dad will probably end up with it, but at the moment
there seems to be no alternative. I saw a solicitor who advised me to just sit tight because I'm in a position of strength.
So I'm not trying to let it bother me too much. My happiest
moments are evenings. I travel back home from Chester now
to be with Graeme every day including weekends, which is a

four-hour round trip. Days are miserable but they do have a purpose. (Remember.)

Diary Excerpt: July 17th, 1998

See. Doesn't time go fast! Only six weeks to go at work (and three days but I won't count them). I've been thinking a lot about sticking my finger up at them. It's such a shame I can't hand in my notice at the end of July. I can't risk working my one month's notice, because I just know they'll make me go to Chester every day and that'll cost £600 [approx. $1,300 CAD] in petrol at my own expense. I know the shit will really hit the fan when I leave at the end of August and never go back.

I'm seeing John on Thursday to sign over the house to him; I felt uncomfortable leaving unfinished business. He is going to sign over the endowment, which I can cash in for £2,000 [approx. $4,600 CAD] so that's my total settlement for eight years together.

Graeme and I are up to £24,500 (approx. $56,000 CAD) now in savings, so with my July salary of £2,000 and another £2,000 from the savings account when the notice is served, and the £2,000 from the endowment, we'll be up to £30,500 [approx. $70,000 CAD], eight weeks in front of target.

So we could have gone earlier, but Graeme's Nan Bea needs us here until the third week in September, because Dick and Barbara—Graeme's Nan's friends who are her Powers of Attorney—are on holidays. Bea is ninety-two years old and lives alone so she needs a family member or friend as a contact in case she has a medical emergency. We have been telling her all about our plans and she is very excited for us and completely supportive and encouraging. She even gave us a money gift to help us along, which was extremely generous of her.

I have been so surprised how quickly I was able to save money when it is not being wasted on rent or mortgage, fashion or dining out. Most of the savings came directly from my salary and Graeme paid for the daily expenses of food and rent from his casual work. It is incredible that you can save for a new life in just six months if you really make a commitment. Even so, it is still difficult to imagine pictures in my mind of what my new life will be; it feels so much more real now. I can't picture it, because I've never experienced any of the things I'm going to see and do, so how exciting is that? I feel so comfortable with Graeme that it's almost scary. I feel sometimes that I lean on him too heavily. He is my whole life and I miss him so much when he's not around. I hate sharing him. He's mine and other company seems so boring compared to the fun we have, which is a good thing, seeing as we are going to be living in a very small space 24/7.

The stress took its toll on me and my historically bad back. I have scoliosis (curvature of the spine) and had major back surgery aged eighteen to straighten my spine, leaving me with a ten-inch metal rod in my back and weak muscles that easily spasm. I'd always had problems with it, particularly when I did long car journeys or became stressed. It was agreed, before I took the job I was presently doing, that I could telecommunicate from my Midlands base, which was ideal for my customers who stretched to the north, south, and west, and not travel every day to the Chester Head Office, a four-hour round trip. Unfortunately, as with many companies in the UK, the style of management tends to be very paternalistic and, if you don't report in everyday to the office, they do not trust you to manage your own time. This left a bad taste in my mouth and was the root of all my ongoing back problems. Eventually, my problem was solved by a particularly bad spasm that left me bed-ridden.

Diary Excerpt: September 14th, 1998

Wow. Time really does go fast—I'm here. As it turned out my time left at work was spent mostly taking sick days and accrued holiday days. I hardly worked at all in August and up until we left I was off for three weeks solid sick leave (in bed). I was beginning to get really worried that I wasn't going to heal this time. I really had pushed myself too far, but it's all in the past now. I went through the usual panic attacks about handing my notice in, and in the end I sent a letter (Graeme wrote a stinker for me). Anyway, it was hassle-free, and I got my one month's notice paid in return for a five-hour handover.

You know the best thing? Here I am now in Durban, South Africa, the sun is shining, the pool is cool, the beer is cheap, AND I'M STILL GETTING PAID.

And so, on September 14th, 1998, we boarded that plane. Mum and Dad were confounded, watching their "successful" daughter standing at the bus stop with just a backpack holding all her possessions. My younger sister wouldn't talk to me, and most of my friends couldn't believe I was really doing it. My older sister, Tina, was the only one who truly supported me and told me to "just go for it." She'd also chosen a more unconventional way to live—she's now the landlady of a local pub.

Diary Excerpt: September 19th, 1998

We've been here a week now and it seems that life just continues, strangely the same, but in a different country. Life is very much more laid back and we've already viewed about fifteen boats, two of which look like they have great potential. I'm getting really excited about doing up our boat, but I already feel impatient. We've got a lot more to look at before we make a final shortlist. It seems so easy to just "chill" where you land, and without some discipline you could just stay in one place spending money. We're moving soon. I feel like I need to see more and we've done very little really. I wasn't very impressed with Pretoria (a city close to Johannesburg), other than with the incredible houses and spaces occupied by the whites in the suburbs. I was expecting a colourful scene of Africa and the promise of Jacaranda trees, but spring was too early and the trees were quite barren.

Diary Excerpt: September 24th, 1998

I feel like we're experiencing the real Africa now that we're in Zululand. We're staying at Cuckoo's Nest in Kwambonambi just north of Richards Bay. The countryside is breathtaking, surrounded by forest and the village is, as usual, very friendly. And of course, it is hot, hot, hot. We saw a great boat yesterday, which we both fell in love with, so we're going to make an offer and see what happens.

Of course, it wasn't quite that easy, but after six weeks of visiting yachts for sale we found the perfect boat. We spent six months in Zululand working on our boat every day, getting her ready for cruising. It was a lot of hard work. We constantly had delays that prevented us from cruising.

Zulu festival of dance, Zululand

❧ Reflections From 2015 ❧

Looking back, this was a really emotional time for me. I'd spent my whole life up to this point not sharing my feelings and avoiding conflict. The English "stiff upper lip" was such an habituated way of life for me that I didn't know any different way of being. It reminds me of the movie, *The Matrix*, where everyone is living in a mundane, grey life with no emotions. I "took the blue pill" and opened up Pandora's Box, facing my loveless marriage head on and testing the loyalty of my friends and family. At the time, I think I probably came across to everyone as cold and uncaring. It must have seemed I was selfishly chasing a dream with no regard for the devastation I left behind.

I remember being shocked by my younger sister and her response to me leaving my husband. She defended him and had no regard for why I was leaving. It was not the British way to leave your husband and family and just run away. My older sister was more concerned about me, even though she was the one who probably suffered the most from my absence. We were becoming more aligned in our values. Mum was the same, with no regard for how much she was going to miss me, just concern for my safety and wellbeing. Dad was just angry; I was letting him down by turning away from my success. John was just angry too, saying, "Why don't you just go travelling for a few weeks and get it out of your system?" It wasn't about me, it was all about him.

I have no regrets—not even signing over the house. The clean break was the best thing, and even though I could have done with my 50 percent of the house when I moved to Canada, it didn't really make any difference to my happiness.

~

Launching Yacht *Khulula*, Richards Bay, Zululand, S. Africa

Open air herbal bath in Impalme, Zululand, S. Africa

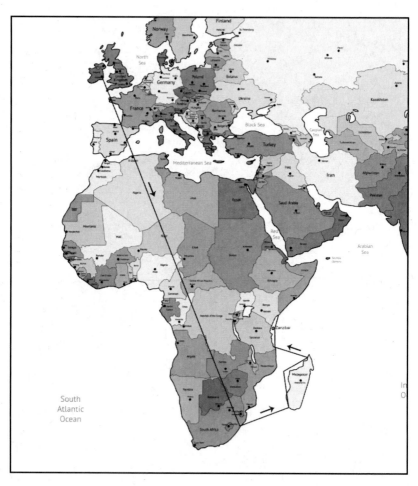

Africa

✢ Chapter Two ✢

Lemurs, Giant Tortoises, and Elephants

"The minute you begin to do what you really want to do, it's really a different kind of life."
Buckminster Fuller

Khulula—Our New Home

Waiting for the transaction to go through for the sailing yacht we had decided to purchase was frustrating. We planned on relaunching the boat with a new name, *Khulula*, which in Zulu means "to be set free."

Khulula was not a pretty yacht, even after we had repainted her navy blue with a clean white deck. She was forty-five feet long and very wide for a sail boat this size. She was made from steel so when we first found her she was not a pretty sight with plenty of rust marks. The main advantage of the big wide deck was that we would be able to accommodate lots of people and we could stretch out and sunbathe with plenty of room. The disadvantage of the flat wide deck was that there was no light into the inside of the boat, other than the small porthole windows along the side. This meant the inside of the boat was dark and cave-like, but it did provide lots of sleeping accommodation. We thought that for a forty-five-foot boat, she would easily sleep eight, and maybe ten in a pinch.

Meanwhile, we had secured ourselves jobs at the hostel where we were staying, not only to distract ourselves, but also so that we didn't have to continue spending our cruising budget on food and accommodation. Fortunately, working at a hostel meant we were able to accompany the managers on the tours to Hluhluwe-iMfolozi Game Reserve and the traditional Zulu villages to learn the ropes so Graeme could take tours himself, and I could sell them to the tourists.

Although iMfolozi (also known as Umfolozi) and Hluhluwe Game Parks were combined in 1989 into Hluhluwe-iMfolozi Game Reserve, they were still considered separate entities when I was there in 1998. They are side by side, and just over an hour's drive from Richards Bay, where our boat was moored. Hluhluwe is the best known of all the Zulu Natal reserves, and it surrounds a deep valley formed by the Hluhluwe River. The park is abundant with Impala, Kudu, and Grey-Striped Nyala: all very distinct species of deer. Large herds of wildebeest (a kind of antelope) are easily spotted, and mischievous baboons are often seen blocking the road as they stop to casually masturbate.

iMfolozi is an undulating wilderness of forty-seven thousand hectares between the White and Black iMfolozi Rivers. It is famous for initiating the program that saved the white rhinoceros, which had become endangered following an increase in hunting to satisfy Far East demand for the horn, reputed to have aphrodisiac qualities. The park now aims to keep a maximum of a thousand animals, and any surplus is made available to other parks. This means the chances of seeing both black and white rhinos in the park are extremely good. Many people confuse black and white rhinos, because their names actually have nothing to do with their colour. The white rhino's name is derived from the Afrikaans word "wyd," which actually refers to the "wide" mouth and the distinctive big square lips that the white rhino uses for grazing. So it should be called the "wide rhino"! It is the second-largest land mammal and can weigh over five tons. The black rhino has pointed prehensile lips used for plucking leaves.

Diary Excerpt: October 1st, 1998

Then on Tuesday we went to the park and I experienced my first wild animals. We followed three male elephants and watched them wrap their trunks around each other and wrestle. At one point, their three trunks were all entwined in each other. You could see they were contented big soft animals that would only harm you if something really annoyed them—then they would show it by standing in your path and seemingly growing in size by flapping their huge ears to warn you (as they did to some tourists blocking their path with their cars).

We saw lots of giraffes, many really close, and they just struck me as being exceedingly graceful and very feminine in every movement. The adult zebra didn't hold the same allure, but the baby zebra we saw did. It must have only been a couple of days old, because it appeared uneasy on its feet and its fur was still downy. The rhinos with their fierce-looking horns seemed more occupied with eating grass than with anything else, but their thick skin looked like an old man's. Even the youngest looked ancient! Oh, and the blue-balled monkeys we saw were amazing—a whole family with the dominant male showing his incredible neon-blue balls! All in all, quite a few days of new experiences with the promise of many more to come!

Diary Excerpt: October 3rd, 1998

I'm sitting on deck while Graeme and the mechanic are still trying to start the engine. As the sun goes down I was hoping for a glimpse of my first African sunset across the water, but alas, the low cloud will probably steal that from me.

I love the sounds of Africa, the singing frogs and birds in an orchestral performance. I love the fact you can see the moon in the day and at night; the tropical storms with the lashing rain, loud thunder, and the sky lighting up. The lightning is amazing to watch because the strikes change direction. One minute they flash vertically down and then the next they flash horizontally—an awesome sight!

I love the open trucks that carry the forestry workers, all the women dressed in layers of colour, tightly packed together smiling and singing. It is amazing to see the road workers who empty out single bags of cement to lay a road by hand, labour being cheaper than machinery. I watched twenty or thirty workers planting individual turf pieces to replace the verge, all bent over carefully laying each piece.

I hate the banks and anything commercial. They would be really frustrating places to work because everyone is so disorganized and unprofessional, and everything takes so long!

The day eventually came when we could take *Khulula* out for the first time in the bay and I stood on the bowsprit and looked back at the boat and watched her on the water, and took a deep breath, to inhale my new life. It felt really right and I just knew I was going to like this lifestyle!

While we were waiting for payments to go through, we continued to work at the hostel and ended up temporarily managing the hostel for several weeks while the owners Karen and Sean visited Cape Town,

When they returned, we rewarded ourselves with a mini holiday to Impalme, which is basically in the middle of sugar cane fields. We stayed in a traditional hut, a large, dome-shaped dwelling with a tiny door and window, a thatched roof, and a dirt floor. It was very cool and quite comfortable. We opted to have an open-air herbal bath: a specialty of the hosts who have their own herb garden. They heated a large, cast-iron Victorian tub using coals. We sat in the bath under the stars, topping up the hot water from the huge cauldron, also heated by the coals. It was a unique experience.

The Zulu Festival of Dance

That weekend, there was a special Zulu festival. We were afforded the enormous honour of being invited as guests to attend the festival on holy ground in the sugar cane fields and to observe the performance. We were very lucky to attend this traditional festival as guests of our hosts who had a special relationship with the local Zulu people. We were the only white people there—just six of us.

Six hundred dancers driving out evil spirits to a mesmerizing beat and close to a thousand worshippers in white gowns sitting on the ground on prayer mats created an awe-inspiring atmosphere. Apparently, this festival only happens once a year; they dance from 10:00 a.m. to 10:00 p.m. and are privileged to dance only if they can afford the traditional costume (at a cost of about five hundred dollars). The individual parts of the costume can take years to collect. An interesting part of the festival was visiting the many traders who had set up stalls to sell the different parts. Each year, the dancer will buy a spear, or an animal skin, or a headdress, until his costume is complete.

The dancers were grouped according to sex and status, and each group danced separately, forming blocks of identical costumes, one hundred or stronger. The unmarried maidens were young, vivacious teenagers; their beautiful naked breasts were anointed with oils and perfumes, and decorated with elaborate Zulu tribal beads. Their striking beaded skirts swung to the beat of the drums, exposing their nakedness beneath. The married women were considerably more conservative in long, decorated black capes, tall beaded hats, and bead decorations. The unmarried men wore kilts, representing the Scottish army that fought in the Zulu war. These costumes looked more like skirts, with white tunics, a green necktie and hard helmet-style hats. It made me wonder how the beautiful maidens would be attracted to these strangely dressed young suitors. The married men wore elaborate animal skins draped across their shoulders, magnificent feather headdresses, and tiny skins hugging their hips and exposing their taut buttocks. Their Zulu spears were thrown into the air and stomped on the ground in a rhythmic beat, representing the warriors, dancing and swirling to the rhythm of the drums.

Each group danced differently, with the warriors being the most animated by the drumbeat. It was quite hypnotic to view them all at once. We were permitted to watch with the spectators, who were very friendly toward us and enjoyed practising their English. It was another unique experience.

This was to be our last overland trip, since our travels from then on would always be aboard our yacht, *Khulula*. We moved aboard at the beginning of November 1998, ready to start our new adventures.

Richards Bay, Zululand, was our base while we got *Khulula* ready for cruising. The harbour had been built in 1976 and is the largest coal terminal in the world. This never seemed to be too much of a problem until it rained; then the deck would get filthy with the black rain from the coal dust. We often saw fierce storms in the bay when fronts came through, with winds gusting to 50 knots and waves coming over the docks.

One particularly bad storm hit when we were in the clubhouse.

A sudden wind started and a huge, dark cloud formed as the wind picked up coal dust from the terminal. As the cloud reached the marina, the boats heeled far over at their docks, the mooring lines screeched under the strain, and unsecured dinghies flew through the air.

Graeme rushed down the docks, struggling against the wind and rain, flickering like someone in an old movie as strobe lights from the lightning lit him up. He had to jump on the boat and start the engine, driving the boat forward to take the slack off the mooring lines and to prevent the strong wind from blowing it onto the docks. Fortunately, these storms were not that frequent and usually predicted by the marine weather station. They certainly seemed to add to the beauty of Africa.

Diary Excerpt: November 12th, 1998

Being on *Khulula* is just great! I've never felt so "home proud"! It was wonderful to start cleaning up (although five days later I'm looking at the job I did a bit more suspiciously).

No one had lived on our boat for five years and it was uninhabitable; not just the coal dust, but old dust, dirt, and dead bugs.

Diary Excerpt: November 12th, 1998 continued

I'm settling into boat life quite nicely, especially now that we've got the stove working and can enjoy home cooking again!

Diary Excerpt: December 5th, 1998

It's amazing how life just settles into a new routine. We work on the boat preparing it for sailing nearly every day. I miss being outside when the wind and rain come, but then the sunny days somehow seem more productive.

Diary Excerpt: December 17th, 1998

Nearly Christmas! We went for our first sail yesterday and it felt really wonderful. It was a festival day and we took *Khulula* out in the bay to watch the formula racing boats from a great vantage point. I just kept looking at the little people on the shore thinking they were looking at the yachts on the water and that we actually had become part of the show.

When we decided to go sailing, I felt a bit apprehensive, but Graeme was in full control and when we had the main up and then unfurled the big genoa sail, our yacht looked really striking in the water, heeled over to the portholes, simply exhilarating and magnificent!

One of our guests said he couldn't find the adjective to describe it, and I quite agreed!

We spent Christmas and New Year's back at the hostel, helping out and celebrating with our old friends, along with some new yachtie friends we had invited along to join us. To celebrate the New Year we watched all the fireworks and a midnight spectacle of red emergency flares that lit up the sky from the deck of the boat. It was quite breathtaking and a great way to celebrate our first New Year's on *Khulula*. As the weeks and months passed we stepped up our work on the boat to get her ready for her first voyage.

Diary Excerpt: March 31st, 1999

Time and money seem to go so fast. We're both really ready to go now. Originally, the end of March to mid-April was our departure target, but we're committed now to be at the hostel until the end of April. Only another four weeks! We still haven't finished painting, but the music system and all other electronics are now installed (GPS, VHF, LOG, depth sounder, etc.). However, the batteries are not properly operational and we do not have a fridge-freezer installed yet. I wonder if we will ever be ready?

Diary Excerpt: May 22nd, 1999

We're cruising! At last!

We were waiting for money to arrive from the UK and we ended up cancelling the transaction and asking a friend to bring some with him when he came out to visit us. We took four crew with us for our first voyage to Madagascar: Chris from Germany, Fabrice from France, and a Swiss couple called Nanno and Nicholas. It was a welcome relief to have another female crew member! The first two crew ended up waiting on the boat for nine days before we were ready to depart, so everyone was really ready to leave!

The first day at sea was very lumpy, very little wind, so we motor-sailed a lot. The dolphins were incredible, we saw twenty to thirty of them about four hours out to sea, and five or six swam right around the front of *Khulula*. It was a breathtaking sight, watching them all jump in sequence and play in the bow wave of the boat.

Our first sunset was so beautiful, all around vision (this was my first sunset from the sea).

The night watch was not so great. The sea was very confused—with some short, low swells and some long, heavy swells—and we had to run the engine most of the time. It was cold and very dark, and I didn't feel at all comfortable. I couldn't even hold a course straight enough for long enough to relieve Graeme! Of course, getting up at 1:00 a.m. and then again at 2:30 a.m. and up again at 5:30 a.m. will take some getting used to!

I already have my first two sailing injuries: the cupboard fell open onto my head while I was asleep, giving me a lovely lump, and then I did something to my little toe. It feels so painful I wonder if I have broken it, but it's probably just badly bruised. So we're on our way sailing; at least, now, we are sailing.

Diary Excerpt: May 25th, 1999

Fifth day sailing. Today the sea has calmed down a bit and the wave lengths are longer, the sun is shining, and again I am enjoying myself. The last couple of days I've felt like I've been in a washing machine, being thrown around like a dirty cloth! I've bashed my little toe again so it's now bandaged up and I'm hopping around, difficult on an angle all the time.

I've got bumps on my bumps, on account of five or six heavy books depositing themselves on top of me while I was sleeping. I have a lovely black bruise on my hip when I did an impression of a flying fish as I attempted to exit the head (the toilet), and threw myself across the boat as it heeled over, hitting my stomach directly into the fiddle rail of the opposite berth, and smashing my hip.

Last night I felt ill for the first time, probably because of the pink scrambled eggs that Fabrice decided to cook for everyone; it was not enough food for a main meal, and left us all hungry and a little seasick! Feeling apprehensive about the future, I want to be alone with Graeme, but feel concerned about just the two of us sailing this big boat when I don't feel self-assured on the helm or being left alone on a night watch (even thirty minutes is a challenge right now). I have mixed feelings about having crew—we can't live without them, I can't live with them. I'm sure things will take their course and we will see what the future brings. This wasn't quite what I expected.

Khulula's big wide spaces below deck meant that in rough weather conditions, we could easily get thrown from one side of the boat to the other. I found comfort in living outdoors on my new home, eating all our meals on the large table at the aft of the boat, and socializing with other boat friends.

Diary Excerpt: May 27th, 1999

We arrived at Tuléar (*aka* Toliara), Madagascar, on schedule; it was our seventh day at sea. It's not the greatest port but I was just so relieved to get the crew off *Khulula* and walk on land again myself, that it didn't really matter that much. It seemed to take forever to get everyone organized, and much negotiation to organize three "puss-pusses" into town. A puss-puss is a hand-drawn carriage for two adults pulled by a Madagascan man running along the ground in bare feet. It felt like we were a school party. We kept waiting around to get everyone together, and then we would lose a couple, find them, wait for them, and lose them again!

We had to do the complicated immigration and port control check-in, notorious in Madagascar because of all the different authorities you have to check in with in a certain order, in completely different parts of town—Port Captain, health inspector, customs and excise, immigration, port taxes—to name a few!

By the time we returned to the boat, the sea had turned into a confused gaggle of waves, with a strong current against a stiff breeze. We had arrived in a flat dinghy with no pump. This provided no way to get back to the boat, so poor Graeme straddled an inflated tube and paddled against the tide, slowly getting lower and lower in the water, to reach the boat and the pump! At one point, we all lost sight of him, but then the anchor light came on and we knew he had made it back safely! As we had no outboard motor, he then had to row back to collect us, once he had inflated all the tubes again.

Cruising Madagascar

We spent a few days at Tuléar getting the crew off *Khulula* and paperwork sorted out before we set off alone to start our adventures as a couple. All went wonderfully well until sunset approached, and then, wham! The calm seas suddenly started to build with swells and increasing wind. Graeme was enjoying this to start with, until he realized we were going to be caught short with no reefs in the huge main sail and no storm jib to assist in "hoving to." This is a method sailors use to "park" the boat in bad weather, by backing one sail against the other so the boat makes no forward motion.

It was suddenly a mad rush and panic. I was being tossed around again like a rag in a washing machine while trying to wrestle a dinner together in the galley, emptying the toilet, which kept flooding, and picking up various articles that were flying around. I was not happy. I don't know what time it started to die down, but I was seriously tired and it was early in the morning.

I couldn't help much. I tried steering for half an hour while Graeme slept by my side in the cockpit, but my shoulders and arms were getting seriously stiff. I think I got a good sleep around 3:00 a.m. until 7:00 a.m., by which time Graeme had got *Khulula* nicely balanced and had lashed the steering wheel with a rope, so it didn't need hand steering. Joy of joys!

Afterwards, I sat happily in the cockpit with a gentle land breeze. Graeme had been sleeping by my side for two hours, and I wasn't going to wake him, since that was all the sleep he'd had for the night. I decided that I would insist on anchoring before dark if we reached an anchorage in time. We both needed a good night's sleep, a good meal, and a good sort-out downstairs. Things had fallen everywhere, and there was a big bowl of washing-up that I couldn't face doing in the rough conditions. I hoped that there were greater things on the horizon.

The Barren Island and a Mouse Lemur

Diary Excerpt: June 9th, 1999

Following a really enjoyable cruise up the West Coast of Madagascar, we arrived today at the Barren Islands. Antananarivo—one of the Barren islands—is really beautiful, with its bright white sand, which makes up for the lack of vegetation, hence the name "Barren."

We waited for the swell to subside, and ended up rowing to the beach at 4:00 p.m. with our fish that we'd caught on the way and the smoker to cook it in! It was so beautiful there, I actually suggested to Graeme that we should have brought the tent, watched the sun go down, and stayed the night. This would have probably been a good idea, since as soon as the sun went down, the surf started to build.

At this stage in our cruising, our dinghy was a deflated Zodiac with no floor and two paddles we'd made out of a packing case. It would have been too dangerous to return to *Khulula* without a moon, so we sat it out until 1:00 a.m., making fires with the driftwood and trying to get some sleep inside the dinghy.

We had just got cozy in the dinghy when a mouse lemur jumped on Graeme's shoulder, much to his surprise, my surprise, and the lemur's surprise. For those who do not know, a mouse lemur has a striking resemblance to a very large rat!

Eventually we got back to *Khulula*, very wet and exhausted, and decided to move on the next day, since the swell was getting worse.

We headed for the next fishing town, Maintirano, located on the Northwest Coast of Madagascar, and quite cut off from any other major town or city. We were hoping to stock up on some basic provisions and cigarettes at this remote location. Again, there was quite a swell, but we decided to just let the surf beach us, which it promptly did! Once on the beach, we saw a unexpected sight. Hidden from any sea view was a red lagoon, about 500 metres across and no bridge! This lagoon had dried out and consisted of thick red mud that didn't look passable.

Excerpt From Letter to Bea: June 21st, 1999

We then continued on our journey and three days later stopped at a most beautiful fishing village called Maintirano. It was the most welcoming place, everyone so very friendly and happy. We anchored about 300 metres off the beach and rowed ashore. I got completely soaked when the surf hit the dinghy, but fortunately I had packed my sarong so was able to change out of my wet clothes on the beach.

We were then faced with having to cross this large dried-out lagoon, which turned out to be thick red mud! Graeme led the way, following some previous footprints, and promptly sank, right up to his knees! It really was quite comical, especially since he had to reach down right into the mud to remove his shoes, covering both arms full length and quite a bit of his stomach in sticky red mud!

I was doubled with laughing and so were the locals, who were watching our antics. The locals led us safely across the lagoon and then to a watering hole where we could wash off the red mud. By this time we already had a number of adults and children gathered around us laughing and smiling and greeting us, and the group grew in size until we had quite a party leading us through the village to the chief's house.

What a wonderfully beautiful place, everything so neat and tidy, each basic hut with a cleanly swept patch of dirt planted with flowers and bushes, and not a single piece of rubbish anywhere to be seen.

Even if we had had a camera, it would never had made it through the dinghy episode, so we have no photos of the village or its people, except the very vivid ones in our minds of well-kept beauty and the radiant warmth and happiness of the people.

We were invited into the home of the chief's family and given hot, sweet coffee served in a large bowl, along with pastries that were similar to doughnuts. A priest who could speak English was sent for following much discussion in a mixture of French, Malagasy, a lot of arm waving, and a little English. We later learned that the priest was a French-Canadian missionary.

We were invited to stay for a wonderful meal of coconut rice, Zebu (a cow with a large hump), and fresh fruit. They also asked us if we wanted a shower. Maybe we smelled a little from our days at sea, but I think it was more a courtesy, because they realized we had a shortage of fresh water on *Khulula*. So we were given a bar of soap and a towel, and took turns using their outside shower. This was all very welcome to us, since we had been eating out of tins and had not had a fresh water shower for some time.

It was not the usual welcome I would expect complete strangers (and foreign to boot) to receive at a foreign port, so we felt really honoured. We were then given a complete tour of the town, including the local school, the church and, much to our delight, the local bar where we were offered a refreshing, cool beer.

Eventually, we told them we had to return to the boat, because we were unsure of the sea conditions. We might have been prevented from rowing back if the swell had gotten much larger. They invited us to join them the next day, but unfortunately we returned to terrible sea conditions, making it an unsafe anchorage. With no means of communication, we could only wave at our new friends on the beach and call goodbye, perhaps leaving them wondering if they had done something wrong. I sincerely hope they realized our situation, which they probably did, since they are also fishermen and understand the sea.

As we approached the north end of Madagascar, we arrived in an area called Nosy Be, which—with its many sheltered islands and bays—is a popular cruising area for yachts. "Nosy" is Madagascan for "island," and Nosy Be is the largest island in this group, with Helville providing a good sized city for provisioning, water, and fuel. We always laughed at the name Helville, wondering how a city had got such a name, but quite honestly it was always Hell going there. Young boys at the harbour always fought over who got to protect our dinghy from theft. We would always smile nicely at one of the boys and choose him to guard the dinghy, but by the time we returned, a little war had ensued and a different boy was guarding it and expecting to be paid again.

Sakatia and Russian Bay are two beautiful places we visited.

Sakatia is a laid-back island with a small resort and diving centre in one corner. There is beautiful white sand and a large variety of fish to see when snorkelling. Russian Bay is renowned for its marine life. It's a natural harbour, three quarters closed in by land. There were turtles, dolphins, manta rays, and fish everywhere. It seems incredible that we were the only people in such a large bay.

Kissaman is a small island—more of a sand spit, really—where we planned to meet up with some friends from another boat. We had a bit of a yachtie party with others we had met in Crater Bay: Norm and Kim, Genevieve and Pierre. A couple of South Africans also joined us. This was my first experience of the yachting community—sharing food and drink on our private party island. I liked it a lot.

From then on, I realized our boat was always the biggest social meeting place in an anchorage, so the parties were always on our boat. Usually sailing yachts have limited socializing space, so *Khulula* was unusual in this respect.

Giant Land Tortoise on Nosy Momoka

Nosy Momoka was our next stop after a sweet departure from Kissaman. I am really struck by the beauty of this island, with its steep, thick jungle and a small clearing at the northern end, where we found a small fishing village, if I can describe half a dozen straw huts as a village. One or two families, mostly older people, lived a simple, happy life amongst the palm trees in paradise.

One thing that struck me was that they actually seemed to realize how lucky they were, judging by the smiles and welcome they gave us. This was quite the contrast to the grey, cold people I'd left behind in the UK.

The following morning, we spotted what we took to be two large boulders on the beach. We grabbed the binoculars to find, to our amazement, two very large land tortoises, probably hundreds of years old. We dashed ashore and approached them, expecting them to pop back into their shells. To our surprise, they actually behaved as though we were the curiosities.

Diary Excerpt: June 29th, 1999

The land tortoises were so beautiful, quite happy for us to be very close to them and touch them. I was expecting their heads to disappear into their shells, but they were far too curious for that! We kept getting closer and closer until I was on my hands and knees looking straight into the eyes of the tortoise and stroking his wrinkled little head. When four fishing pirogues (a "pirogue" is a small boat, like a punt) arrived with supplies for the village, one of the locals came over to show us that you could tap the tortoises on the back of their shells and then stand on their backs for a ride! Well, I thought that was a bit cruel, but obviously the tortoise was quite used to living side by side with the locals on the island, which is why they were not shy of us. I wanted to take one back to *Khulula*! It wouldn't have even fit in the dinghy.

The hidden bay of Andranira was, quite simply, stunning. We couldn't see the entrance from seaward. The small entrance was not visible until I felt we were going to run straight into land. We really had to trust the GPS. That only added to the beauty, since we were completely enclosed by steep rainforest and cut off from the world—at least, that is what it felt like.

We spent a couple of days here, completely on our own, using the last of our oranges to squeeze fresh orange juice and cooking potato and tuna bake with the last of our provisions. It's such a shame we had run out of cigs, rum, and fresh fruit and vegetables, because we could have stayed there much longer.

At the time, I was a heavy smoker, and I never realized how much my life was run by cigarettes.

Islands of the Famous Lemurs

We started our next round of exploring at Nosy Komba, following another trip back to Helville on Nosy Be to stock up. Nosy Komba is famous for the black lemur, which has bright orange eyes and a large, elaborate tail. The villagers keep a kind of sanctuary for the lemurs at one end of the island, for the benefit of tourists, of course. We sat around feeding the lemurs our old bananas out of our hands. It is not really an enclosure; it's a place the lemurs visit to be fed by the tourists. It wasn't exactly the same as seeing one in the wild, but we tried that first and had no sightings at all; they were all in the feeding enclosure, I suspect.

The island has a nice feel to it, despite the influence of the daily tourists encouraging the locals to sell their wares, and it does have the advantage of a fresh water supply. We paid for a local to fill up our containers with fresh water and carry them to the dinghy. Graeme then rowed the containers back to the boat, and the helper lifted the heavy containers from the dinghy up to her deck. It took the whole day to ferry enough water to fill our 100-gallon tank on the boat, so we make sure we are very careful with our consumption of water. The only other way we could top up the tanks is by collecting rain water, of which there wasn't much at that time of year.

Nosy Tani Kely was our next stop, with a beautiful palm-fringed beach and a colourful reef close to the shore. It is a great place for snorkelling, with great visibility and a good variety of coral and huge shoals of multi-coloured fish. It was nice to have the option of snorkelling from our anchorage, climbing down to the water from our boat. This was really the first snorkelling I had done from the boat, so I was quite nervous to start with. It was going to take some time for me to gain enough confidence to snorkel alone, but Graeme could not see anything without his glasses and did not have prescription goggles. It always amazed me that he spent so little time in the water, considering the sea was our life.

Nosy Iranja, otherwise known as Turtle Island, has a large sand isthmus that connects it to a neighbouring island at low tide. It was a nice walk across to a perfect oasis, although signs of building could be seen on both sides. I suspected that the turtles had already moved to Russian Bay, because we saw no sign at all of their presence. This was the first time I had experienced a sand spit, and it highlighted the nature of the tides. I suddenly realized we would need to quickly return to the boat, as the incoming sea was rapidly covering the spit. Indeed, the turn of the tide actually made rowing back to *Khulula* quite difficult, and, at one point, I was convinced the current was going to take us past the end of the island, where we would be carried out to sea. It was necessary to paddle really hard against the current to keep the dinghy heading toward the boat.

Diary Excerpt: July 17th, 1999

The following day we headed back to Helville and felt a little sad that this marked the end of our visit to Madagascar. As luck had it, Chris, our crew member whom we were picking up there, had met a local Madagascan girl, and wanted to spend a little more time with her. Lily was a sweet nineteen-year-old with strange coarse long hair; I later discovered the hair was a wig that she thought made her look more Europe-an and sophisticated. Chris offered to pay us for Lily's food and lodgings for the next three days, proposing we visit a few more islands together, which we readily agreed to.

For Lily, it was an interesting experience and an opportunity to learn English. For us, it was an opportunity to spend more time with a Madagascan girl and understand her perspective on life. I eventually persuaded her to remove her wig. Chris hadn't even realized it was a wig, although he had been sleeping with her for the last three days. She looked so vulnerable with her sweet, heart-shaped face, beautifully framed by her own, much lovelier, short, dark hair.

In reality, she didn't turn out to be quite so sweet. She harassed poor Chris, who thought she was genuinely in love with him and not just a prostitute who was demanding a three-day rate from him. I'm not sure who I felt the most compassion for: Chris, because he really had fallen head over heels for the sweet Lily; or Lily, because she saw Chris as just another paying customer. Well, we had a lovely time until it was time to drop Lily off. That is when another side of her sweet personality started to show through, demanding huge sums of money that were way beyond Chris's means. Chris eventually did pay her an amount he could afford, but with a broken heart.

The British Madagascan Consulate From South Africa

Nosy Mitsio was our next port of call, via a small island we spotted on the chart called Tsara Bajina. As we approached Tsara Bajina, we were quite surprised to see an orderly row of umbrellas on the beach, and what looked like a large thatched roof amongst the palm trees. This was the first example we had seen of turning a beautiful island into an exclusive holiday resort at two-hundred dollars per night. It was very tastefully done, with obvious attention to nature conservation, and the management was very welcoming to the scruffy yachties. We bumped into the Madagascan consulate (who was English, but based in Durban, South Africa) and his wife, and invited them to join us on a cruise to Mitsio the following day.

Mitsio is a really spectacular sight: the famous rock formation called "church organs" really lives up to its name. It is steep, too, right up to the sheer face, so we got the yacht pretty close and saw individual "pipes" formed by the basalt—a real piece of natural artwork. There was a lovely anchorage in a nearby bay with nice snorkelling, white sand beach, and local fishermen willing to trade a large Red Roman fish for two t-shirts.

We had delayed our departure from wonderful Madagascar for a few days, but it was time to cross the ocean again to East Africa, calling on a few islands on the way.

Giant Land Tortoise, Nosy Momoka, Madagascar

⅋ Reflections From 2015 ⅋

Looking back at my experience of Africa, I realize I learned a lot about different cultures in a short time. I was appalled by the daily murders and violence in South Africa. Disappointed to see so much discrimination, I actually became racist myself against the white Afrikaans. When it is "in your face" every day, it can happen so easily. I saw so much violent racism from the whites against the blacks that I began to feel hatred myself. It took a year before I even realized my "ears" reacted to the Afrikaans accent, and I'm still sensitive now. Fortunately, I met a number of "nice" white Afrikaans in my continued travels, and I soon recognized my own discrimination.

How can humans be so cruel? Why does such discrimination exist when we are all one humanity? I lived in a safe cocoon in England with no violent crimes and no blacks actually in our village. I learned so much in Africa about human behaviour, because I witnessed my own.

Travelling through Madagascar was like travelling through a time machine to a world one hundred years earlier. The people were poor, but kind and friendly. Only when material wealth came into the picture did I ever experience violence or anger.

During these first few months of travel, I was constantly fascinated by new people and new cultures. Adapting to life in *Khulula* seemed pretty easy, and it was a life of adventure with little conflict.

❧ Chapter Three ❧

Zanzibar, Maasai Mara, and Malaria

"Life tends to respond to our outlook, to shape itself to meet our expectations."
Richard M. Devos

The great thing about cruising is that you can change your mind whenever you want. Once we left Madagascar, our original plan was to visit Mayotte, a French island to the northwest of Madagascar but, given the state of our finances, we decided that this was not a good idea and decided to head for Aldabra, north-northwest. Of course, we changed our minds again a couple of days into the passage as the increasing swell was hitting us beam on and driving the first mate insane. This constant thrashing of the waves onto the side of *Khulula* builds up a sideways momentum, which means we were constantly thrown from one side of her to the other, making sleeping, cooking, and reading almost impossible. So we quickly consulted the chart again and decided to head for Glorieuses, just halfway to Aldabra. The Glorieuses is a small group of French islands, only occupied six months of the year by a French policeman, two military men, and a meteorologist.

When we arrived at Glorieuses, we found a really beautiful island, but it was not a great anchorage and it didn't look possible to row to the beach. It looked a lot more accessible once it was low tide, so we said we would try to swim ashore. Chris got in first and thought he saw a shark, and that made us decide to not swim. Instead, we took the dinghy. Chris did some snorkelling over the coral, and I did some hanging over the side of the dinghy. The coral was white and really stunning with a lot of different fish. We decided not to attempt to go any further because of the surf and returned to *Khulula*. The reef was between the boat and the shore, so we would've been in danger of bursting the dinghy on sharp coral or scraping ourselves if a wave had tipped the dinghy in the surf.

Within a few hours, we received visitors at our boat: a French policeman, two military men, and the weatherman in a large skiff. To start with, they were very formal, demanding to see our passports and interrogating us about why we chose to stop at this island. Once we explained our innocent need for a night's rest and offered them some "*Khulula* spirit" (rum), their moods quickly changed. They invited us ashore to visit their weather station and military headquarters, and we readily accepted, hopping into their skiff, which had two powerful outboard motors. The four strong men plus Graeme and Chris still struggled with the boat in the surf, and I was the only one who escaped without getting too wet.

We then jumped onto the back of a tractor they had waiting for us for the two-kilometre ride across the island, through the dense interior of the jungle, to their base. The interior of the island was really beautiful. Thick palm trees let the sun slice through, but provided shade for the sand road. When we arrived at the other side of the island, there was a clearing with the meteorology building and the officers' mess, which was where they kept the beer. We got the grand tour of the meteorological building—from where they transmit weather reports to London twice a day using a surprising amount of technology for a small island—and the officers' accommodation. That's basically all there was on the island. The only thing that stood out was a really beautifully kept graveyard for the original inhabitants. Each grave was bordered by clean white pebbles, and the same pebbles were used to represent the cross, in the centre of the grave. A small gravel path led to each grave, again with a border of clean white pebbles. I guess this upkeep is what the policemen and military men did all day.

When they returned us to our boat, and we thanked them for their hospitality, they said we were much nicer than their last visitor, who demanded a tour of the island and then had an argument with the policeman because he was not given permission to go ashore. This then escalated into an even larger argument when he demanded to know how much the island would cost to buy. When the policeman inquired who this person thought he was, trying to buy French land, the visitor announced that he was a famous movie star. I instantly recognized the name, but none of the policemen, military gents, or met officer had ever heard of any of his films, nor did they recognize that he was famous, so he was promptly asked to pull up the anchor of his super-yacht and leave French territory.

We spent the evening there and left the following morning, changing our plans once again when we realized it might be impossible to go ashore at Assumption or Aldabra Islands, and heading instead for Mafia Island. Probably the main reason we changed our mind was the large swell that was still hitting us on the beam, starting that rocking momentum going again and driving me completely insane.

Mafia Island and the Boy Who Ate a Banana Without Peeling It

As it happened, we could not go ashore at Mafia Island because of high winds, although we did receive a visitor from the island who paddled for several hours, against the wind, to check us out. It turned out the poor boy was a little mentally challenged, and we invited him aboard for a rest. In the meantime, the whole village had to send out a rescue party to come and collect him. He was very happy to be sitting aboard and kept pointing to things, which we assumed he wanted. There was obviously some problem, because when we offered him a banana, he started to eat it peel and all, as though he had never seen one before. When the village men arrived at our boat to collect him, they were making "crazy" hand signs to us as a way of apology. We smiled and gave them a few gifts as gratitude for removing the boy, who had happily settled in and was showing no signs of wanting to return to his island.

We rested for two days and, once the wind died a little, set off northwest for Zanzibar, Tanzania, on the island of Unguja on an overnight passage. However, the winds died completely and so in the late afternoon of the following day, we made landfall on Tanzania's mainland at Dar es Salaam, a little south of Unguja. We did not want to arrive in Zanzibar at night-time, so we pulled into the bay for a short stopover to get our feet on earth and have a cold beer.

Chris was only on *Khulula* as crew to mainland Africa, so it was time for him to depart. His last words to us as he left were, "You'll still be here in eight weeks."

His prediction rang true when one event led to another, almost too many to mention, but first the engine broke down and it took four weeks for the parts to arrive. The bill was so high, we blew all our savings and we had to find some way to make more money so we could continue cruising.

We met some ex-pats, who were all aid workers at a small store that had tables outside. They had christened this "the corner bar," and it was right outside the bus stop for the "dala dala" minibuses into the city of Dar es Salaam. We made friends with many ex-pats who got involved in helping us get our engine parts and helping us pay for them. Several were keen fishermen who paid a small fortune to go on fishing trips, and so a deal was struck that they would contribute to the parts fund in exchange for fishing trips to Latham Island to the east, once the engine was working. We also planned to take them all on a "booze cruise," so they were always keen to see us waiting at the bus stop to get the latest news on our boat repairs. We became locals ourselves, since every time we tried to get into the city, we would be spotted at the bus stop and invited into the bar to be bought drinks.

We enjoyed our time there, especially the trips on the "dala dala," where we met many colourful locals, women, children, chickens, and goats all squeezed into the small space of a crowded van with small windows. Often sliding doors were left open to accommodate the men who hung out of them.

We also spent some time with Alex, Fansar, and their little one, Tina, on the sailing yacht *Ice*. Alex was of European descent and Fansar was from Madagascar. Alex had been a live-aboard yachtie for three generations, making little Tina the fourth generation of kids to be raised on a boat. Alex was quite a character: a grown man of thirty-two who acted like a teenager being exposed to the pleasures of a city for the first time in his life. He would come home excited, clutching a pair of Levi jeans he'd bought at one of the stalls or telling stories until the small hours of the morning of the discos he loved to visit. He was often seen paddling his surfboard back to the boat at sunrise. His dinghy had been stolen, so this was the only form of transport from the yacht for the whole family.

When we eventually left Dar es Salaam, we planned an outing to the beach with the family, and both yachts headed for a small island. Alex was always up to crazy games, so he immediately rushed into the waves to play on his surfboard as we sat on the beach with Fansar and Tina. We saw him get tossed in the surf on the reef and watched in horror, as he tried to get away from the sharp rocks, unable to do anything to help since he was so far away. Eventually, Alex righted himself and started to paddle back to us from quite a long way out. When he arrived back, blood was all over him and he casually spat a tooth out of his mouth onto the beach as though it was no big deal. What a character; so typical of the many people we met during our travels.

Winning a Local Competition in Dar es Salaam

Excerpt From Letter to Bea: September 20th, 1999

Through the friends we met, we found someone who could fix our fridge-freezer. We've been without refrigeration since it stopped working two weeks after we left South Africa. We've got used to not having it, but when you have guests who are paying, they do expect cold drinks at least!

It came about because Lady Luck shone on us again and we won a local photographic competition, quite by accident! A man with a camera took our photos while we were sitting in the corner bar, and we thought nothing of it, since he also gave us some promotional hats and pens. It turned out to be a competition by a cigarette company, and we happened to be smoking his brand of cigarettes at the bar! We didn't think anything more of the incident until everyone we met told us that they had seen us in the national press and that we had won 100,000 Tanzanian shillings (about two hundred dollars US), so we rushed to the office to claim our prize! It doesn't sound much, but it was to us, and we treated ourselves to luxury foods like instant coffee, cheese, and Worcestershire sauce! It is very expensive to shop in Dar es Salaam (because the goods are imported especially for the aid workers who get paid big salaries), so you have to be careful what you buy, and instant coffee at ten dollars a jar had been crossed off our list for some time!

So we resumed repairs on *Khulula* and we've now renovated the wooden sailing dinghy we bought in South Africa just before we left. At the time it seemed it was destined never to float, but Graeme gave it his usual care and attention, and now we feel like we have more freedom to go places we could never go before in our semi-inflatable rubber dinghy we'd had to row everywhere! It is so wonderful to have the freedom to sail in the dinghy a long distance and we visit other yachts a lot more often, now that distance is not a problem. We're so proud of our "little yacht" and I call it "My Baby."

Stoning for Thieves Still Goes On

We took such care of the dinghy, but our worst fear was that it would be stolen, and we always left it tied up when we went into town. Theft is a real problem in mainland Tanzania, despite the tough sentence given to anyone who is caught. Graeme witnessed this when he visited the city one day and saw a live stoning of a man who had been accused of theft. He was shocked to see this kind of punishment still used, thinking this kind of sentence belonged in medieval times. With this knowledge, we were very careful not to shout "Thief!" after that.

One day, Graeme had visited the city of Dar es Salaam alone and I was alone on *Khulula* in the cockpit when I noticed our sailing dinghy being paddled away from the shore. My first thought was that someone was moving it or using it to reach their own boat anchored out, but then I realized it was being stolen. I didn't want to shout "Thief!" because of the consequences, but at the same time, I didn't want our one and only dinghy stolen.

I reached for a wooden whistle that I'd bought from one of the Maasai Mara and blew loudly, standing on the deck, pointing and waving my arms in the direction of the thieves. This got enough attention from the local fishermen to understand what was going on, and they then started to shout at the young boys. The boys realized they had been caught in the act and changed direction, rowing the dinghy back to the dock. I was pleased to see through the binoculars that they ensured the dinghy was well secured before they ran off.

I think they realized they had been given a chance, and I realized our relationship with the local fishermen was good enough that they helped out. Only the day before, when I was going through our provisions and spotted a few weevils in some pasta, I had given it away. The weevils are harmless, but I couldn't afford to keep them on board, since they would contaminate other food in storage before I had a chance to eat up the pasta with the weevils. It seemed sensible to me to give this excess food to the fishermen for their families, and they were very grateful.

The East Coast of Africa offered us great sailing, good consistent winds, fishing, and regular sightings of large groups of dolphins. The amazing sailing pirogues performed acrobatics, which I thought should be categorised as "extreme sport," particularly as most sails seemed to consist of roughly sewn rice sacks, or even plastic bags. It is very unusual to see motors on any of these fishing vessels in this part of the world. I was always amazed to see the rough wooden boats with their outriggers powered only by handmade sails. The crew would jump from the boat and balance on the outrigger like a windsurfer to catch the wind in the sails and give themselves more speed, whizzing past our comparatively sophisticated yacht and waving at us.

Mtwapa Creek Near Mombasa

Mtwapa Creek is a beautiful anchorage on the Mtwapa River; well-marked from the ocean, but easily mistaken if approached from the north. You sight the second markings first, which guide you straight across the reef. I experienced this confusion firsthand as I nearly guided our yacht over the reef on our first entrance, because I mistook the markings. Once inside the creek, anchorage space is restricted, but easy access to the village compensates.

We found Mtwapa to be a delightful local village with good fresh produce and friendly, colourful Kenyans. The women dress in bright layers of clashing patterns and colours from head to toe with matching slings for the beautiful children they carry on their backs or hips. I loved walking into the village to buy fresh vegetables and fruit from the market stalls, and always delighted in watching the women carrying their purchases on their heads.

Despite my being a lone, white female amongst a sea of African faces, they were always very friendly, smiling when I brought my own plastic recycled bag to carry the groceries. I couldn't communicate with them, but lots of smiles and sign language usually helped. I would just follow what the locals did, selecting the fruit and vegetables, and then waiting for the assistant to write down the total. I am quite sure they charged me more, but since this was the only local place I could buy fresh crops, I was happy to pay whatever price they chose to charge me.

The incredible thing about this village is that it had the very first internet café I ever saw. The fact that this African village was offering public internet access, even though it was slow and expensive, seemed such a disparity. Next to the internet café was a hairdresser, and I noticed that the Mtwapa women would spend a good amount of money on their hair, winding their afro frizz into elaborate corn rows and braids at the expense of their groceries, if necessary. Next to this shop was the government water tap, where people would pay to fill their containers with fresh drinking water. There were many Maasai Mara men eager to help us carry our twenty-litre containers the two miles to the anchorage to fill up our water tank with fresh water. We negotiated with two young men a reasonable day's wage for the task, and it took them most of the day to deliver the water to our boat. We invited them aboard when the job was finished to enjoy a cold beer, listen to Bob Marley music, and share our stories. We always loved the opportunity of this kind of interaction with the locals to learn more about their culture.

The Dala Dala Minibus to Mombasa

The overcrowded dala dala into Mombasa from Mtwapa was very cheap and a real cultural experience. We were likely to be standing with our arms or legs draped around various body parts of other sweaty people or, if we were lucky enough to get a seat, we provided a lap for someone else's child, chicken, or shopping bag. It's all done with a big smile and the Swahili greeting "Habari." I spent many happy days on the dala dala, and I always found it a great way to get to know the locals, since passengers are often left waiting for as long as an hour before the driver decides to leave the bus stop. The dala dala probably seats around twelve passengers, but it will never leave until it has at least twice this number of people inside and the same number dangling or balancing on the outside. Some people found this frustrating, but I always found it an enjoyable experience.

Back at the anchorage, Kenya Marineland has an excellent restaurant that was great for a treat, and their own Maasai Mara, who always befriended the yachties. While they dance for the tourists who visit the restaurant, they will smile, and share a drink with the yachties, and tell stories of their lives back in the mountains. Most of them have come to Mombasa to dance or make crafts for the tourists so that they can save enough money to buy enough goats for the dowry for their bride. Some get caught in consumerism and end up spending their goat money on new sandals or Walkmans.

Excerpt From Letter to Bea: October 1st, 1999

Now that we are in Kenya, we have an address at our first port of call—Mtwapa Creek, Kikambala. We have been made very welcome here and it is a beautiful anchorage, very lush and green with all the facilities we need, including hot showers (what a treat!), fresh water to fill our tanks and do our laundry, diesel, and a very nice village with a good market about a mile's walk away. It also has a nice restaurant and bar, all the facilities provided free of charge on the assumption you will spend some money there (too expensive to eat but we do treat ourselves to the odd glass of red wine!). We intend to stay in Kenya a couple of months so we will spend the next few weeks checking out the other areas, Kilifi Creek and Lamu Island in the Lamu Archipelago.

While in the area of Mombasa, we didn't miss the ebony-carving community of Wengi. We heard them shouting, "Wengi wengi" at the dala dala station in Mombasa, so we just jumped on board to check it out. A large, rough courtyard in the middle of the area was full of men and women of all ages whittling away at elaborate Maasai Mara statues, plaques, and various animal carvings. The women carved delicate jewellery, spoons, and letter openers, and the children were busy covering up any mistakes with Kiwi boot polish. We had to look closely and carefully, but we haggled a good souvenir here. We bought a few carvings to hang on *Khulula's* walls, promising ourselves that we would start collecting souvenirs for ourselves and possible trading items for the future. Alex had told us how he bought carvings and jewellery from Africa and traded with them in other countries, so we thought this might be a good money-making idea. We considered that African items might be of interest to European tourists in Asia, where we were planning to visit next, or a trip home to England might offer another opportunity to sell.

Zanzibar

Zanzibar is a great sail from Mombasa, and it is rich in culture and spices. We anchored right next to the night market: a hustle and bustle of locals and tourists devouring magnificent displays of freshly caught lobster, crab, fish, and squid. We tried out their "pizza," which is a cross between a kebab and a filled pancake—delicious! If you're addicted to good food, like we are, you could put a lot of weight on at less than a dollar a go. We washed it down with sugar cane juice extracted using something that looked more likely to mangle your laundry dry during wartime. Climbing up the old stone wharf steps, slick with algae and refuse, was always a challenge from the dinghy. As with many markets that are set up alongside the water, that area provides a convenient disposal area for old cooking fat and scraps, as well as acting as the local urinal. Our approach needed care to ensure a large pot of hot oil wasn't about to be emptied into the sea, or that a local vendor wasn't about to urinate directly into the dinghy. Often, we would return to the dinghy and have to remove scraps from inside before setting off.

Old Stone Town in Zanzibar was a fascinating place to get completely lost in. The narrow streets were fragrant with spicy smells and bustled with activity. We saw the famous Zanzibar Doors from various ages, as well as their reproductions. Apparently, the giant spikes on the heavy doors were to discourage elephants from trying to turn in the narrow streets and destroy the front doors.

Social life can be restrictive in this Muslim-dominated town, and we were visiting during Ramadan, which is the Muslim festival of fasting, when they cannot eat, drink, or smoke during daylight hours. It seemed incredible in the heat that they are not even allowed to drink water during the day. They were not very friendly to the tourists they saw taking pleasure in any of those activities. It was best at that time to head for the north of Zanzibar for some serious chilled-out beach life.

Diary Excerpt: October 23rd, 1999

Zanzibar has lived up to our expectations; Stone Town was fascinating and the famous street market food was incredible. We were anchored right next to it! After a week of exploring and topping up our trading items of batik and some bead jewellery, we left again for the sanctuary of a beach on the north tip of the island. Ras Nungwi was a beautiful beach, with white, white sand and a collection of nice bars and people. We met three Americans, Jim, Jay, and Lioness, who joined us as paying crew to explore Pemba and gain their passage back to Mombasa. Good company and good crew.

Ras Nungwi is a great anchorage outside the cyclone season, with its white sand beaches, turquoise waters, and backpacker-style bars.

Pemba

From there we decided to head to the islands of Pemba nearby.

Pemba is an isolated island with many small islets surrounding it. Good snorkelling, breathtaking scenery, and little else made it definitely worth the visit. We certainly did have some exciting times navigating the area with the limited charts available. We quickly found out that charts are not that accurate when they mark the depths and positions of reefs, and I clearly remember getting the yacht quite stuck when we literally ran out of water. I was hanging over the side of the bowsprit, looking down into the clear water, watching the depth getting shallower and the reef getting closer to the bottom of *Khulula*. We could not steer her in reverse exactly the way we had entered the reef, so the only way out was to jump into the water with a snorkel and navigate our way around the reef. At one point, we had four divers in the water shouting instructions to me that I was relaying to Graeme at the helm. We were always extra cautious when we entered these islands, and the challenge of navigating the reefs was perhaps another reason we never saw any other yachts in the area.

Mkoani, Pemba seemed like a never-ending round of immigration and charges with little of interest. We spent most of the time in very basic, hot huts, looking across at the customs officers and getting our passports checked and stamped painfully slowly. The officers would write so slowly and then go into a kind of trance while they tried to remember what they were supposed to be doing next. We headed for a small nature reserve island called Msaki, which looked beautiful, but they wanted to charge us thirty dollars to anchor and five dollars per person to stay there.

Looking back now, I think it would be worth that much, but we were on such a tight budget we would never have considered spending that kind of money just to anchor. So we moved onto Wete, a small fishing town with a good market, and we managed to get some beef, although we questioned whether or not it was Zebu, which is the cow-like animal with a large hump. People were very friendly, although immigration was the usual pain. We then headed for the northern tip and the most incredible white sand beach. It was mainly uninhabited except for a small fishing village and the odd white Peace Corps doctors and teachers. We chilled out very nicely for a couple of days, cooking fresh lobster bought from the fishermen on the beach.

Excerpt of Letter to Bea: November 1st, 1999

We picked up three American chaps north of Zanzibar and they cruised with us for seven days around Pemba and back to Mombasa. We found a stunning white sand beach on the

northern tip of Pemba (two miles long and deserted), and
the local fishermen visited our yacht every morning with
their catch; we ate like kings! Octopus and lobster cooked
on the beach with coconut rice (made with fresh coconut,
of course) and salad. What an incredible treat. We bought
seven lobsters between the five of us for under five dollars!

So we continued to cruise from Mombasa north to Kilifi and
Lamu, and south to Zanzibar and Pemba, picking up paying
crew when we could to top up the cruising kitty and carry out
the necessary repairs to get ready for our trip across the Indian
Ocean.

Excerpt of Letter to Bea: November 29th, 1999

We are now settled in Kilifi Creek, twenty-five miles north
of Mtwapa Creek, but expect to keep commuting between
the two. Mtwapa is much prettier, more lush with a lot more
colour from the flowers, but Kilifi is the home of quite a few
other yachties and it makes a nice change to have "like" people around you. We also have the facilities of a workshop
with electricity to do some more work on *Khulula* and also
a place where we can dry out the boat to check the bottom.
It looks like it's not going to be too difficult to earn money
with paying crew either. We just did a trip for seven days
for four people to Lamu, which is a group of islands a hundred miles north, including Manda Toto Island. It was a very
good sail up there and only took seventeen hours, but two of
the girls got seasick and one of them got off the boat at Lamu
and didn't want to get back on! Still, the two Danes were
very happy and would have stayed with us longer if they had
more time.

The journey back was against the current with heavy rain
and lightning, and no wind, so it took twice as long, arriving
back at Kilifi at 4:00 a.m. It seems that the "short rains" have
arrived at last, which I think is a good thing for Kenya, as

there are many stories in the newspapers of areas struck by famine because of the droughts. When it rains, it really does rain, then it passes and you're left with no wind, and a very still hot atmosphere.

We Meet Other Cruisers

We've met some really nice people called Nick and Sue from Ripon in England on the yacht next to us. They have been here for three years, because Sue had an unexpected baby. Little Jo is now seventeen months old and quite a character, running around the boat and playing in the sea all the time; he seems very happy.

Gary and Jen are Australian and had been there for a couple of years. Gary had been working for the UN on food distribution for famine areas and earned quite a lot of money doing so. The UN pays him "danger money," since he had to go unaided into the jungle for periods of time, lead an expedition team of locals to find the food dropped by helicopters, and then carry it to the various famine areas that need relief. Jen was always frantic with worry when he left on an expedition; I told Graeme in no uncertain terms that no money was worth that kind of worry. They had sailed from Australia in a tiny twenty-six-foot boat, and were saving for a larger one. It made us feel very lucky to have found such a big boat; we admired her all the time and thanked our lucky stars.

Graeme was in the process of designing a self-steering wind vane for *Khulula* so that we didn't have to hand steer the wheel twenty-four hours a day; the wind vane should make passages more comfortable. I was in the process of becoming truly self-sufficient for our trip to Chagos in the middle of the Indian Ocean, as there is nothing there at all. Jen was showing me how to bottle and can meat and vegetables, and I was busy brewing rice wine. We had three months at Kilifi before we set off again in February, so I made the most of the spare time.

Don't Get Malaria in the UK

We found out after we left Kilifi that bad luck befell Nick, Sue, and little Jo. First, Sue visited England and came down with malaria while she was there. In East Africa, that would not have been a problem, since the FDA was testing a well-known cure for all strains of malaria in Africa, but the FDA had not yet approved it and it was unavailable in the UK. This wonder drug, called Duo-Cotecxin, was readily available, as was a simple blood test to check if you had malaria in Kilifi, but it was not available in England.

Unfortunately for Sue, malaria is a tropical disease, unfamiliar to the hospitals in England, so she kept being referred to special centres for tropical diseases until it was almost too late. This was very frustrating for her, since she recognized immediately that she had the symptoms for malaria and kept insisting this was what she had, but the doctors would not agree. In England, it took two weeks to get the results of a blood test, by which time her organs had started to fail. She did eventually make a recovery after a lengthy hospital stay, but swore to take Duo-Cotecxin tablets with her if she ever made a trip away from East Africa again. The other yachties took her advice, and we all added Duo-Cotecxin to our medical boxes.

But Getting Malaria in East Africa Is the Safest Place to Get It

I came down with malaria a little while later in Tanga, Tanzania, and I was very grateful that I was still in Africa. I had a really uncomfortable night, and I felt really uneasy when I woke in the morning. I told Graeme I didn't feel good and had a really pounding headache. We decided it would be wise to visit town and get a blood test for malaria. I took a Duo-Cotecxin tablet anyway, since it is harmless to take, being a two thousand-year-old Chinese herbal remedy from the bark of a tree. It starts to work immediately on killing the parasite, but the longer you leave it, the less effective it can be. The blood test was very easy, cheap, and safe. I waited in the little lab behind a shower curtain while the technician immediately tested my blood for the parasite.

When I walked into the waiting room and told Graeme I was positive for malaria, he went for a test with two other yachtie friends who were with us. The problem with malaria is that if someone near you has it, it has a good chance of being passed on, since the mosquito can bite the infected person and transmit it immediately to the next person with the next bite. The following day, we told everyone we had come in contact with at the Tanga Yacht Club to go and have a test, and found that this was the site of infected mosquitoes. It's worth bearing in mind next time you hear of someone close to you that has been infected.

Sometime, after Sue recovered from malaria and returned to Kilifi, a terrible accident befell Nick when he was helping someone in a house with a light fixture. The electricity in East Africa is not to be trusted, with bad wiring and no safety standards, and Nick received an electric shock that instantly killed him. We heard that Sue and little Jo returned to England, their dreams shattered.

A reminder to live life to the maximum, because you never know what is going to happen.

Diary Excerpt: December 30th, 1999

So Christmas has come and gone already!

After Mtwapa, we stayed in Kilifi for a couple of weeks. It was nice to see other yachties again, but we soon got tired of the long hikes into the nearest market to get provisions. We were beginning to think about the Millennium and wondering if we could take advantage of the occasion to get some special paying crew to do a trip, when Bruno, a local crew member on a German boat, suggested Tiwi Beach, a resort that was popular with backpackers. We spent the day talking to the backpackers, most of whom had already made special millennium plans, but we did meet Bronwyn and Emmet who were really keen. If only we could find more people to share the cost.

The following day, we met in Mombasa and found "the boys"—Jerker, Rasmus, Tobius (brothers), and their friend Robert—from Finland and Sweden. They were a great comedy act and made a really great ten-day trip to Pemba and Zanzibar. It was good sailing and everyone got on and joined in really well. We had a fabulous dolphin show the first morning we arrived at Pemba, with fifty or sixty playing in the bow wave for a good half hour. The guys wanted to swim with the dolphins, which we didn't think was possible, but they did all jump in, and indeed, did swim with the dolphins!

We stopped for a day at Njao Gap and then on to the Hotel California of Funzi Island (Pemba), a real paradise offering great snorkelling, a white beach, and clear water, with an incredible sunset silhouetted by tall palm trees. Everyone really enjoyed themselves!

We made a quick stop at Mkoani for customs and immigration, which this time tried to wangle fifty-five dollars out of us! Considering we paid less than a dollar per person the last time, we were not happy and complained until they accepted fourteen dollars for all of us with much negotiation!

The fishing village of Mkoani was as delightful as I remembered it last time. Then to Zanzibar, where everyone agreed Ras Nungwi would be the place to celebrate the Millennium.

Millennium 2000 Celebrations

We took a night sail to Stone Town to do immigration business and get diesel, and for the benefit of the guys who were on a tighter time scale and had not visited Stone Town. Everyone was in really high spirits and looking forward to returning to Ras Nungwi for New Year's Eve.

The celebrations had pretty much started before it became January 1, 2000 at the International Date Line, and by 6:00 p.m., we were in full flow, dressing the guys in my clothes and forming quite an array of breasts from coconut shells. Even Emmet wore a dress, although he and Chris changed back into normal clothes before going ashore. What a party we looked! Rasmus, in my polka dot Lycra dress, looked nothing short of an attractive woman with his long, thick blond hair. Toby sported the most magnificent Marilyn Monroe breasts in my halter neck top, and Jerker looked plain gay with his bald head. Graeme was definitely the belle of the ball, wearing my white velvet bodice top with firm coconut breasts and his green underpants—he got free drinks all night! We had quite the party and a memorable experience.

Bruno, from Africa, who came along as crew for the trip after his job had finished on the German boat, managed to spoil things a little by stomping his feet and demanding to stay with his "brother and sister" Julie and Graeme for the rest of his life; he threatened that if this couldn't happen, the mafia might have to intervene.

The East Africans still maintain a very paternalistic relationship with the whites, and much prefer the lifestyle they led when the English aristocrats gave them their own quarters in their homes for their families in exchange for light cleaning, cooking, and gardening. Their life under the British rule and the Queen provided them all with more money, food, and better health care. They seemed to aspire to this way of life again, always trying to find work with a family to provide for them. We often came across locals who asked us when our Queen would return to rule them. Unfortunately, the present president does very little to help the underprivileged, keeping the riches for himself and his own family.

It soured our relationship with Bruno a bit, but he had been spoiled by everyone on the boat and not asked to do any work, and he didn't want his life to change. When we returned to Mtwapa, we helped him find another job as crew on a different boat, learning a lesson about providing employment for the locals.

Diary Excerpt: January 27th, 2000

This will be our last trip in Africa, as plans are underway to cross the Indian Ocean, the grand plan being to head for the Seychelles, Chagos, and then Thailand. I'm really looking forward to visiting those places, but still feel quite apprehensive about the sailing. Will I ever get used to it?

✵ Reflections From 2015 ✵

Looking back, I remember East Africa as being quite a different culture from South Africa or Asia. The children in East Africa wanted to reclaim the "good old days" of British rule. The children saw the whites as targets for handouts. I was asked on several occasions by young and old, "Why did your Queen leave? Can you tell her we want her back? Things were much better then." The children in Asia were all entrepreneurial. They wanted pens and to learn English so they could educate themselves and make money with tourism. The East African children just wanted handouts and to be looked after. I can see how tourists visiting for the first time can easily fall for the begging children wanting charity.

I don't think I realized the significance at the time, but I observed a culture yearning for a return to paternalistic British rule at the same time as I was questioning the very same system I had been raised within. I considered myself a rebel to this paternalistic system, but here I was witnessing the positive aspects of British rule. I wondered what my life would have been like if I had not had the advantages of being raised in England.

Looking back on this time, I also see it as a time of change around my attitude toward my own health. I had started to shift my own stance, becoming more aware of my body and listening to symptoms. This literally had saved my life when I got malaria. Previously, the symptoms would have been lightly dismissed as the flu, but with my heightened awareness of my own body and trust of my inner voice, I had the strong message it was malaria and acted quickly.

I recently had a conversation with my neighbour who had had malaria ten years earlier, and he refused to believe I had no repeat symptoms. He could not believe that I self-diagnosed in the first day, wiping out all the parasites before they had a chance to multiply. Most people have so many parasites in their body by the time they are diagnosed that they will get repeat symptoms for the rest of their lives.

I really saw a change in my beliefs around "medical experts" during this period. I started to question whether the "experts" were right to break my back— the back of a fit, healthy, eighteen-year-old— to straighten my spine from the scoliosis I had had since birth. If I'd had this healthy attitude when I was eighteen, would I have questioned the doctors? Would the outcome have been different? I realized that I knew very little about what they had actually done to my body.

Reflecting back, I see how this experience led to my strong feelings of connection to people who are passionate about educating others on mind-body awareness. I have now assisted potential authors in this field to help them get their knowledge out to the world by writing a book on their knowledge. I would never have guessed at the time that these experiences would be guiding me to my purpose.

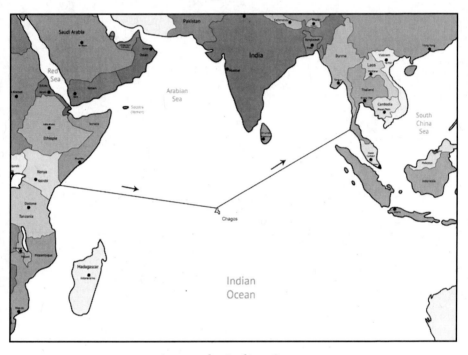

Across the Indian Ocean

⚜ Chapter Four ⚜

The Indian Ocean and Six Months at Sea

"There is nothing so desperately monotonous as the sea, and I no longer wonder at the cruelty of pirates."
James Russell Lowell

Preparations in East Africa

By the time we had arrived in East Africa, we had made up our minds to head east and north east across the Indian Ocean to Thailand. I had already learned a lot from other yachties, particularly in South Africa, but then the hard work really began. *Khulula* did not have refrigeration, so all the food we took had to last for six months without refrigeration; that needed some careful planning. We needed to take into account water and propane gas supplies for six months, and storage for the maximum amount of diesel possible to see us through the doldrums, when there could be days without any wind. The reason we were going to take six months was that we intended to stay in Chagos, which were uninhabited islands, for the maximum time of three months.

Excerpt From Letter to Bea: January 28th, 2000

We will take 1,600 litres of water from Mtwapa (Kenya), 31 litres of propane gas, 800 litres of diesel, 100 kilos of flour, 75 kilos of sugar, 50 kilos of rice, 50 packets of 250 g pasta, 5 kilos of coffee, 2,000 tea bags, 20 kilos of onions, half a ton of potatoes, 10 kilos of garlic, 10 kilos of mostly green tomatoes, 12 kilos of margarine, 20 litres of cooking oil, and over 500 tins of canned vegetables and other foods. I'm also taking 300 fresh eggs, which I have to individually coat in Vaseline to prevent any air from entering the shell; this prevents bacteria from entering the shell too. I have arranged to collect these from a farm that guarantees freshness.

It takes quite a long time to calculate what you need. For instance, if you want fresh bread every other day, that's how you calculate how much flour, yeast, etc., you need. Then we had to find the best place to buy our food supplies (we try to find bulk wholesalers), decide how to get it back to *Khulula*, and decide where to store it all. And you asked in your last letter what do we do for entertainment!

I've just filled twenty 20-litre barrels with all the rice and flour, etc. and left a white trail of handprints and footprints all over the boat! Tomorrow, I start more serious bottling—we've now successfully bottled nine jars of fillet steak. (See? Why do we need refrigeration?) And I want to try some more jam (mango this time), and pickle some eggs and maybe onions … so much to do! What would we do without our pressure cooker? I guess we would need a fridge!

I met quite a few other yachties at Tanga; we all swapped recipes for preserving food. It's very entertaining—women spend an evening swapping ideas and recipes while the men discuss boat maintenance and winds and currents! Certainly more entertaining than discussing what was on television or what I did in the office!

We've become quite friendly with a couple who are going to the same places as us. We spend many evenings sharing stories of where we've been and what we've seen, and tips on where we're going—plus trading charts, looking at their photos, etc. We're never bored and certainly don't miss television or radio, not when we have a complete arena surrounding us of a constantly changing back garden!

We also read a lot (when we have time), and now have a completely new library of thirty or forty books swapped with other yachties. We've actually met about twenty or so other yachties also going to Chagos (some already left, some already there), so we'll have lots of friends when we get there, as well as make new ones, no doubt. We're looking forward to learning all about fishing (fresh fish every day in Chagos). We're not very good at catching, but there'll be plenty of other yachties to teach us all about spearfishing and trawling and line-fishing, as well as crab hunting and coconut harvesting. Because Chagos is only accessible by yacht, it is quite a community. We expect up to fifty yachts to be there by the time we arrive. Even so, when we want to be alone there are many islands where we could lose ourselves.

I never imagined that the first leg of this passage would take thirty-five days.

Coëtivy, Seychelles—Indian Ocean

We could not make our first landfall of Praslin in the Seychelles, since the wind was pushing us south and further away from this destination, so we headed for the most southern atoll of the Seychelles, called Coëtivy; it became our first stop five days after leaving Kenya. We suspected we would not be allowed ashore, because the official check-in with immigration has to be done six hundred miles north on Mahé, the capital island, but a captain we met in Africa had told us they were very friendly to him when he visited and they allowed him ashore.

Excerpt From Letter to Bea: February 8th, 2000

Graeme celebrated his fortieth birthday anchored off one of the most southern Seychelles islands called Coëtivy; it is a private island owned by a prawn farm with two hundred inhabitants employed by the factory. Unfortunately, we were not allowed ashore but we had a nice rest for five days while waiting for the wind to pick up. A couple of boats came out to visit us and one man promised to post our letters—but never returned. The Island Manager did not want us on his island and I think perhaps he saw us visitors and told his man not to return to us.

All I wanted to do was walk on land, but I had to wait another thirty days until we got to Chagos before I would get that privilege.

Reading this letter jogged my memory, but I couldn't remember why they wouldn't let us ashore, so I emailed Graeme and this was his reply:

"The trip to Chagos is easy ... nothing happened. We drifted in the right direction for thirty days; we baked a different dish every day, I got a bottle of Guinness on my birthday at Coëtivy, but they wouldn't let us land unless we had weed to sell and loose women on board. We caught an ugly fish. Memory jogged?"

He was right. It did jog my memory, but I definitely remember feeling very indignant when the first boat arrived and asked if we were "a couple." It seemed like an odd question at the time, but after we had several more visitors asking the same odd question, we eventually befriended a native long enough to ask him about it. The riddle was finally laid to rest when the local quite nonchalantly explained that the "last boat" that had visited these islands had a single female crew member who had been at sea a bit too long and was at that age of sexual experimentation. The captain had made it quite clear there was to be no "hanky panky" between them, so I guess she was quite sexually frustrated by the time they arrived at this island. The locals were happy to oblige and solve this young lady's problem, so they automatically assumed the next boat along might need similar help

Also, our helpful previous captain had a little "stash" on board, which he happily shared with the locals so that he wouldn't have to throw it overboard before making customs and immigration landfall in Africa. They expected the current captain—Graeme—to show the same generosity (even though we did not possess a "stash").

It was an easy mistake to make. This island, the most southern atoll of the Seychelles, is six hundred miles south of the capital island, and is not on a yacht's normal course across the Indian Ocean, so they are quite cut off. The previous yacht with the frustrated crew and generous captain had visited eighteen months earlier.

They must have been full of anticipation and then disappointment when they saw our yacht drop anchor.

Incidentally, we had met this yacht in Africa, and we would like to pass on our gratitude—for misleading us into visiting this "very friendly island"—to Jamie the Australian who may be reading (and laughing) should he ever get a copy of this book. He had lived very nicely off this island for three weeks, staying in different huts every night and making the most of the hospitality, promising to send another boat soon to visit them. His misguidance had persuaded us to alter our course to rest here, assuming we would receive a warm welcome too. It was a lesson well learned and, despite being a funny story, it is evidence of how a yacht can innocently influence a whole remote island and affect the reaction the next yacht will receive. It also reminded me of the inhabitants of the French-owned island Glorieuses who didn't want to entertain us because of the attitude of the very famous movie star who had visited them previously.

The Indian Ocean—First Leg, Seychelles to Chagos in Thirty Days

We waited as long as we could for the winds to come back, but they never really did, so we spent the next thirty days drifting in the right direction with the current.

Excerpt From Letter to Bea: March 13th, 2000

I was pleased to see land after five weeks. We had very little wind and it was a very wearisome journey; there were days when we just bobbed in the middle of the Indian Ocean, a thousand miles from the nearest land. Our only company were dolphins and flying fish and nothing but blue, blue sea for twelve thousand feet down. It would have been nice, many a time, to take a dip, but the sharks in that depth probably wouldn't turn down an opportune snack! Many other yachties do swim in the deep blue; personally, I didn't think it was worth the peril and so sea-water showers suffice when we needed to cool down.

We saw some magnificent sunsets and sunrises. The best was on a very tranquil day when the sea was like glass and the sun as it set turned the water an incredible crimson. For a complete 360°, all shades of scarlet, ruby, amethyst, violet, and pink reflected off the soft feathery clouds—it was truly stunning. That same night the sky was so clear the stars were extraordinarily bright, the Milky Way like a giant white bridge, and the whole sky literally twinkling. We sat for two hours watching the fantastic light show—we were so lucky!

We often had dolphins visit us and one day we even saw a whale—the spray of water and its back arching out of the water. It was quite a sight because of the absolute size of it—not the kind of thing we would want to get too close to our boat! I can only guess it was at least twice the size of *Khulula*!

Being at sea for thirty days was a once-in-a-lifetime experience. I was personally quite spellbound by flying fish and some of their antics, by the way they hurtled across the waves, leaping from the apex of the white water, trailing water droplets, spreading their horizontal fins, and taking flight above the waves for more than 130 metres. Seabirds often stopped by for a rest on the boat, including a particularly large bird who struggled to stay on the safety line by wrapping his webbed feet completely around the rope and then rocking forward and backward with the motion of the boat, desperately trying to stay put on his semi-stable perch as long as possible! We tried many strategies to get him off the safety line, not only because he was making quite a mess, but because I was being distracted by him on night watch.

I also remember, quite vividly, the utter darkness of night watches, particularly when cloud cover obliterated the horizon and stars made me feel very inconsequential in a colossal cosmos of blackness. I used to hate night watches and, as the setting sun touched the horizon, I was always left with a sense of the impending darkness that was about to descend like a prowler in the backyard. On nights like this, I seemed to plunge into a black hole, with only a red glow from the compass light mesmerising me into a hypnotic state as I tried to stay on course. Time would slow right down, making an hour or two seem like an eternity. I was forever checking the time and playing games with myself to avoid the realization that only a few minutes had passed since the last time I checked. When the time eventually arrived to change watch, I would carefully note how long it took Graeme to respond, and I would try to figure in an extra five minutes to make a thermos flask for his watch, which meant my shift finished five minutes early to make his flask up. I never came to a fair use of the time between shifts to eat or drink; it always seemed such a waste of precious sleeping time.

Moreover, I recall some of the strange UFO sightings in the sea, as well as in the sky. One particular episode I put down to giant squid signaling each other across the ocean with their bright, effervescent lights at regular intervals. Phosphorescence is a phenomenon that is produced by plankton. This chemiluminescence is common to marine animals, believed to be a protective reaction to danger, and is likely to be the sanest explanation for the large bright spheres I saw.

One day as dawn broke I spotted a strange sight, which looked a bit like the tops of palm trees floating on the horizon; they gradually formed into a group of sand spits topped with palm trees. After five weeks at sea, we had finally sighted Chagos: a breathtaking landfall of ten islands surrounding a lagoon approximately four miles in diameter.

Salomon, our first landfall, has become a yachtsmen's Mecca, being one of the only places left on the planet that is totally uninhabited and quite inaccessible. The total Chagos Archipelago is actually scattered over an area of 54,389 square kilometres, with a total land area of only 60 square kilometres. Salomon and Peros Banhos atolls lie to the north, with Diego Garcia, the largest island, to the south across the Great Chagos Bank. The archipelago was first discovered by the Portuguese, and then settled in 1776 by the French, who used it primarily as a leper colony. It became British in 1814, and in 1970 the US began leasing Diego Garcia as a military base.

Today, the only people here are the US military and a handful of British administrators on Diego Garcia, and there are no people on any of the other islands. Since Diego is quite a few hundred miles from the most northern islands where the yachts visit, we never saw anyone other than yachties and coconut crabs. We did receive one visit in the three months we were there: from representatives of the British Navy who stamped our passports.

At its peak, the population of Chagos was mostly Portuguese fishermen and lepers from Mauritius, who were known as the Îlois. At the beginning of the 20th century, there were 450 families in residence who were soon depleted by the spread of leprosy. The islands were then known as "The Oil Islands," named for the oil extracted from copra, the dried meat of the coconut.

When the US took control of Diego Garcia as a military base, the population of all the islands was sent back to Mauritius, causing quite a stir amongst the islanders, some of whom were fifth-generation Îlois. Eventually, after many court battles and human rights protests, the deported islanders were compensated by the British government, but they are still not allowed to return to the islands to visit the graves of their loved ones. As a result of being unpopulated for nearly forty years, each anchorage off the islets has pure white sand beaches overgrown with lush palm trees; it was a real picture postcard of unspoiled splendour. No fishing is allowed in the waters, so the coral is pristine and the fish are abundant.

Laundry day, Bodum, Chagos

Bodum—Situated in the Salomon Atoll—The Island of Ruins

Bodum—an island in the Salomon Atoll—still has some ruins of the last inhabitants, making for captivating exploring. I think what made it more fascinating was the way the jungle had completely taken over the ruins and added an almost supernatural magnificence to the place. Although it was nearly forty years since the last people had lived there, the old wells still provided brackish fresh water, ideal for showering or doing the laundry. All that remained was the front wall of the church, an overgrown graveyard, and an even more overgrown school house.

The inland area of the island had very few ruins; the large palm trees entirely dominated the interior. The only inhabitants were outsized coconut crabs, which have front claws the size of my forearm and stronger than the human jaw. They were evident by the large piles of coconut husks outside their hideouts, and we saw them up close by coaxing them out of their dens with a stick poked into the entrance.

The view from the beach belonged on a postcard: crystal clear water, well-preserved coral gardens, a startling diversity of multi-coloured fish, and palm trees swaying in the breeze. This place really was seventh heaven, and we were delighted to be able to sail everywhere in our dinghy—a little Mirror with a red mainsail and spinnaker that we'd purchased to have aboard—and investigate around the shoreline.

Hunting coconut crabs, Île de la Passe, Chagos

Île de la Passe—The Island of the Colossal Coconut Crabs

The small island of Île de la Passe, situated in the "pass" of the Salomon atoll, is rarely visited and has the largest population of coconut crabs that we had ever seen. The jungle was more dense here, but a glade had already been cleared. We adopted this glade as our base camp for a few weeks. Our group consisted of Mercedes and Ronan (English and French), Kevin and Sue (South African), Tommy and Sandra (German), and ourselves. We made a good amalgamation of diverse desert island skills, so we pooled our resources to share the major meal at our encampment every day. Tommy was an exceptional fisherman, and always had a good catch of coral trout, red snapper, or grouper. Sandra was an extraordinary bread maker, baking in a cast-iron pot on the campfire by stacking hot ashes on the lid and around the pot. Every day, she came up with a new recipe: fresh coconut, onion bread, garlic bread, and more. Mercedes made the most inconceivable ginger beer, of a quality that I still can't reach, despite having her recipe. Ronan was dependable for the larger fish catch, yellowfin tuna, by trolling with his dinghy. Sue had a hoard of remarkable pickled vegetables, and was the best at sprouting mung beans for the salad, while Kevin made some really mean brews with orange peel and anything else he could get his hands on.

Graeme and I became the "pub," offering interesting fruit wines, made from a bag of out-of-date dried fruit, and rice wine, which I had become quite the expert at brewing. Graeme became the authority on harvesting the heart of the palm: the only fresh vegetable, apart from sprouts, available to us. We really enjoyed this time together, and it holds fond memories for us all.

Mercedes and Ronan, Tommy and Sandra, and
I enjoy being onboard Khulula at Île de la Passe.
Ronan shows his injury from a triggerfish.

Takamaka and Fouquet—A Visit by the "Millennium Round the World Yacht Race"

The two most strikingly beautiful islands in the Salomon group
were the sites chosen for the "Millennium Round the World
Yacht Race" beach barbecue. I think all the yachties at Salomon
were surprised to see four identical sixty-five-foot racing boats
anchoring for a few days' R&R, obviously stocked up with cold
beer, meat, and probably fresh vegetables. Everyone made it
clear to them that our diet of fish, rice, coconut, and homemade
wine could be supplemented with a few of the luxuries on
their boats in exchange for our island knowledge. We showed
them how to recognize and harvest drinking coconuts, eating
coconuts, and heart of palm, and how to find the coconut crabs.

We also supplemented their barbecue with fresh fish of all
varieties, lobster, octopus, and squid. We were invited aboard
Spirit of Diana for roast lamb dinner the following day, much
to our delight, and left with multivitamin tablets, a bottle of red
wine, and what was left of a large bottle of scotch whiskey.

Peros Atoll—The Impenetrable Islands

Much quieter than Bodum, Peros Atoll was larger, but has a restricted number of wells and very little sign of any habitation. Most of the islands were impenetrable because the palm trees were so dense, but still offered the same beautiful, clear waters and marine life. One morning, we woke to find a large manta ray with a two-metre wing span swimming around the yacht. For over twenty minutes, we watched it elegantly gliding and somersaulting for our entertainment. From the sea, whichever island on whichever atoll looked pretty much the same as the rest, other than the density of its palm-trees: very flat, with bright white beaches and crystal clear turquoise waters.

Excerpt From Letter to Bea: May 18th, 2000

The islands are so beautiful and abundant with birds and fish and coconut palms and coconut crabs; these are pre-historic giant crabs that feed exclusively on coconuts that they break open with their huge claws. I have never seen anything like it! We went hunting with friends that we met up with again here, Ronnie and Jenny (whom we originally met in Tanga). Jenny is quite incredible; she is Thai and like a little monkey climbing trees to harvest the coconut—completely fearless. Also, she just stands on the back of a crab, grabs its huge claws, and ties them with palm leaves to immobilize them, then marches it straight to the beach fire. Absolutely delicious!

Ronnie and Jenny also showed us how to harvest heart of palm, which is a wonderful crisp white vegetable, a cross between a radish and white cabbage, and makes a very tasty salad. It is the base of the palm tree and you have to keep trimming the husk to get to the heart. You get quite a large heart from a small palm tree and it is the only fresh vegetable you can get on the islands. We still have onions, garlic, and potatoes that we bought in Kenya, but, as it is six weeks since we bought the tomatoes, they need using quickly now for cooking and the potatoes are going quickly, too. Still, we can catch plenty of fish and crab fresh every day. It really is quite a life living on a desert island and we feel very privileged to be here.

By the time we left we had learned so many island survival skills that we would have no problem competing in those survivor series they have on television. Graeme was often seen marching into the jungle, machete in hand, to hunt a coconut crab and chop down a young palm tree to get to the heart of palm. We also feasted on quite a variety of fish from line-fishing off *Khulula*, as well as lobster (usually speared by someone else).

We were invited along one day to watch some other yachties spearfishing and I found the whole experience quite frightening! The sound of the spear in the water attracts sharks and they will happily circle around while you hunt for the fish or lobsters. I had already been warned about the sharks and told not to panic under any circumstance, but to either ignore them or growl or be aggressive toward them. Well, when one of the spears found a large grouper fish, one of the sharks decided he wanted it for dinner and chased the swimmer to the surface! I'm afraid I panicked and starting splashing in the water to get back to the dinghy! Jenny came to my rescue and I nearly drowned her struggling to get out of the water! Everyone found my reaction quite amusing, but at least I distracted the shark away from the swimmer! Needless to say, I didn't go along to watch the spearfishing again. There was an incident a few years earlier when a spearfishing yachtie lost an arm to a shark. I heard the tale told around the fires and just assumed it was one of those fishing stories; now I wasn't so sure!

I even collected clams on the beach, small, but very tasty! But we soon ran out of the fresh vegetables we brought from Mombasa, and our only other vegetable was bean-sprouts, which were ready every two or three days with continuous sprouting of the mung beans we bought in Africa. They made an excellent salad with the heart of palm and onions and garlic, which we still have. As the weeks went by more and more bartering took place amongst the yachts, some trading cigarettes for garlic, beer for rice, or flour for salt. It made for an interesting barter market over the VHF radio every morning. Coconuts were aplenty and we learned which were best for drinking (young and green and usually still on the tree), and eating (older and usually fallen). A delicious meat can even be found in the sprouting coconut.

I continually brewed and *Khulula* became quite popular for our varieties of home-made wine. I managed to produce eighty litres from one kilo of dried fruit, which was definitely the best! My other specialty was rice wine, made from rice, sugar, and yeast with a handful of raisins. Each yacht had its own speciality. We met an English girl married to a Frenchman who made the most excellent ginger beer. Mercedes and Ronan became good friends and we were sorry to go our separate ways. They arrived from Thailand enroute to Africa, so we had lots of stories to swap. The last few weeks we were in a group of four yachts and the eight of us met every day for communal meals. It worked very well as everyone produced one dish, so there were four dishes each meal to share.

By the time we left, the sea was a lot cooler and, with days of rain, there were fewer opportunities to snorkel and swim. That was a shame, because the coral was quite spectacular.

Addu, Maldives, Indian Ocean

Eventually, the change in weather and lack of provisions alerted us that it was time to move on to the next leg of our journey across the Indian Ocean to Thailand, but first, we took a small detour north to Addu in the Maldives for a little limited provisioning and refueling with diesel.

Excerpt From Letter to Bea: June 15th, 2000

It's incredible that Addu (the most southern atoll of the Maldives) is only three hundred miles further north of Chagos, yet considerably hotter. We're really pleased to be exposed once more to shops and the little luxuries like fresh eggs, vegetables, and chicken, which are really special.

The people are very friendly, mostly Sri Lankan and East Indian, working in the four textile factories here, one of which is a Victoria's Secret. We've made friends with the cafeteria management who cater all the meals for thirteen hundred employees. Tonight, we are invited for dinner. They have also offered us the use of their bicycles so we can visit some of the other islands in the atoll. They look quite beautiful, but thirteen kilometres to the furthest island is a bit too far to walk (that would be twenty-six kilometres in one day), so we'll try the bikes and see how far we can get.

We were very impressed by the islands we visited; each was connected by a causeway to the main island with the factories. The streets were spotlessly clean, with the little yards in front of each small house freshly swept and tidy. The children waved and smiled, and the adults shyly acknowledged us with polite greetings.

We only visited two of the other islands, because we were so distracted by another little store we found that sold frozen buffalo; also, they had just received a new shipment of fresh vegetables. We didn't have enough cash to buy all the fresh produce we would have liked, so we proposed a trade for some of the canned produce we had on our boat. They were very pleased to make the exchange, and we agreed to bring canned vegetables to exchange for apples, oranges, and potatoes. Each day, we walked to the island with another backpack of cans and exchanged them for fresh produce.

The rules and regulations were quite strict on the island,

the people being austerely Muslim, and the locals did not like to be seen socializing or spending too much time with "the white boat people." In fact, the one evening we convinced the cafeteria management to visit our boat for a return meal, we had to sneak ashore in the dark to collect them from the beach, because it was declared illegal to visit a foreign yacht.

Second Excerpt From Letter to Bea: June 15th, 2000

We are both very well, although we were conscious of the fact that our diet in the last three months has lacked a lot of vitamins and minerals you get from fresh vegetables and meat, also rainwater lacks the minerals you usually get from groundwater, so that doesn't help (but it tastes so sweet). We were fortunate that the Millennium Round the World Yacht Race called in at Chagos. They were all British and very kind to us, donating vitamin supplements and a very nice bottle of red wine. We're not sure which we were more delighted with! Obviously, the wine is long gone, but we're still taking the "one-a-days."

We're stocking up for the journey to Thailand—we expect it to take a couple of weeks—so I'm busy again bottling meat. We should be able to get cabbage and potatoes to see us through, and maybe some fruit for the first few days, but it doesn't keep. We'll probably be in Thailand by August. We're both really looking forward to a different culture and seeing some three-dimensional scenery after these flat islands!

The Indian Ocean—Second Leg, Maldives to Thailand

This time, I thought I would keep myself occupied at sea by writing a daily diary, which I could then send to all my friends and relatives when we arrive to give them an idea of what it is like being at sea for long periods of time.

We calculated our distance to Thailand by using an early, handheld GPS instrument called a plotter; it gave us our latitude and longitude and we then plotted our position on our charts and used a ruler to figure out the distance yet to travel.

Diary Excerpt: July 12th, 4:00 p.m.

We have 1,583.94 miles to travel from Maldives to Phuket in Thailand. A perfect sea and a perfect sail! After some delay leaving the island of Gan in the Addu Atoll in the Maldives, we're on our way!

If sailing were like this all the time, we wouldn't want to worry about how long it will take to get anywhere. It's truly beautiful with a cooling breeze, a gentle swell, and just the sounds of the sea. We were delayed by our anchor getting fouled on an old anchor chain on the seabed and, having spent six hours yesterday trying to retrieve it ourselves, we eventually had to pay for a diver— $40! That leaves our funds at the grand sum of $150 for arriving in Thailand! Hopefully, money will meet us there from England, but we're told it's cheap in Thailand anyway, so I'm sure it won't be a problem!

Diary Excerpt: July 13th, 9:29 a.m.
Khulula Crosses the Equator!

We're bombing along at 8 knots with a 30 knot wind and no rain. We didn't see a sign or a dotted line or a join mark at the equator, and we've crossed from winter to summer, so where's the sun? You'd expect something to mark the crossing at the middle of the earth, wouldn't you?

Diary Excerpt: 5:30 p.m.
Same Day—1,487 Miles to Go

Lying ahull in the rain, again. The same thing happened last night at about the same time—no wind—so you put the sails away; then comes gusting wind. You say, "Sod it, I didn't want to get wet anyway."

Anyway, it's dinnertime. Tuna curry tonight and last night buffalo stew, compliments of my busy bottling while in Addu. Quite marvellous, bottled meals. Who needs tins or refrigeration? I've bottled buffalo, chicken, fish, soup, and curry. I'm just adding a few vegetables (potatoes and cabbage because they last best), garlic, ginger, onions, herbs, and spices.

Presto! We're actually eating better at sea than we did on land! I got the idea from another yacht, a posh one whose inhabitants made meals, froze them, and then whammed them in the microwave at sea. But hey—that's the normal way, and *Khulula* has its own bottling and brewing factory, so who needs gadgets? Other than the pressure cooker, of course!

Diary Excerpt: July 14th 10:30 p.m.
1,390 Miles to Go

I'm writing in the moonlight on watch. The sky has cleared and the wind has gone completely, so we've been motoring most of the day and probably will for most of the night. We saw a really beautiful 360° sunset from flaming reds to purples and pinks. The almost-full moon looked like a bright white ball against a cerise sky. The sea is so tranquil, the colour of gunmetal; it reflects the moon and the colours of the sky like a mirror with not a ripple to spoil the picture. I had a baking day today, so we had fruit scones with homemade mango, apple, and strawberry jam and our last tin of cream—yum, yum! We've got English muffins for breakfast (or watch snacks), which take less time to bake than bread (and we only have half a bottle of propane to last us, so gaseasy meals are important).

We both managed to do some reading today and both enjoyed fresh water showers (compliments of all that bloody rain). All we need now is some wind! Thank God for the diesel we bought in Gan. It was a wise decision to blow the last of our money to fill up the tanks (five hundred litres), so we could motor through the doldrums until we pick up the trade winds. Bobbing and drifting can drive you nearly insane when you haven't got the luxury of motoring (like the Mombasa-to-Chagos passage). Sailing, though, is much more comfortable (you don't get slammed so much by waves), so the sooner the winds blow again the better.

In case you didn't realize, we don't have autopilot, so we hand steer 24/7, along with various techniques to enable me to write at the same time (i.e. steer with the feet, tie the wheel if the boat is balanced). We take turns to be on watch. Usually Graeme does three hours and then I take over for two hours to allow him to sleep (and that is every twenty-four hours continuously). For this passage, though, we made some new rules: if there is no wind and we're tired, we go to sleep and let the boat drift. If it's squally and horrid outside, we close the hatch and let the boat drift. If we both get really tired and there is wind we "hove to"—setting the sails for a controlled drift. After all, what's the rush?

Diary Excerpt: July 16th 3:40 a.m.
1,291 Miles to Go

We've been drifting since I came off my last watch at 12:30 a.m. We had a good day sailing all day and the wind died on Graeme's first watch. We motored until 12:30 a.m., then decided there was no use driving when we could be sleeping! Graeme still stayed up on watch though, keeping a lookout for ships, etc., because we don't have radar. If he sees we're in any danger, he can always change course by starting the engine. A really huge container ship passed close-by yesterday morning. It is evident that we are in shipping lanes at the moment.

We were rewarded with a royal dolphin show last night,

just before sunset. They are attracted to the bow-wave of *Khulula* and play a dare game, diving across the front of the boat as it crashes into the waves. These were particularly playful, small with long noses and tri-coloured bodies (lightest on the belly). They are called "spinners," because of the way they leap really high out of the water vertically and then spin several times in the air. They played with us for a good twenty to thirty minutes and then all dashed off, leaping out of the water.

Shortly afterward we had a catch on the fishing line (tuna, of course) but unfortunately lost it just as Graeme was trying to land it. It's not easy when you're sailing along trying to land a catch two metres from the waterline. A real shame, since we seem to have mastered the art of tuna biltong—sundried and cured tuna—great, tasty snacks. Our recipe recommends soaking small strips of raw tuna for twelve hours in soy sauce and coriander and then hanging them up in the sun and wind for two days to dry, then munch—yum, yum! Oh well, maybe another time.

It looks like the wind is on its way back, so I'll give Graeme another half hour to make sure it's blowing consistently, then we'll set off again.

Diary Excerpt: July 18th 3:45 p.m.
1,039 Miles to Go

Hooray for the trade winds! We're really making good progress now.

After a couple of frustrating days in Sri Lankan waters seeing nothing for days on end and enjoying the solitude, we suddenly had far too many frequent visits from Sri Lankan fishing boats. These were big, ugly, loud wooden boats that made a beeline for us and tried to scrounge cigarettes, beer, or anything else a rich white yachtie would have! They come really close, holding up fish, and coconuts, which they want to exchange for "white" goods, and they won't go away until some trading has taken place.

On one occasion, we had three racing toward us to see who could get the closest and do a trade. Nice enough chaps, but you can do without the open market at sea! However, we did exchange some of our valuable possessions for a big yellowfin tuna (which is now drying in the sun for biltong) and a packet of lemon-puff biscuits! We were only 120 miles off Sri Lanka, so it did get quite busy! Now, we seem to have passed the main fishing grounds so, hopefully, no more visitors!

This is great sailing, 7 knots in the right direction. Only problem is it can get quite tiring and it's bloody hot. We've rigged a shade but it's still scalding!

Diary Excerpt: July 19th 7:15 p.m.
927 Miles to Go

We are definitely in the trade winds now; the only problem is being physically able to sail for twenty-four hours at a stretch! It's pretty tiring on the helm in good winds like these, so last night we tried to get the most out of it by doing a 2:1 watch—I get the two-hours' sleep, one-hour watch; Graeme gets the one-hour sleep and the two-hour watch. It worked until about the third watch around 3:00 a.m. when we were both suffering from sleep deprivation and short tempers. For tonight, we've decided to take the night-off, at least until our bodies tell us they have caught up on their sleep.

The moon is coming up later each evening cycle and it's not due tonight until 9:00 p.m. It's pitch black outside, but I found that once my eyes adjust, the stars get quite bright. We're still in shipping lanes—we're south of the mouth of the Bengal Basin—so we have to keep a watch all night. At least, we're not on the helm so we can write and read.

The sea in this area is quite strange, olive green, really a very dark green. I've never seen a sea like it. We've sailed over five thousand miles at sea and have only seen the bright blue variety, so I wonder what could be causing it to turn green? We did wonder if it's air pollution from India. We have seen some very strange colours in the sky and the moon with four or five halos of green and pink! However, we have been told that the sea in Thailand is emerald green, so what causes that? Still, I'm sure emerald green looks much nicer than olive green.

It makes us think: we're so out of touch with the rest of the world that there could be nuclear fallout on land and we wouldn't know about it. Imagine arriving on land and yachties being the only survivors in the world. We'd survive pretty well with all the provisions we carry (usually enough for a year's supply of tinned food and staples), but what a shock it would be to arrive on land and find that civilization had died out.... Mmm, the things you think about at sea ... they remind me of a movie.

Diary Excerpt: July 22nd 5:40 p.m.
683 Miles to Go

We're still making good progress, but both very tired! We've taken to stopping whenever we both feel we need more sleep and this tends to mean around twenty hours underway a day. We've now put the clocks forward one hour; we thought it was about time as it was getting light in the morning around 4:30 a.m. and, being at sea, we can decide for ourselves when to change the hour. We will need to put them ahead another hour before arriving in Thailand (Greenwich Mean Time plus seven hours).

The sea has returned to its beautiful crystal blue (it's particularly beautiful at the moment). We're both really looking forward to getting back to land and things are beginning to run a bit short. It looks like all the tank water has gone, so we're on our emergency 100-litre deck water now. Propane gas is likely to run out in the next day or so, half a tub of margarine (which is okay, because we can't cook bread with-

85

out propane gas and anyway there is not enough flour left). Sugar is down to half a tub, but there are still 15 litres of home-brew (ginger beer and pineapple wine), so our "spirits" are still high!

Diary Excerpt: July 26th 7:00 a.m.
304 Miles to Go

We're both extremely tired and fatigued. Days and nights have blurred into light and dark. We're so tired that if we're not steering, we're sleeping. There is no time for anything else, because as soon as it's your turn for a break from the helm, all you want to do is sleep! We're both looking forward to sleeping more than two hours at a time! No opportunities now to stop and rest, as we're constantly having to keep watch for the busy Straits of Malacca traffic.

We've passed so many really high container ships. The size of some of them is quite incredible; they're like small islands! One particularly large one we passed close by at night actually cut its engines to let us pass, since we were travelling so slowly. Fortunately, sailing vessels have the right-of-way, so if ships are in our path, they have to change course (which most tend to do rather than stop). We do hear stories of container ships that keep a poor watch and run down a yacht without even knowing they've done so.

We also met another yacht at sea, the first time ever, so we motored over to say (shout) hello! They are also on the way to Phuket, although they are making better progress than we are. Their rig is more suited to this wind, which is blowing mostly from behind; their sails are goose-winged to catch the wind. We've not spotted them since, so we're calculating they are presently further east and north, and will certainly arrive before us. They did throw us some old bread, which we were quite grateful for since we've now run out of propane gas and sugar, and are down to 80 litres of water.

Graeme is trying to be very inventive with food by creating combinations you can cook in a flask of boiling water; instant potatoes are proving to be very popular. We have an electric kettle that we can boil when we switch the engine and generator on, so it's quite a task every time we want to boil the kettle!

We are expecting to see land today at Sumatra, and then it's into the busy Straits of Malacca, which we will cross to get to Phuket, Thailand. The straits are notorious for busy shipping and horrid weather, so we'll see what it has in store for us! So far we've been very lucky with the weather. This being the rainy season for Thailand, we expected lots of rain. None so far, touch wood. I expect once we get closer to land, we won't be so lucky! You can already see the clouds building, so it won't be long before we're sitting in the rain on the helm!

We have both said we will not do another long ocean passage without auto helm (or extra crew), whatever the cost! Hopefully two or three more days and we'll be in the land of eight-hour sleeps, cold beer, and decent food!

Diary Excerpt: July 28th 1:40 a.m.
142 Miles of Torture to Go!

This is really horrid! We are in a patch of very turbulent sea, which is bashing *Khulula* around so much we cannot steer under sail or motor; it's really frustrating. We've still been pretty lucky with the weather but the wind is now "up the bum," which is impossible for us to sail on. Seems such a waste of good strong wind, but it only sends us in the wrong direction, so we keep having a break. Graeme is asleep and I'm on watch until 2:00 a.m. We had anticipated arriving first light Saturday morning, but that won't happen if we don't start making some progress!

Diary Excerpt: 4:45 a.m. Same Day
Still 139 Miles to Go

We've covered three miles since 1:40 a.m. How's that for progress? Now, we've got the weather as well! High winds and squalls!

Diary Excerpt: July 29th 8:50 p.m.
11 Miles to Go!

So close and yet so far away! After a very exhausting night of hourly watches on the helm to make the most of the squally wind, it was touch and go whether we would make the anchorage before nightfall. We made the decision at 3:00 p.m. to abandon all hope. Despite only being fourteen miles offshore, we had no wind and were only achieving a pathetic 3 knots (making it four and half hours to our destination). The entrance is not that easy, with reefs and shallows, so we don't want to navigate in the dark. We're hove-to, drifting toward land, and we'll plan to sail at first light. It's extremely frustrating being able to see land and all the goodies that await us and not being able to get there!

We virtually have no food left (at least food that we don't need to cook) and yesterday, the engine decided to stop working, hence the reason we can't motor to our destination. So we can't even boil a kettle! Graeme had a tin of cold vegetable curry for dinner, straight out of the can, but I couldn't face it and decided to wait until we get to land tomorrow!

Diary Excerpt: August 3rd
Anchored in Ao Chalong, Phuket, Thailand

To finish the tale, it took even longer to get to land than we expected! We rested on July 30th, and set off again at 3:00 a.m. on July 31st. The wind died and then changed direction, which meant making land was extremely difficult since it was blowing us away from shore.

We eventually dropped anchor at 5:00 p.m. that day, exhausted, frustrated, and ready for that beer! It had taken us twenty hours to complete the last eleven miles without an engine, so the warm welcome, a great meal, and several cold beers were very much appreciated, before settling into our first full night's sleep for seventeen days!

Never again.

✒ Reflections From 2015 ✒

I don't think I realized the significance of the solitude of water during the thirty-five-day Indian Ocean passage at the time. Julia Cameron quotes in The Artist's Way: "Until we experience the freedom of solitude, we cannot connect authentically."

I could not have said that at the time, but I identify with this new self-expression, and it has certainly stayed with me to this present day. I was aware of being in the moment and really living each moment. Time stretched to the point where I was unable to escape myself. These vivid moments are still with me today: the white bridge of the Milky Way, the phosphorescence and the flying fish, the colour of the ocean.

I believe this experience contributes to my ability today to be very present. People comment at my workshops on how present I am. In conversations, I am in the moment, and this is reflected in my personal distaste for cell phone calls that take people away from the person they are engaging with; they seem so intrusive.

I believe this period of time in transition really contributed to my desire in the present day to create community. Community is very important to me, and this represents my choice to live in a marina environment in a float home. Water people are different, because they have presence and they value community.

In my publishing business today, I make it a priority to create a family of authors who collaborate and support each other in a career choice that is usually associated with the proverbial lonely writer.

~

Indochina

✤ Chapter Five ✤

Land of Smiles and Sea Gypsies

"There are two choices. You can make a living or you can design a life."
Jim Rohn

Phuket—Our First Landfall

Ao Chalong, Phuket, was our first landfall in Thailand, and the thing that struck me more than anything else was how hilly the islands were.

They call Thailand the "Land of Smiles," and this I would completely agree with. Following our long, hard journey to get there, the smiling welcome was warm and indisputable. I insisted we set off for shore almost immediately, beckoned by cold beer, fresh meat, vegetables, and cigarettes. This turned out to be no easy task, bearing in mind we had just done a major ocean passage. Our dinghy was lashed to the deck, and the rig was lashed to the safety lines. We only had our sailing dinghy, which relied on wind to push us along, or short paddles when there was no wind. We didn't even have proper rowing oars. It would be an effort to get the dinghy in the water, and then rig it up with the mast and sail, ready to go ashore.

"It's worth the effort," I told Graeme. "There's a little wind, and if we get becalmed, we could always paddle."

"Have you seen how far we are from the shore?" was Graeme's reply. It must have been close to a mile, because this was a shallow bay that dried out.

"I'm not spending another evening without food. Let's just do it."

So we did, and we paddled some of the way. We headed for a

bar/restaurant called Suda's Bar & Restaurant, which had been recommended to us by a couple we met in Chagos.

"They are really yachtie-friendly there, with great, cheap food and beer, fast Internet access, use of the basic shower and laundry, and a cruisers' board for information," Mercedes had told us.

Sure enough, Suda's welcome was incredible. We must have appeared quite dishevelled and had no Thai Baht to pay for anything, but despite this, we were given credit and a warm smile. "Don't worry about the money, we're used to cruisers here who have just arrived from another country and spent many days at sea. Help yourself to anything on the menu and we'll start a tab for you. Welcome to Phuket," said Suda with a big smile.

This ended up being our home base for over two years, and we returned Suda's goodwill many times over when we brought tourists, other cruisers, and guests to her establishment to buy food and drink and pay for the laundry or Internet. This was the kind of businesswoman who knew how to run a successful business, but from her viewpoint, she was just following the Buddhist way of life: giving unreservedly.

Generally, we found this to be the case in the whole of Thailand. Everywhere, we met generous, warm, trusting people who didn't understand the concepts of lying or deceit, bad manners or duplicity. Suda ended up giving us two weeks' credit while we waited for money from the UK, and we could have just sailed off anytime and disappeared, but it didn't cross her mind that we would even consider doing a thing like that.

I once left my purse in the market and didn't miss it until several hours later when someone approached me in Suda's Bar and asked if this was my purse. They had walked over a mile in the heat and headed for the farangs' bar where they were likely to spot the stupid white farang who had left her purse behind. "Farang" is Thai for white person.

And so, with Ao Chalong becoming our home base in Phuket, we started to explore the surrounding cruising ground.

Phang Nga Bay and *The Man With the Golden Gun*

After seeing only flat islands with palm-trees for so long, the high limestone outcrops ringing the South Andaman Sea to the west of us were fascinating. Phang Nga Bay was an incredible inland sea of these outcrops, forming small islands and great sheltered anchorages.

Diary Excerpt: June 14th, 2001

Koh Phanak in Phang Nga Bay is a steep island with a really deep, high cave leading to an inland "hong" accessible at different tides. At high tide, it is necessary to dive under the undercut at the back wall of the cave. It's easy to spot because you can see the light shining up through the water.

Apparently this hong and many others were discovered in World War Two when the planes flew low looking for prisoners of war who hid in the caves. They could see the hongs, because they are exposed to the sky. Apparently, "hong" is Thai for "room," so a hong is a room inside the mountain. This whole area was full of hongs, so we would have plenty of exploring to do. We had a small, handwritten guide of clues of where to find the entrances. This guide was given to us by some other cruisers we'd met in Chagos.

The first time we came to Koh Phanak looking for the hong, I was nervous paddling the dinghy through the cave. It has a high roof and we were soon in complete darkness. All we could hear and smell are the bats. As we entered the cave from the sea, the cave takes a turn to the right, so this then blocks the light from the entrance. You just keep rowing in the dark, using flashlights until the cave dead-ends and you spot the light from the "hong" shining up.

"How do you know how far you have to dive before you come up inside the hong?" I asked Graeme, as he was contemplating diving under the undercut to investigate.

"I don't know, but I'll just feel my way and push myself against the roof until I reach fresh air," was Graeme's brave reply.

He lowered himself into the water, and I watched him disappear through the hole in the cave. An anxious wait inside the dark cave alone was interrupted a few minutes later.

"I got through to the hong, it's a massive inland lake with steep jungle cliffs surrounding it. We'll come back at a lower tide so you can explore it with me."

And that is exactly what we did, when we had some friends visiting us a few weeks later. We entered the cave at mid-tide, which gave us enough water in the cave to row the dinghy to the end of the cave, but it was low enough that the gap in the wall was exposed and we could see through the gap to the other side. This meant I didn't have to dive under the undercut, just swim, taking care not to catch myself on the sharp oyster shells that lined the ceiling.

"Wow, this place is amazing—an inland lake that can only be entered from a cave," I exclaimed.

One of the islands is named after its hong, so it is called Koh Hong ("Koh" meaning "island," so it is an island with a room). This hong—a large inland lake—is reached via a large open cave that you can enter by dinghy from the sea at hide tide.

Diary Excerpt: June 21st, 2001

Koh Hong is one of the most striking hongs we visited for the first time with Liz and Kendra. As we paddled through the large open cavern entrance, the emerald green inland lagoon came into view. It was surrounded by high sheer limestone cliffs from which kingfishers were diving. We tied the dinghy to an overhang, lowered ourselves into the emerald water, and floated, looking up at the blue sky. We swam to the far side of the hong and disturbed a giant water monitor that must have been six feet long; it's easy to mistake a water monitor for a crocodile, but there are no crocodiles in these waters.

There is another Koh Hong in the area, which is also a beautiful setting. This hong is now quite open since the original high cave has been eroded by the sea, leaving two giant limestone outcrops in its place.

Kendra and Bronwyn (crew), and Graeme inside the inland lake of Koh Hong, Thailand

Diary Excerpt: June 29th, 2001

Koh Hong, Krabi, is where we spotted our first "cartoon bird," which we decided was either an extinct species or maybe one not yet discovered. The colourful bird had a large head with an oversize beak, which made it look a bit like a hornbill. It was very downy, and vibrantly coloured scarlet and orange with a comparatively diminutive body and petite feet that seemed to defy gravity, the way he was balanced on a twig. After much research we concluded it was some kind of kingfisher, but couldn't place this particular species.

Koh Khai had a fabulous overhang on a cliff face, which created a canopy of stalagmites and stalactites forming itself into an ingenious fairy-tale palace complete with staircases, little castles with turrets, and courtyards. Colossal crystal waterfalls cascade down the cliff front, frozen mid-flow, and shimmer as though the water still glistens.

The first time we visited Koh Khai, it was low tide and we had to use ropes to climb up to the canopy to explore it. It was a tough climb for me and a couple of our friends. We didn't want to rappel back down, so we edged to the rim of the canopy and looked down to the ocean to see if jumping would be a better option. As we all stood on the rim looking down (maybe thirty feet), a monster sea snake surfaced and surprised us with his size. It must have been over five feet long and as thick as my calf. We didn't know they got that big in this area. Unsure what it actually was, we debated for some time before we decided it was safe to jump!

One of the most legendary islands in Phang Nga Bay is nicknamed "James Bond Island," since this was the site where the movie, *The Man With the Golden Gun*, was filmed. It is a steep limestone protrusion that appears to have exploded out of the ocean and literally drips with implausible, external stalactites covered in thick green vegetation.

Since Thailand only issues thirty-day visas, we had to leave every month to renew our visas. Most yachties seem to see this as an annoyance and tend to hang around Malaysia instead, which issues two-month visas. We found the visa limit a great opportunity to compel us to explore new islands and hidden lagoons, and to spend time in the crystal clear waters and abundant coral gardens that aren't that close to Phuket. Some of our favourite places in this part of the world are on the "visa run," so we always looked forward to having to leave!

Long-tailed boats used for tours at Koh Phi Phi

Islands on the "Visa Run"—Koh Lanta—Muslim Floating Fishing Village

Most people are familiar with the beaches on the West Coast of Koh Lanta, but few visit the small Muslim floating fishing village on the southeast corner of this island; we did. It was a really beautiful floating village, bursting with flowers and complete with inland banana plantations. The people were really gracious. Each walk through the village to buy a fresh chicken or the fishing catch of the day or to just watch the children playing was most enlightening.

Koh Muk—the Emerald Cave and Lost Land of *Jurassic Park*

This was the most incredible hong accessed through a striking cave given the name Emerald Cave. The sun reflects on the water inside the cave, illuminating it and giving people the appearance of their bodies glowing when they swim through it! The cave itself has amazing stalactites and stalagmites dripping from the ceiling and walls in iridescent apricots, greens, yellows, and ambers. The light was at its best when the sun was low and the tourists had already gone home.

We swam through the tunnel and as we approached the bend to the left, everything went utterly black. We couldn't see our hands in front of our faces, but we kept swimming. After only a few seconds of darkness, we saw the bright light of the hong directly in front of us. We swam to the exit cave and emerged into what I thought looked like the lost land of *Jurassic Park*. This enclosed lagoon had a white sand beach and gargantuan vegetation that belonged in a completely different era. The shrill drowning noise of the cicada insects inside this hong echoed against the sheer walls, and gave a unique aura to the place. Each plant had grown enormous, unspoiled by human intervention.

The first time we visited Koh Muk, I was petrified about swimming in the pitch black, but one of our friends swam with me, holding my hand the whole way.

Another time we visited and jumped off the yacht into the sea to swim to the entrance, and swam into a mass of jelly fish spawn. They were not poisonous, but it was like swimming through jelly. It was a very disconcerting experience.

Koh Rok Nok and Koh Rok Nai—Home of Christmas Tree Worms

Koh Rok Nok and Koh Rok Nai are actually two islands; we anchored between them. The water is crystal clear, and the coral is quite diverse, particularly with the strange polyps that reminded me of the little multi-coloured lemmings I used to display around my computer. They are actually called Christmas tree worms, so the real name is just as good. They are all very vivid colours like orange, scarlet, and neon blue, and they seem to have little ornaments that make them twinkle.

We usually get a really good deal from the fisherman there, once landing a large bucket of tiger prawns, squid, and two large coral trout for the equivalent of less than three dollars.

Some of the many backpackers working crew on the ten-day visa-run trips from Thailand to Malaysia

Koh Bulon—Phosphorescent Swimming at Night

Koh Bulon is a small island with one very small bungalow development and not a lot else. It has exquisite beaches, white sand, and clear waters. There was very little ambient light from the shore, so it was a great place to go night snorkelling in the phosphorous. With no moon, the whole sea sparkled as we swam in the dark water; it felt like we were swimming through the stars. We even "speed snorkeled" by dragging a rope behind the dinghy and holding onto it while we snorkeled in the sparkling water.

Koh Butang—Tarutao National Marine Park

Koh Butang is a tiny island that didn't seem to get any visitors, has no inhabitants, and boasts the most incredibly varied coral gardens I have ever seen. I can only describe snorkelling off this island as soaring over a rich rainforest with visibility so clear, I could see the "forest floor" itself. The coral was so high in places, with visibility up to 30 metres, that I felt I was viewing a mountain range. Each way I turned, I discovered a new plant, species, or colourful fish. I was particularly in awe of the huge sunfish—shaped like a giant multi-pointed starfish—which must have been three feet in diameter and neon blue and black.

The next island is Koh Lipe. It has a couple of small bungalow developments right on the beach with a choice of three or four restaurants. The restaurants put their tables on the white sand beaches where we could watch the sun go down and eat under the stars. It was a fine, carefree, tranquil island with clear water and dazzling white sand. Visitors can take a walk over to the other side of the island and stroll around the traditional Chao Ley (sea gypsy) village and watch the residents building wooden, long-tailed boats for fishing, weaving traps, or mending nets.

Koh Adang—Home of Pirate's Falls

This was the neighbouring island. It had a striking forest trail that we ascended up to the precipice, where the views of the Butang Atoll are breathtaking. There was another trail up to Pirate's Falls, which used to be really beautiful before they dammed it to provide fresh water to Koh Lipe. That's progress for you. On the west coast, the beaches were pure white sand, absolutely bare except for huge boulders that dominate the beach. They were quite spectacular to see and fun to clamber over. The panorama there was very similar to the Similan

Islands of southern Thailand, which are also dominated by their gigantic boulders.

Chao Ley Sea Gypsies in Koh Phetra, Thailand

Koh Tarutao—The Largest Island of the Fifty-One-Island National Park Tarutao Archipelago

The densely forested former penal colony of Koh Tarutao had many walking trails leading to streams, pools, and lookouts. The scenery was breathtaking in the rainforest, with many strangler vines hanging in twisted shapes. There were many species of wildlife, but this was the only place in Thailand we came face to face with a large, aggressive wild boar. The other islands, particularly the Butang group, lived up to their national park status with stunning coral reefs that look like forests from the surface.

We once anchored there, only to be moved on by a large dinghy whose crew claimed to be filming a survival game show. They told us they had the authority of the Thailand government to ask yachts to move on if they thought we might provide an easy way out for the competitors on the island to get luxury goods or even a ride. We compromised and moved to an anchorage that was further from shore, but we dragged anchor because the anchorage was not as good. We guessed this island was remote enough to provide a good base for the television program, especially since wild pig could be on the menu. I recently saw the third series of *Lost*, and I swear "Jack" used that same beach of Koh Tarutao when he was in Thailand.

Koh Kradan is now known as the "love island," since eighteen couples got married here under the water on Saint Valentine's Day. I'm not sure if this happens every Saint Valentine's Day, but the island seems to be quite famous for it now.

The fish there were amazing, and the little tiger fish constantly nibbled at my toes as I swam through huge schools of them. I was completely surrounded by all varieties of fish when I swam, so I can see that it must have made a great scene for a wedding.

Mu Koh Phetra—Bird Nest Island

Also known as Bird Nest Island, Mu Koh Phetra is a very steep island that had only one place to land our dinghy. We had heard that the sea gypsies (Chao Ley) who live here can be quite belligerent and territorial about their birds' nests, and it was not recommended that visitors go ashore. Birds make their nests high on the steep cliffs from their spittle, and the Chao Ley risk their lives to harvest the nests on a strict seasonal rotation that allows the birds to continue nesting there. The nests are sold as a delicacy and served as Bird's Nest Soup in high class restaurants.

We did visit the Chao Ley on the island and they made us very welcome, showing us an example of the birds' nests and trading a large fish for two packets of cigarettes. They did, however, make it quite clear that we should cook and eat the fish on our boat and not on the beach. This was communicated with the help of sand drawings since we could not speak Thai and they could not speak English.

Another Money-Making Opportunity

One of our priorities when we reached Thailand was to find a way we could make a living without compromising our lifestyle. We had taken paying crew to Madagascar and for the millennium in East Africa, so we decided we would use this as a model to design a life. There are many charter companies in Thailand and Malaysia that offer luxury exploration of the many islands, providing staterooms with all the amenities people would expect in a hotel, maid service, and dining under the stars. These companies are all licensed by the Thai government and provide all the necessary insurance and health standards you would expect. We were not competing with these people. We were not even running a business (that would be illegal); we were simply inviting adventurous travellers to join in with our lifestyle and experience everything we would experience.

As paying crew, their contribution would pay for their food, bed, maintenance of *Khulula*, diesel, propane, and water. We calculated the cost to cover all expenses incurred and only did ten-day trips or more, so that they could truly appreciate this way of life. They played a completely active part of the daily boating requirements, from helping to provision (we would go down to the market en masse and buy several weeks' supply of fresh food) to cooking, cleaning, and boat maintenance. The only additional money we made on top of this was from the later introduction of a bar, since we soon realized it wasn't practical for everyone to bring their own liquor aboard. We kept an "honesty tab" and crew simply paid for what they drank.

Whenever a special occasion came up like Christmas or New Year's, we would invite friends to join us and pay to be crew instead of spending their money on a package holiday. We often invited backpackers we met, but were always mindful to not compromise our way of life. We were sharing our home with relative strangers for ten days at a time and, with mixed personalities, this could easily lead to disaster in a small space.

We joked that crew had to pass "the test" before they were invited, but neither of us could really define what the guidelines were; we just both had a sense for good people. I still email many of these crew today: Philly and Dan from Ireland, Ronald and Cathy from South Africa, Ellen and Joyce from Holland, Kim from Vancouver, Glen from the US, Tom and Annabelle from London ... we have all lived our separate lives for over five years, but still keep in contact.

Ronald and Cathy were inspired by our lifestyle and now get away when they can and hire a bare boat to cruise alone. Tom and Annabelle ended up buying a yacht in Thailand when they got off our boat and continued their travels west on that vessel and sailed up the Red Sea. Only a few weeks ago they sent me a funny story of their voyage from Greece via the French canals back to the UK, where they left their boat in storage. So we touched people's lives, showing them a different way to live.

For Christmas, December 2000, we decided to take a trip north close to the Burmese Islands and, with a mixed crew of six, we experienced the unique Thai islands of Surin and Similan.

The Surin Islands—Nomadic Sea Gypsies from Burma

This marine national park is the Thai island group closest to

Burmese waters, mostly uninhabited except for a few park rangers and nomadic sea gypsies. The Surin consist of two main islands with offshore islets and rocks with many sheltered anchorages. As was the case with many of these Thai islands, we really needed to visit a few times in different weather conditions to truly appreciate all they had to offer. However, our first visit was over the Christmas period and we couldn't have chosen a more isolated paradise to celebrate in. It had white sand beaches with the consistency of fine flour, clear turquoise waters, and stunning coral gardens. On Christmas Eve, we watched the sun set on a secluded beach with a fallen, sun-bleached tree providing our "cocktail seats." I think it was so extraordinary just because we were the only people there to share a special moment in a truly beautiful place.

Koh Surin Nod—Christmas Day

We spent Christmas Day in the larger bay of Koh Surin Nud enjoying its glorious, extensive white sand beach backed by abundant vegetation. A few locals challenged us to their version of Hacky Sack, played with a small hard woven plastic ball and the only rules being that you have to keep the ball in the air using your head, shins, or forearm. The locals obviously don't bruise as easily as the farangs, since we all found it pretty hard going.

Graeme returned from the yacht with homemade Pina Colada (coconut cream, fresh pineapple, and Thai rum), which we sipped lying in the sea with an inflatable drink holder. A perfect day. Once the Christmas festivities were over, we set sail south for the Similan Islands, reputed to be one of the top dive sites of the world, and therefore, frequently visited by dive operators.

We had some of the best sailing we've experienced in Thai waters, a fairly consistent northeasterly wind blowing 20 to 25 knots and occasional gusts to 35 knots to add a little excitement. Since *Khulula* is a heavy boat, these are perfect conditions for her.

Similan Islands—One of the Top Dive Sites in the World

This group of nine main islands with rocks and islets derived its name from the Malay word "sembilan" meaning "nine." The Similan Islands are a popular dive site even though they lie sixty miles north of Phuket and can only be visited in the northeasterly wind season, from November to March.

After the privacy of Surin, we all felt a little crowded when we arrived at Koh Similan and struggled to find a bit of solitude. However, the snorkelling definitely made up for this and we mostly managed to avoid crowded waters. We found a small bay first thing in the morning opposite the main anchorage on the most northern island (Koh Bangu), which turned out to be an exceptional snorkelling site. There, the colossal boulders that litter the shorelines, finely balanced one on top of each other, also lay in chaotic heaps beneath the water to depths of 35 metres. Soft coral and tropical fish of every conceivable colour, pattern, and size created vast walls of colour that we swam through.

We moved further south to Koh Miang and found a lovely spot in turquoise waters backed by gigantic boulders. The water clarity was such that it was difficult to believe the depth sounder, which was showing thirty feet. Not trusting the instruments, I jumped in the water expecting to see the keel close to the bottom, but instead I was surrounded by thousands of brightly coloured fish that were suddenly attracted to our boat. I had never seen such a variety of fish in such a small space. The large triggerfish, with their strange bulging eyes that look as though they are halfway down their bodies, seemed to be the leaders of the school. I shouted to everyone else to jump in and it felt like we were swimming in a very crowded aquarium. We spent two days exhausting ourselves with snorkelling before we moved further south to Koh Huyo, the most southern of the Similan Islands to celebrate New Year's Eve.

Koh Huyo—New Year's Eve 2001

It suddenly felt like we had returned to the Surin Islands. Again, we were on our own, and what a fantastic place to ring in 2002. The long white powdery beach was completely empty—four miles of emptiness—and, with its palm trees and scattered boulders, it really was a picture postcard. As the evening progressed, we were treated to the most magnificent moonrise. The gigantic orange globe crept out of the water on the horizon: a sight not many had previously witnessed.

Before the moon rose higher, I urged everyone to jump in the inky black water with their snorkels and masks to witness the phosphorescence. The waters in Thailand were particularly good for seeing this phenomenon on dark nights, and the waters around Koh Huyo were particularly spectacular.

I'd like to describe it through Philly's eyes because this was her first time: "It was like swimming through the stars, like millions of tiny fireflies in the water."

We all had great fun diving down and watching the glowing bodies as we disturbed the phosphorescence.

Phuket—Vegetarian Festival of Body Piercing

We had heard stories of the vegetarian festival that takes place in Phuket town and decided to visit to see for ourselves. The festival is based on a religious fasting period where the Thai are not allowed to eat meat or take part in any other gratification of the flesh in training for a meditative pageant of ghastly body mutilation. The theory is that the fasting and the period of meditation allow the devotees to mutilate their bodies with large spikes without experiencing any pain. They then carry these spikes through the streets in procession.

The grisly demonstration held no bounds on the imagination, and many devotees had long spikes that went through one cheek, into the mouth, and out the other cheek. Other attendees supported the weight of the spike at each end, because it was decorated with whole pineapples and watermelons. Other devotees pierced their faces with everyday items such as a satellite dish, a child's bicycle, and a flag pole. The most macabre sight was the self-mutilation by axe of the tongue: the devotee walked down the street with his tongue stuck straight out and carved it back and forth with the axe. His attendees tried to stem the flow of blood by constantly dabbing his chin and neck, yet his ceremonial apron was still soaked red. Another devotee wielded an axe in each hand, swinging it over his shoulders to an imaginary drumbeat, while taking big slices of flesh out of his back.

I found the whole display quite distressing and had to take sanctuary in one of the many food stands with a cold drink and a sit down before I fainted. I didn't return the following year to watch this festival nor recommend that anyone else visit.

This festival has nothing to do with Buddhism, but instead has some strange significance in the animalistic religion and the power of mind over matter.

Phuket—Songkran Festival

This water festival is full of "sanuk," which is the Thai word describing everything that is fun and enjoyable and gives pleasure. It celebrates the coming of the rainy season and is celebrated by everyone throwing water over everyone else. During this time, I learned not to wear anything that I did not want to get wet in public, because we were guaranteed to get water thrown over us. If we were riding a motorcycle down the street, someone would step off the curb with a bucket of water and throw the whole bucket over us. If we were on a tuk tuk (a three-wheeled motorized open Thai taxi), other people on the road would throw water into the tuk tuk. Even at the market, everyone was throwing water around with giant water pistols, buckets, and even hose pipes. I found it was best to get into the spirit of things, rather than to avoid getting wet. It was a good opportunity to cool off in the hot climate.

Malaysia—Langkawi

Langkawi is a beautiful Malaysian island, very close to the Thai border, and well worth a couple of days' motorcycle hire. There were many stunning anchorages away from it all at the north end of the island—at Hole in the Wall—so named because of the relatively narrow entrance to the mangrove forest from the ocean. Hole in the Wall is actually the Kisap River, on the northeast coast of Langkawi.

Once inside Hole in the Wall, we found we could explore the many branches of the mangroves by dinghy. The various waterways led to little known caves, home to bats; we viewed these at close range. Some of the caves had been enhanced to make access easier, while others seemed less accessible. Exploring the mangroves in silence rewarded us with spectacular sightings of fish eagles, brahminy kites, various monkeys (watch out for the spectacled long-tailed macaques as they forage for crabs), colourful kingfishers, hornbills, and giant monitor lizards.

We were fortunate enough to watch an entire family of spectacled long-tailed monkeys running along an old electric wire strung across the water. Despite our shutting off our engine so we didn't startle the family, the monkeys panicked as they saw us below in the water and started to scamper across the wire hastily. It was a real scene to see the monkeys falling off or catching themselves with their long tails before they fell in the water. One mother was dangling by a hand and tail with a very small baby clutching her chest. We watched in dismay as the baby lost his grip and tumbled into the water below, screaming all the way. The mother instantaneously let go of the wire and dived into the water after her baby. In the meantime, the audience of the other monkeys on the shore was making an implausible racket, pointing and screaming at the baby in the water. A large male launched himself into the water from the bank and started to swim anxiously toward the mother and baby, while the baby coughed and spluttered and swam to the family on the shore. I had never realized monkeys were such good swimmers, but they obviously don't choose to go in the water unless they have to.

We felt quite culpable that we had led to this catastrophe, but all the monkeys got safely to shore and then screamed at us from the trees for causing the calamity. This was another example of how our presence had disrupted the delicate balance of nature.

Maidens Lake

Situated on Telok Dayang Bunting, the freshwater lake Maidens Lake is reputed to be high in minerals and have healing qualities. Certainly after ten days of saltwater, we were pleased to see it. Our clandestine access was via an old timber staircase that climbs the lowest point of the mountain and back down to the lake. It was worth the exertion to have the solitude of that end of the lake, out of sight from the new tourist jetty.

The emerald green lake was enclosed by steep jungle, and the sounds of birds and frogs rebounded off the water. We spotted many monkeys in the branches and they were quite used to the tourists who handfeed them. We also visited a catfish pond that was tightly packed with giant black catfish, their whiskers sticking out of the water. The tourists were encouraged to sit on the edge of the pool and put their legs in the water so that they can be tickled by the catfish as they swim around their feet. It was quite entertaining to watch everyone shrieking when they did this.

On the same island is an interesting cave accessed through the mangroves by foot. We climbed deep into the cavern through water sometimes waist high and the ground was a little slippery. Graeme later explored further into the caves with the stronger members of our group to find three large caverns accessible through hard climbing and bat-dodging! Needless to say, I did not attempt that one.

Other anchorages off the surrounding islands provided tranquil beauty with steep rain forests, fantastic sunsets that lit up the limestone outcrops, and plenty of sightings of giant fruit bats, which erupted from the roofs of the rainforests as the sun dipped into the sea.

The Ideal Life?

We easily settled into life in Thailand and Malaysia. Every six weeks, we did a visa run to Langkawi in Malaysia, taking paying crew who were usually backpackers. We would make enough money to maintain *Khulula*, buy fuel, food, and drink. These were our only expenses since the boat was paid for and we anchored for free instead of staying in marinas. We had no insurance and we provided our own electricity, refuse disposal, and propane gas for cooking; therefore, we had no taxes or bills to pay.

It seemed that things couldn't get much better since we didn't want for money. *Khulula* provided a lovely home and we had a constant change of scenery and new guests to alleviate boredom.

Life was idyllic, or so I thought, until Graeme calmly announced one day that he didn't love me anymore and would like me to leave *Khulula*. We had been sleeping apart for some weeks because of the hot climate and I was feeling very "unloved." I knew he was avoiding talking about our new sleeping arrangement, so I eventually asked him directly if he still loved me. This was the answer I got.

I did not see this coming. I saw no other "signs" other than this change.

My idyllic life suddenly fell apart and I was homeless, penniless, jobless, and stranded in Malaysia. Of course, this wasn't exactly the case, since Graeme wasn't so cruel as to force me to leave until I had decided where I was going, but my pride and a broken heart made me want to leave as quickly as possible.

James Bond Island, Phang Nga Bay, Phuket

🥀 Reflections From 2015 🥀

I have fond memories of my time in Thailand and Malaysia, and looking back, I know this was largely due to my growing sense of purpose. During this period, I started to find my own purpose in being of service to other people. We were introducing our backpackers to a new way of life lived without material belongings; we were teaching them the importance of community.

As I reflect back now, I see that I treated these guests with the care of a mother, managing their quarrels and upsets in a confined space, as well as tending to those who suffered from seasickness. I believe it was this experience of leading a community that armed me with the skills I use today while I mother my authors who are giving birth to their own books.

Reflecting back on this time on *Khulula*, I realize I had started to really try and understand what my "purpose" was. I was the leader of a community; everyone always said how positive, helpful, and compassionate I was when we took charter guests on our boat. Always mindful of the small space we were living in, I rallied around, organizing their cooking and cleaning duties, encouraging them to all eat together and to try "new" things. I was always on the lookout for those "firsts." I helped several people overcome their fear of the sea and even helped several nonswimmers to snorkel using life jackets. I was always "the Scout Leader," leading a group to hike to the waterfalls or swim through a cave. I encouraged group discussions about living a different type of life, and I even helped a British couple buy a boat so they could live their dream of sailing the ocean before starting a family.

The heartbreak I felt when Graeme ended our relationship was just as much to do with this loss of purpose as it was to do with the loss of my partner, my home, and the lifestyle. I did not realize it at the time, but I was completely reliant on Graeme. This was not healthy, and this parting was a significant time in my life when I discovered my own personal style of self-expression. As Julia Cameron writes in *The Artist's Way* "In order to have self-expression, we must first have a self to express."

This was clearly not going to happen in a co-dependent relation-ship.

Chapter Six

The Second Enlightenment

"When men come to like a sea life,
they are not fit to live on land."
Samuel Johnson

Contemplation in Inland Malaysia and Northern Thailand

I had no idea what I should do. It had never occurred to me that I wouldn't be with Graeme for the rest of my life, living in Thailand and Malaysia or wherever *Khulula* happened to sail.

"Why don't you go backpacking?" asked Graeme. "It would do you good to be on your own for a change and it will give you time and space to decide what you want to do with your life."

It seemed very strange that my best friend was giving me advice on how to cope with my breakup from my lover, who happened to be the same person. No wonder I was so confused.

"Well, I guess I could try it for a short time and see how I like it. I could go to Penang first, since we've been there before so at least it is familiar. I could go to the Cameron Highlands and visit the tea plantations that Kendra and Elizabeth told us about."

And so this was the beginning of my lone travels, in the hope that I would discover a new life, without my best friend, my great love, and my loving home, *Khulula*.

It may have appeared I was taking this in my stride, which was the mask I was trying very hard to wear. My pride would not believe that this was really happening to me. I felt like I had been thrown overboard. I had sacrificed so much to go on this life journey with Graeme, and now he was calmly announcing he wanted to continue it without me. It seemed like I was living in a movie set or something; this could not have been real life. I had nowhere to go, no job, no home, no friends, no family, and certainly no Plan B. I was also in Malaysia.

My first trip alone to Penang was a very tearful one as I watched *Khulula* at anchor disappearing, even as my ferry picked up speed. I had spent so much time living on a boat that it was going to seem very strange sleeping on the land in foreign beds. I'd always hated being alone and here I was more alone than I had ever been, and suffering from a broken heart with no friends or family for support.

I just swallowed back the tears and put myself on autopilot. I really had no choice. All I could think of was running away and escaping from the hurt I felt every time I looked at Graeme and *Khulula*. As the ferry slowed down for the port of Penang I wiped away the tears once more and put on my brave travelling face.

Penang is a bustling multicultural town with heavy English, East Indian, and Malaysian influences. The streets have huge open drains where the giant rats dash in and out, and garbage is strewn everywhere. The men always spit openly in the street and the pollution of the public buses is awful. Of course, I'd been here before with Graeme, so I knew how to dodge the spit, the open drains, the rats, and the garbage by walking on the road and avoiding the many hand-drawn rickshaws.

I headed for the main part of town that my guidebook advised was the backpackers' area and secured a single bedbug-riddled cot in a small dark room with no windows on a street called "Love Lane." How ironic!

It was pretty different from *Khulula*, I'm telling you.

This was obviously not the place to be when I was feeling lonely and sad, even though I tried for a few days to visit the local temples and attractions alone. I sat most of the time with my head buried in the guidebook, drinking cold beer, chain-smoking, and trying to figure out this backpacking game. I decided to head for the cooler mountains of the Cameron Highlands and the famous English tea plantations. It was pretty simple to arrange the bus once I decided to go there, and the following morning my transfer taxi was waiting to take me to meet the bus.

As soon as the bus started to wind through the mountains, immediately, I felt better and started chatting with some of the locals on the bus. Once I arrived at my destination, I headed for the particular backpackers' lodge I had chosen from the guidebook and started to explore the area. I was surprised how many single travellers there were, so I quickly started conversations and didn't feel so lonely. I was actually a bit of a novelty, since most were gap-year travellers, a good ten years younger than me, so they liked my stories of living on a sailboat. Then I met a lone female traveller from California, a few years older than me, so we joined up to visit the tea plantations together.

Cameron Highland hill tribe children, Malaysia

One of the ideas I had was to find a new career, but my heart wasn't really in it and I was just marking time. I walked the hotels and hostels in the Cameron Highlands, hoping to secure a job in this breathtaking area with its wonderful climate of cooler mountain air and the rich green fields of tea. I loved the locality with its multicultural Indian and Malaysian food, dense rain forest jungle, and fun backpackers. I soon discovered, though, it was not that easy to work in a foreign country without a work permit, despite the heavy English influence in this area.

That first trip lasted three weeks before I rang Graeme from a phone box and begged to return and discuss our future. I just wouldn't believe that this was what he really wanted and secretly hoped he had missed me. It became apparent, though, that Graeme wanted a permanent split, and so I planned to make the most of a bad situation by returning to *Khulula* and packing a bigger backpack to visit all the inland destinations I had heard all our backpackers discussing when they were aboard *Khulula*.

One of the many temples in Penang, Malaysia

I had never travelled alone and that short trip had shown me it wasn't so bad. It was the best plan I could come up with until I figured something else out, anyway. I needed some kind of distraction to stop the constant tears and the heaving of my heart. Staying close to *Khulula* was not the answer, because that hurt even more. I wanted to prove to Graeme that I would not be beat, that I was strong, and that I would survive without him. My short-term plan was to visit inland Malaysia, Northern Thailand, and then continue on to Lao and Cambodia. I had no time scale and limited funds; Graeme had agreed to let me have all the money we had left in the bank and to borrow $10,000 from a friend to give me as my share of *Khulula*.

I just hoped that at the end of this time I would have a new life plan.

The only thing I knew for sure was that I could not return to England to live with my mum and dad to listen to them say, "I told you so." It would have been like returning home with my tail between my legs.

I headed across Malaysia to Taman Negara, a dense jungle area whose name means "National Park" in Malay. Originally, it was the King George V National Park. I decided to take a three-day hike into the jungle. A Malaysian guide, Bok, assured me he would help me out if I struggled with my back and he even lent me some sturdy hiking boots that another backpacker had left behind.

I set off with two other lone female backpackers who were going on the same trip: Martine from Singapore and Anya from Germany. I soon realized that single travellers always tend to join up so that they're never really travelling alone.

On the way to the jungle in Bok's car, we stopped at Lata Rek and cooled down in its waterfall, before arriving at the jungle base camp where we prepared for the first trek to the animal hide. Bok set off in the lead, carrying everyone's camping gear and food, while we three girls followed behind. I was almost surprised that he kept his bargain seeing as he was quite a large lad with plenty of extra weight, instead of the usual hiking guide image I had imagined. He was a jolly fellow though, happily walking along at a good pace loaded down with all our packs and telling us all about the National Park and the local hill tribe people of this area.

Tea plantation, Cameron Highlands, Malaysia

Diary Excerpt: June 5th, 2002
Beware of Jungle Leeches

Thank God for the socks I bought and the wise move to tuck my trousers into those socks! Thank God for the hiking boots that Bok provided; hiking in my reef sandals would have invited the leeches to a party! Martine attracted a really big leech that was frantically trying to burrow itself inside her skin. Bok reacted hastily and grabbed the leech by the tail, just before it disappeared; we were all aghast at the sight.

He then took the cigarette he was smoking out of his mouth and burned the end of the tail of the leech; it let go instantaneously. First lesson of the jungle.

We arrived at the basic hide, which had a number of cots and an open wall at one end from where we were supposed to spot the animals. Bok announced we were going on an evening hike through the jungle, which I quickly declined, being terrified of leeches I couldn't see and of the dark! This meant I had to stay behind alone, but I still preferred this option to trekking out there in the pitch black! My heart was pounding, watching them disappear into the jungle, each with a small flashlight.

I was left alone in the hide and was instantaneously bombarded by giant insects attracted to my candlelight; I shone the light around and spotted giant ants large enough to carry me away! The black ants are honey ants and have large honey sacks on their backs; Bok says they are very tasty, so I decided not to be intimidated by them. I decided they must have felt way more scared of me.

Since I'm alone, I'm overwhelmed by the sounds of the jungle. So many diverse songs of insects, frogs, and birds, all in competition to make the loudest sound! Despite the "jungle DEET" I'm wearing, I'm definitely being eaten alive and it's really hot and humid. I'm sweating like a pig and although it's 8:30 p.m., it feels hotter than it did in the day.

Now it's really dark and I mean black, and the girls are out there somewhere. I'm just watching a striking moth, which I mistook for a small bird because of its size, and it keeps rebounding off the ceiling, spellbound by my candlelight. It is so large that it makes a reverberation like a hammer and when I shine my flashlight onto it, it glows bright orange near its mouth, but has a pure white furry body, and quite plain brown wings. It must be at least twelve inches across in size. There is a really adorable frog on the wall, which makes an exquisite sound and I remember from the exhibition at the base camp that this is a flying frog. I have never felt so aware of nature; I don't seem to be afraid of the dark anymore.

Bok left something cooking on the camp stove and it smells appetizing. Surely they should be back by now? It's almost 9:00 p.m., so they've been gone more than an hour. I wonder if they got lost. They said they were only going for a twenty-minute walk to try and spot the phosphorescent mushrooms and any night animals around and I'm beginning to feel a little concerned.

One and a half hours later, two very exhausted girls trampled back to the hide clutching the glowing mushrooms in their hands, which really were quite spectacular, glowing bright orange and yellow. They said they looked miraculous on the jungle floor. I was still glad I didn't go; they both said they were worried about the leeches and the walk was much longer than they'd anticipated. Martine had borrowed a pair of my socks so she could tuck her trousers into them and she said she was really glad she had, since it was too dark to spot any of the little monsters.

This morning, we had a lovely walk over a suspended rope bridge hanging thirty metres (about ninety feet) in the air from the canopy floor. It was not a place for anyone who suffered vertigo to try, particularly as it swung considerably as you walked on it. I loved to see the jungle from this height, viewing the tops of trees, instead of the trunks, and watching the colossal beehives that hang from the treetops, their honeycombed surfaces buzzing with activity.

The tallest variety of tree in the Malay Peninsula grows in this variety of rain forest jungle—the tualang. It stands at 173 metres tall (that's over 500 feet tall). On the rope bridge, I was looking at trees 60 metres tall (180 feet), and that seemed really imposing from where I was standing. I can only imagine the tualang. It only flowers once every ten years, and it loses all its leaves, all at once, every year. Regrettably, because of the infrequent flowering, the tree is now threatened with extinction, since it established in a cooler climate that is now considerably warmer—the last ice age did not affect the Malay Peninsula but it did lower its temperature. The base of the tualang has high buttress roots for support, and because its root system is not deep, many old trees are rotten and hollow inside.

Suspended rope bridge with Anja and Martine,
Taman Negara National Rainforest

An enchanting, if short, river trip was another highlight, although our canoe struggled upstream against the small rapids. Bok skillfully steered us to a natural gravel sand bank that created a deep water pool we could bathe in. After making camp and building a fire, the girls set to making dinner over the campfire. The fishing was unsuccessful, so Anja and Martine created what they could with the dry ingredients that Bok carried. He had set up a small tent for us all to sleep in, but it had the effect of creating a greenhouse, so Anja opted to sleep in her sleeping bag by the fire on the beach, while Martine opted for the hammock, strung up across two trees.

I opted for the tent, which was not very comfortable since

I had to lie on the hard ground—I hadn't thought to bring a sleeping mat—and use my backpack as a pillow. By morning, a swarm of bees wanted to make my tent into their new hive and it was quite a dash to open the flap and escape before they swarmed inside. Apparently, it was the honey season and lots of bees were around; the constant buzzing was really irritating, as opposed to terrifying. I used to be terrified of bees, but, again, accepting nature banished another of my previous fears. I didn't let them stop me from performing my morning duties and, after I had dug a hole for a makeshift toilet, I took a cool shower in the river.

For our return journey back to the base camp, we built rafts out of bamboo poles and drifted in the current down the river. I got the impression the poles had already been trimmed and cut to the exact size required, so all we really did was tie them together. It was a wonderful way, though, to complete our trip into the jungle.

The Perhentian Islands—Snorkelling Guide Extraordinaire

From Taman Negara, I continued across to Malaysia's east coast and caught a ferry to the Perhentian Islands. I walked the beach with my heavy pack looking for accommodation that I could afford and soon discovered that many backpackers worked on this island in exchange for shelter, food, and sometimes tips. Without too much trouble, I secured myself a job as a customer service coordinator for a small resort that catered to Kuala Lumpans on four-day trips from the city. The deal was that I got free accommodation and food in return for greeting guests and organizing any leisure activities for them.

After a couple of weeks, I also became the snorkelling guide, working with parties of forty-plus nonswimmers. The workload started to get really hefty, considering I was getting no pay. I brought in another couple of backpackers to help me, on the same deal, but it became apparent pretty quickly we were being taken for a ride. It was nice to stay in an air-conditioned room, but the food was not that good and we hardly got any spare time to benefit from our environment.

One thing was that I did get a lot of pleasure from watching the giant monitors that visited the kitchens every day to be fed scraps. From the safety of my balcony, I was fascinated to watch these six-foot-long crocodile-like lizards eating the scraps. I often escorted guests across to the other side of the island and saw many of these giant monsters lying in the shade of a tree or under a hut, which I—as tour guide extraordinaire—would point out to them.

On the way over to the other side of the island, people had to walk through an area of dense jungle where the trees overhung the path forming a kind of ceiling. If people looked up into this ceiling, they would see giant black spiders hanging from their webs just above their heads. Women backpackers who had been happily walking down the path, not looking up, would erupt in screams when someone pointed upward. This usually happened when we were halfway down the path so that the women couldn't quickly escape. It was always fun to point them out to my guests as part of the tour of the island.

I Plead to Be Urinated On

The job came to an end when I had an accident on one of the snorkelling trips; this alerted me to how badly organized this resort was. I was accountable for over forty nonswimmers, despite not being such a strong swimmer myself and having no lifesaving skills. We were trying to track a couple of giant sea turtles. We spotted the turtles and I jumped into the water to follow them while the boats with the other snorkelers followed me so everyone else could jump in and watch the turtles. I was so intent on following the turtles underwater that I didn't realize I'd swum into a giant pod of jellyfish. I was completely covered in the finger-sized jelly fish, which immediately injected me with their toxin. As I thrashed around in the water trying to get the jellyfish off—they had stuck to my skin all over my face, neck, and body—a boat picked me up and dragged me out of the water. It wasn't my boat, but one from another resort.

No one had vinegar, which immediately neutralizes the toxin, so I was shouting for anyone to urinate on me, as this has the same effect, but no one would. In the meantime, I was going into shock and imploring someone to urinate in a jar or container so I could use it to neutralize the toxin. Everyone was too embarrassed to help me and didn't realize how ill I was. All they did was drop me at the nearest resort to try and seek medical help.

At the resort, no one knew what to do and so I asked for directions to the kitchen and shouted for vinegar. Eventually, they understood what I wanted to do with the vinegar when I explained to them how it neutralizes the toxin. It took me over a week to recuperate from the welts all over my face and body, and this is when I decided the job wasn't worth the pay. I'd spent enough time on the islands anyway, so this became a good opportunity to force myself to move on.

Even though I was now on the east coast of Malaysia, it wasn't that far away to enter Northern Thailand via Hat Yai. In fact, it seemed quite common for people to take this route, so I wasn't short of other lone backpackers for company.

Diary Excerpt: July 11th, 2002

As I left Malaysia, I made a note to remember how helpful the Muslim men were when they saw me struggling with my backpack. In Thailand though, you don't even have to struggle, because they actually anticipate that you need help! Back in the Land of Smiles, I stepped off the ferry at Satun and saw a big welcoming sign "Welcome to Thailand" with small words underneath—"Except Drug Traffickers"—which always brought a little smile to my face. I always wondered if thieves and murderers were, therefore, welcome, too.

I didn't need to worry about how I was going to get to Hat Yai or carry my heavy backpack that I couldn't actually carry alone. As I dragged it off the ferry, I dumped it, knowing it would be safe, and went to check in with immigration. A motorbike taxi approached me and asked in broken English, "Where you go?"

"To Hat Yai," I replied.

"No problem, I take you to bus," and with that, he grabbed my large backpack and grinned at the surprising weight as he launched it onto his shoulders and led me to his 100cc moped. He somehow balanced the huge bag between his knees, resting his chin on the top of the pack so he could see the road, and I delicately sat side-saddle with my other bag on my knee. You must ride side-saddle if you're a female wearing a skirt; plus, it is very impolite for a woman to sit astride the pillion of a motorbike taxi, so I had become quite an expert at the art.

Both of us finely balanced, we trundled off for the twenty-minute ride, which cost me less than a dollar. He chatted along in his broken English, asking me questions, as my legs, which were dangling with no foot support, began to numb. He took me to the minibus stop and unloaded my big pack, pointing to the minibus, which was just about to leave. My timing was really tight and they wouldn't let me on that bus, because my bag was too big and the last seat had just been sold.

I was devastated. I was in the middle of nowhere, my only friend, the motorbike taxi, had already left, and if I missed my connection for the train, I would miss the night train I was planning for my overnight accommodation. I pleaded and I begged, not realizing all the seats had been sold, until a Thai lady stepped forward and handed me her ticket. I was amazed. She just smiled at me and said, "Take ticket, I wait, you miss train."

I carefully put my two hands together and made a low bow, the traditional thanks, which also showed her I understood she is "making merit," a religious practice for improving karma in Thailand. Even so, do you think someone in Canada or America or England would do that?

I got to the train station with ten minutes to spare and there was a queue at the ticket booth. A couple of Western girls turned to me and told me the train for Bangkok was booked solid for the next three days. The next three days!

I approached the ticket booth and prayed they could somehow squeeze me in. They had only one first-class ticket available and I didn't have enough cash to pay for that— it was double the cost of the second-class ticket. I quickly looked at the two Western girls and asked them if there was an ATM machine nearby. They said, yes, there was. I left my bags where they were and ran to the ATM to get more cash. It would cost me more than the difference between the ticket prices to stay in Hat Yai for three days so it was worth it.

By the time I returned, the ticket lady had already instruct-ed a guard to put my bags on the train and she quickly took my money, pointing at the guard who was running down the platform with my bags. I followed him and he took me directly to my first-class carriage. You don't tip Thais; they are insulted by it because they are doing their best for you anyway to make merit, which is much more important.

I'd paid for first class, so I had high expectations. When I was shown the cabin, I smiled to find a young Thai woman with a sick baby covered in spots. Oh, no!

I went to get some fresh air and chat with the conductor who told me all about his family and then inquired where my husband was. How many children did I have? How old was I? We chatted about Buddhism and he was soon plac-ing his hand on my thigh and planning an evening of Thai whiskey on the train! I was given coffee, invited to share his dinner, and learn all there was to know about this sixty-two-year-old conductor!

As he got increasingly friendly, I decided it was a good time to retire to my cabin (with a lock) for a short rest. I headed for the dining car, dodging all the Thais gambling and laughing, and realized even the second class carriages are really loud tonight. It was probably a good thing I was in the private first-class carriage, even though I was sharing it with a spotty baby. At least I'd get some sleep! Thai babies do not cry, not even when they are ill; babies only cry for attention.

It's now 9:30 a.m. Everyone has been on the train for fifteen hours, some longer. The gambling games are still going on, getting more frantic, the bids higher and higher, and some carriages are completely blocked with everyone crowded around games going on at a table. I quickly counted over 1,000 Baht (approx. $20 US) on a table, so the stakes were now high, but everyone was still smiling and laughing, and covering their tables with shared snacks of sunflower seeds and monkey nuts.

I was using an old *Rough Guide to Asia* to plan my travelling and I'd set myself a budget of ten US dollars per day, including accommodation, travelling, and food. This was quite feasible if I stayed in the cheapest huts and ate street food from the stalls. The *Rough Guide* gave me a good selection of accommodation in this price range. It was also a guaranteed way of meeting like-minded backpackers, because they would be staying in the same places.

I came to love the Thai railway system and found it extraordinarily economical and comfortable. Second-class accommodation usually provided a restful sleeping berth for the long journeys, saving on a night's accommodation at either end of my destination. In fact, it was an experience in itself, watching the porters make up my berth with crisp white sheets and pillowcases.

On the first Thai train journey I ever took, I walked through the cars while my porter was making up my berth. I was inquisitive about the non-sleeping cars in third class, where I found a deafening, confused tone of hilarity and cheer, and I could hardly pass down the corridors crammed with crowds of Thai people, teeming around several tables where ferocious gambling was taking place. It was quite astonishing to see such a good-tempered ambience when so much money was swapping hands; piles of the distinctive pink 500 Baht notes were randomly thrown on the tables. The Thai people do like to gamble and spend lots of money on their national lottery, but they always do it with a smile and geniality. On that occasion, I was glad I had opted for the second-class carriage with sleeping berths, and returned to a quiet atmosphere of Thai families and travellers settling down for a good night's sleep.

Obviously, if the train is full, it is wiser to book the private first-class carriages, as I had on this occasion!

My starting point from which to explore Northern Thailand was Bangkok, and from here I decided to visit Kanchanaburi and the Bridge of the River Kwai, which was only two hours away by bus.

Kanchanaburi and the Bridge Over the River Kwai

Although many people visit because they are familiar with the historical tale of *The Bridge on the River Kwai*, they stay because the surrounding countryside has much to offer. I decided to take a tour with Toi's Tours for around 550 Baht (ten US dollars), which was a fun trip in an air-conditioned minibus with a safe driver.

Elephant Ride Through the Jungle

The first stop was the elephant camp for a forty-five-minute ride aboard a bamboo chair mounted on an elephant. The elephant trainers carefully select the weight of passengers to match the size and age of the elephant, and they treat their animals with great respect. I was riding with Michaela from Jersey, and we ended up with the smallest, youngest elephant, who had a big personality. We giggled as the mahout—the elephant trainer—was trying to convince our elephant to walk through mud. He simply didn't want to get his feet muddy and always screeched to a halt whenever we approached a mud puddle. As we ambled toward the river, the incline was steep, and it was quite difficult to hold onto the back of the chair to prevent myself from falling forwards, but our elephant appeared to be in a rush to wash his muddy feet in the river. The ride seemed longer than forty-five minutes and was very enjoyable. We clambered off our elephant onto a bamboo platform and headed to the river to do some river rafting before we visited the waterfall.

Sai Yok Noi Waterfall

The next stop was Sai Yok Noi waterfall. One of the most impressive I have seen in Southeast Asia, this waterfall is set in lush jungle and cascades from a great height, forming strong falls of water that people can bathe under. I was one of the first to clamber up the rocks to stand right underneath the torrents of water cascading down, and experience the cold water pounding my body. It is quite unusual to be able to get so close to a falls and this is why this place is so special. This is maybe one of the first places I understood my oneness with nature; I recognized that I didn't feel lonely. I decided that maybe this travelling alone was good for me after all.

Hin Dat Hot Springs

We made a short stop for lunch before heading for Hin Dat Hot Springs. As we crossed the river, we got the first sight of two steaming pools set in a tropical jungle: an exquisite paradise waiting to be sampled. We were instructed to first take a dip in the chilly river before plunging into the closest of the natural hot spring pools, which maintains a constant temperature of 35° Celsius. After fifteen minutes, we climbed into the second pool, which at 55° C is like a hot steaming bath. We then repeated the process at least three times. This very therapeutic experience left us feeling exhilarated and rejuvenated for the final part of the day trip to visit the Death Railway.

The Death Railway

The 257-mile-long Thailand-Burma railway started construction in June 1942 and was planned to be the crucial link between Japan's newly acquired territories in Singapore and Burma. With an almost impenetrable terrain and only basic picks and shovels for tools, this rail route was responsible for the deaths of 16,000 Prisoners of War (POWs) and 100,000 Asian labourers by the time it was completed fifteen months later. Thirty-eight POWs died for each mile of track laid and so it was nicknamed the Death Railway. The route is very scenic and the short train journey took us through a ninety-foot cutting through solid rock at Wang Sing and the Wang Po Viaduct, where a trestle bridge nearly a thousand feet long clings to the cliff face as it curves with the River Kwai Noi. The thrill of hanging out the windows as the train slowly crossed the viaduct felt a little like a helter skelter ride as I stared down into the abyss below.

The following day, I attended the River Kwai Bridge Festival of Sound & Light, which celebrates the anniversary of the bombing of the River Kwai Bridge, and watched an open-air theatre group of more than two hundred performers re-enact the story of the POWs, with the help of old news footage showing the actual events projected onto a giant screen of water across the river. It seemed amazing that I was watching a spectacular light and water show in this part of the world, complete with translation headphones so I could hear the story in English. The light and sound spectacular featured some of the latest computer-generated technology with four-dimensional speakers and pyrotechnics including more than two thousand fireworks to mimic planes bombing the bridge and destroying it. It was really well-choreographed with lifelike explosions and bombs falling from the air, leaving the bridge shrouded in smoke.

The cottages where I stayed were set in beautiful gardens; there were more expensive cottages right on the river front, but I was still within my ten-dollar-a-day budget, although the trip obviously exceeded that. From there, I decided I wanted to head further north, so I returned to Bangkok to catch the overnight train for Chiang Mai and the northern territories of Thailand.

The Little Town of Pai
and Sleeping in the Garlic Fields

I had heard a lot about the mountain area of Pai, so I decided to take the two-hour minibus trip from Chiang Mai into that area. It certainly turned out to be an especially peaceful and reflective place, and I slept the first night in a very rudimentary bamboo hut deep in the garlic fields. With no electricity or water and a dreadfully simple mattress, this was one of the cheapest and most humbling experiences I'd had so far.

The following morning I could hear the quiet; the river flowing; the low mumble of farmers planting garlic; the birds, insects, and frogs. I set off back to the main area for a shower and breakfast, and spent over an hour trying to navigate across the fields. When I peered across the fields, each group of bamboo huts looked identical, and it was impossible to tell which group belonged to the farmers, and which had been adapted for the tourists with hot water showers and electricity. I stopped to ask the Thai farmers for directions, and they just laughed and waved in their normal polite manner, directing me to nowhere in particular.

This is an important lesson to learn in Thailand: the people will lose face if they refuse to help or are not able to help a stranger, so it is better for them to point you somewhere so you appear to be grateful and satisfied. This can often mean that you end up more lost than you were before you asked for help, but they gave you help, which meant they had made merit. In my case, they pointed me to a road, which ended up quite a distance from the huts where I was staying.

This concept is also known as Kreng Jai or "awe of heart," which is sometimes translated as "consideration" or "deference," but neither of these words does justice to the connotations of "Kreng Jai." If one is in "awe" of others' feelings, this carries with it an implicit obligation to respect others' feelings. This involves two aspects: the first of which is to avoid imposing on other people, and the second of which is to avoid confrontation that suggests dissent.

The farmers felt this obligation to respect my feelings and avoid confrontation by providing a solution to me. If they had just shrugged and ignored me, they could have possibly incited a confrontation. Kreng Jai is a unique form of Thai behaviour that is also influenced by respect and obedience to elders, trust in their wisdom and protection, and the need to return favours received. The underlying ideas are the principle of mutual dependence and reciprocity and the principle of being practically and morally indebted. It is the recognition that people need each other if they want to go on living. Behaviour is also influenced by respect or fear of the powerful, respect for superiors, and consideration for foreigners, mostly because they are an unknown quantity.

Once I started to spend some time around the Thai people, I began to understand this philosophy more, and it was very evident around families who obviously mutually respected and considered one another. Even small children are never ignored as they are in the Western world. Indeed, the very notion of pushing a child in a pushchair in front of the parents would be unacceptable, since the child is dependent on the parent, and the child is quite alone in the front that way. This is why you rarely see Thai babies or children crying: everyone in the extended family gives each other mutual support rather than using outside services such as kindergartens or nurseries. If a woman has to work, her mother or her sister or even her cousin may take care of her child. In turn, the child is taught respect for superiors and so the tantrums you see so much in the Western world are also absent here. A child is never put in front of a TV or a computer game to occupy it when the parent is occupied. The child joins in with every daily activity, observing its mother folding the laundry or riding on a farming woman's back.

The whole philosophy of life in Thailand is very different from that in the Western world.

The Tranquil Mountains of Pai

Diary Excerpt: November 9th, 2002

The mist lifting from the mountains in the early morning light has a peaceful effect on body and mind. Everyone feels relaxed and tranquil in this environment.

Heidi is peacefully playing her guitar crossed-legged on the bamboo floor overlooking the River Pai; she has discovered her passion for music. Everyone gets a chance to reflect on life here, so it should be a good place for me to stay a while.

That is one of the great things about Pai: you can choose how close you want to be to the locals' way of living. Right next to the huts I was staying in were the beautiful upscale Rim Pai cottages, with individual hardwood accommodations, nestled in the trees with their own private balconies overlooking the river. This was where you'd find en suite tiled bathrooms with flushing western toilets and comfortable beds (and still only for twenty-five dollars a day). Personally, I'd choose the bamboo hut with shared toilets and a simple shower any day. Hot water was supplied by electric heaters, which was most common, but I did see a giant cauldron heated by coals—a novel way to bathe in the open-roofed showering hut. Scooping the boiling water into a bucket certainly involved some careful mixing with cold water before tipping it over your head!

Diary Excerpt: November 19th, 2002

The mist has almost completely lifted from the mountains now, exposing a bright blue sky and a bright warm sun, with a chill still in the air. I'm here in November, which is one of the best times to visit Northern Thailand with warm sunny days and cool nights and mornings. Late November to February is the cool season and March to May the hot season, so I ended up here at the right time.

Exploring the area was easy and convenient; I chose how much I wanted to spend and how I got around. The simplest and cheapest transport was by motorbike for around 150 Baht (approx. four US dollars) a day with insurance. If I didn't fancy doing it alone, there were always plenty of other travellers I could join in with for the day. If time was limited or I wanted to visit with a guide, I could choose from many of the tour companies that offered everything from a five-day trek across the mountains, staying each night in a different hill tribe village, to an elephant trek that ambled through the local jungle. I was lucky enough to meet up with a group of other backpackers who shared the cost of renting motorbikes, so I rode pillion passenger with one of them. Most of the single travellers I met were on a tight budget so there never seemed to be a shortage of people asking around to share costs. I often wondered how different this travelling experience would have been if I'd had a limitless supply of money to spend on accommodation and excursions. I suspect the experience would not be as rich as the one I was having.

Many of the guesthouses supplied giant rubber tires or a simple bamboo raft so that you could drift down the river. Whichever you choose, you are guaranteed to get wet in the chilly water. Pai Adventure Rafting organized trips, which was a safer option given some of the dangerous currents and fast overflows. I got hours of entertainment watching other backpackers getting dunked in the fast-flowing brown water, while sitting on the balcony and sipping cold beer. Many of the backpackers were there for a truly relaxing experience, and there were many natural hot spas where you could stay a few days at the natural hot spring bungalows or Thai Pai spa camping. You could choose an exhausting day of clambering through giant caves and visiting waterfalls, or opt for a traditional Thai massage or book yourself into a course and learn how to do it yourself!

There was so much available in Pai to keep you occupied— learning Thai cooking, reflexology, Reiki, or yoga. I think some backpackers may have forgotten to simply relax and enjoy the special ambience and beauty of this wonderful place.

The huts where I was staying often ran unpretentious Thai cooking classes where a group of backpackers stood around a couple of Thai girls who shared their culinary secrets. I still cook some of my favourite authentic Thai dishes from a handmade recipe book written by one of the Thai girls and translated by a backpacker.

I also attended modest yoga classes held on the high balcony of the restaurant by a backpacker who made money for her travelling by asking for donations (which were plentiful). She easily made enough money for accommodation and food and beer, and probably enough for travelling too, since most people donated a few dollars a session and she attracted around twenty people per session. I did wonder whether I could come up with a money-making activity like this so I could just keep travelling and living this way as long as possible.

I wondered whether I should write a book.

The Hill Tribe People of Northern Thailand

One of the motorbike trips to explore the area took us to visit a remote village tribe of Karen long necks. I was very humbled by this experience and felt really privileged to meet and talk with the tribal women. The villages of northern Thailand's mountain people are home to a number of distinct ethnic groups, the main ones being Karen, Hmong, Lahu, Yao, and Lisu. There are approximately 300,000 Karen in Thailand, making them the most populous minority group. They have lived in the area far longer than any other mountain people, perhaps two hundred years or more, and originated from the neighbouring country of Burma (now called Myanmar), home to more than four million Karen. The Karen hill tribe can be divided into several subgroups, the largest of which are the Sgaw Karen and Pwo Karen. The Long Neck tribe is called Padung, and is divided into two societies called Ee-lu-phu and Kai-phu. I could not ascertain which society wore the brass rings around their necks and which stretched their earlobes with giant rings, but it was very evident in the village that two societies existed. The children of both societies were in mixed classes and were being taught English as well as their traditional language and customs.

Long Necks Wear Many Bronze Rings Around Their Necks From Age Five

Members of the society that wears many tight bronze rings around their necks are initiated from the age of five, with the rings being added five at a time by being coiled around their necks and tightened. Another coil is added every few years until the age of sixteen. A woman I talked to was carrying eleven pounds of rings on her neck and wore them constantly. They clean them daily with lemon juice and wear cloth around the chin area to prevent chafing. They also wear one set of rings on their calves, and one girl was suffering from water retention that caused considerable chafing. The pressure of the weight of the brass actually squashes the collarbones and ribs, and to remove a full stack would cause collapse of the neck and suffocation. They were proud to be carrying on the tradition, although there was no headman pressure to do so. Women not wearing the rings comprised a small percentage, but were evident.

The Padung people are famous for producing the best mahouts (elephant handlers); probably attributable to the fact that the elephant and his handler grow up from childhood together, and the elephant is very much part of the family.

Many of the women weave scarves and wall hangings to provide funds for the village for education and medical supplies. Prior to the intervention of the Thai government, their traditional cash crop was opium. The government intervened with big incentives to encourage cash crops and handicrafts that are more legal. The girls I talked with were weaving and selling their handicrafts; they seemed very warm and friendly with big smiles and were eager to practise their English. I hoped their culture and traditions would not be affected too much by the Western tourists who visit, but it did appear to be controlled by the simple fact that they are difficult to reach.

A Silk Factory

After a few weeks, it was time to move on again and I headed back to Chiang Mai, via minibus, to visit a silk factory where visitors could see the process from the silkworm right through to the dyeing and weaving of the silk. It was a very educational and informative experience, and it is a very important industry for Thailand.

How Is Silk Made?

The silkworm goes through seven stages of its life cycle before it hatches into a butterfly. The first is the egg stage, which lasts ten to twelve days before tiny worms hatch, progressing to small maggot-sized worms within five or six days. By stage five the worms resemble caterpillars and grow for a further seven or eight days, feeding on mulberry leaves, before commencing the weaving of their own cocoons in preparation for transformation. Cocoon weaving takes nine to ten days to complete and, in a factory setting, the progress is monitored closely in order to pick the optimum time to terminate the natural life cycle of the worm by exposing it to light. The cocoons resemble oval marbles of yellow, fibrous material that—for Thai silk—are about the same size as an almond. Japanese silk cocoons are around the same size but slightly rounder and white in colour. The cocoons are harvested by placing twenty to thirty in boiling water to soften the fibre so the end of the yarn can be identified. Each cocoon will harvest between eight hundred and a thousand metres, and is hand spun to uncoil.

Once the yarn has been processed, it is ready for dyeing in giant vats. The many beautiful colours are achieved by carefully mixing the dyes, and for the more complex designs, different colours are alternated across a single yarn. The yarns are then dried naturally in the sun on giant frames. Once dyed, the yarn is hand spun from bamboo spools and either coiled further onto smaller spools or hand stretched across giant frames in readiness for the weaving machine.

Setting up a weaving machine takes a whole day, and as many as 120 rolls are hand stretched in the right combinations of colours to achieve the desired colour or design. It takes four thousand individually threaded yarns to make the basic framework for the machine set-up and each cycle of the bamboo-weaving frame can weave just two hundred metres of four-ply cloth. The weavers work ten hours a day and in that time complete only eight to nine metres, depending on their skill. It is not surprising, therefore, that Thai silk holds such a prized reputation throughout the world for its quality and wondrous colours.

Modern manufacturers have tried to simulate the feel and texture of 100 percent Thai silk, but the real thing is not that difficult to distinguish from artificial silk if the two samples are laid side by side. However, if you really want to test the theory, you can do a simple burn test to ascertain if it is the real thing by holding a lighter to the fabric and allowing it to burn. If it is 100 percent silk, it will not burn and it will smell of human hair as the flame extinguishes itself. If it is artificial silk, the flame will continue to burn and the fabric will smell like melted plastic.

Thai silk is available in three different plies according to its end use.

One-ply is generally used for shirts, blouses, skirts, and scarves;

Two-ply is for dresses, jackets, and trousers;

Four-ply is for suits and upholstery.

The price of silk directly relates to how many yarns are used to achieve the thickness required and the labour required to weave either plain, mixed, or patterned designs.

Chiang Mai, the City of the Hill Tribes

Chiang Mai is a beautiful city. Every day, I saw Thai women busily cleaning the streets with a simple grass brush and a pan. It must have been very satisfying for them, since they seemed to have constant smiles on their faces. The construction workers also seemed to enjoy their work. The women and men laughed and sang while they toiled in the midday heat, dressed in many layers to protect them from the sun and the dust.

The gas station was usually only visited by motorbikes, since this is the main form of transport in most of Thailand, and gas is sold by the bottle, usually in a Sangsom whiskey bottle, the most common way to measure gas out of the large drums of gasoline.

The evening market in Chiang Mai is a colourful, cultural event, a chance for many of the hill tribe women to sell their crafts and the local farmers to sell their produce. As usual, the sight of fresh meat sold in the sun with no refrigeration took some getting used to, but it still didn't stop me from tasting the many barbecues and snack stalls that line the streets with delicious Thai delicacies. I did, however, manage to avoid trying the many deep-fried insects they like to eat in the North. They made for a ghastly display, with giant bugs and maggots alongside grasshoppers.

One option for me to move on from Chiang Mai was to take Thai Airways internal flight to Mae Hong Son. This amazing flight only cost 850 Baht (about twenty-two US dollars) and flew low over the mountains, allowing passengers to spot the small settlements of the Hill Tribe people from the air. The mountains were exceptionally striking, and there were lakes and waterfalls meandering through the passes. Mae Hong Son is also the name of the main province for the area and many of the hill tribe mountain treks start from there.

The town is extremely beautiful, with a large, very ornate Wat (temple), called Wat Jong Klang and Jong Kham. The Wat borders a stunning lake in the centre of town and, in the evening, the reflection on the water shimmers with the many lit candles.

Mae Hong Son is the furthest northwest corner of Thailand,

close to the border with Burma, so now my travels turned east again to Chiang Kong and the River Mekong.

Bamboo sleeping hut in the garlic fields

Long-neck tribe, Northern Thailand

✑ Reflections From 2015 ✐

Living in Thailand for two years gave me a unique insight into a different culture and different belief systems. You cannot gain a real understanding of what this means until you have actually lived it and seen firsthand how it affects the day-to-day life of the people. Thailand is called the "land of smiles," and I certainly never saw road rage, shouting, anger, or aggression from the Thai people. This seems to come down to their Buddhist beliefs about being "reborn." It is important for them to "make merit" so that they return in the next life with a higher status. Their greatest "fear" is to be reborn as a dog, and they believe that if they do not make enough "merit" in this life, that could happen.

What a great philosophy; their whole life is about doing good so they can return and do even more good. I often wonder why the "fear" of not going to heaven in the Christian faith does not have the same effect in that religion. I think it all comes down to learned behaviours of consequence, and what I witnessed in Thailand was a unique way of living that results in happy, loving, compassionate, helpful people.

I easily adopted this way of being, myself, and I think it has deeply affected the way I live my life today.

～

Chapter Seven

Luang Prabang—City of Temples

"Seek and you will find. Don't be willing to accept an ordinary life."

Salle Merrill Redfield

Journey Down the River Mekong

I left Chiang Mai with another lone female backpacker called Linda, also from England, and we spent six tiresome hours on a minibus to Chiang Khong. We had the reprieve of a comfy bed at Chiang Khong before being rudely awakened at 6:00 a.m. by the yapping of dogs and the constant cock-a-doodling of the cocks. That day we would continue our journey to Luang Prabang, Lao, by slow boat down the Mekong River.

A woman I met later in Lao explained to me some of the interesting facts I didn't know about the country, such as the origin of the name. It has been called Lao People's Democratic Republic (PDR) since 1975 when it became independent from French colonial rule; previously, the country was called Laos. These days, the rest of the world still calls Lao PDR "Laos," which is politically wrong. Lao PDR rarely refers to itself as Laos. The people and the language are called "Lao people" and the "Lao language," respectively. It is okay to shorten the name to Lao, but whenever you do this outside the country, you'll find people trying to correct you by saying, "Oh, you mean Laos," with a heavy emphasis on the "s."

It sounded so romantic, to take a two-day slow-boat trip through beautiful countryside down the Mekong River into Lao. The reality was different. We were hustled into the minibuses before we had a chance to finish our breakfast properly, and quickly paid for the sandwiches made up for the trip ahead. Eventually, with all the packs stacked tightly into the van, we took the five-minute ride to immigration to check out of Thailand. Before we knew it, we were loaded into another van for another five-minute journey to the Chiang Khong Port on the Mekong River.

Walking the plank to get on the slow boat going down the River Mekong to Lao

The ferry across to Lao was by long-tail boat, long wooden canoes that use long propellers to drive the boat. The engine is exposed and could be from any type of previously used machinery that required a diesel engine, so they are never the same size and usually result in a noisy ride. These boats are used all over Asia by the fishermen as well as for the tourist trade and are usually decorated with garlands of colourful ribbons and fake orchid garlands, to bring good luck. It is unusual to see a long-tail boat converted for use with a quieter outboard motor, since this is a much more expensive way to run the boat. Besides, "quieter" isn't necessarily "better" in Thailand.

As we reached the shore, we loaded the packs again, hauled them on our backs like donkeys, and trudged up the hill for Lao's immigration and the transfer to the port for the slow-boat. Around sixty people crowded onto an old, long, wooden narrow boat, completely enclosed by a low roof, not high enough for Western people, with open wooden frames for windows.

A full boat

Diary Excerpt: December 2nd, 2002

Everyone jostles for his or her own bit of space, and Linda and I sit straight-backed on a little wooden bench with a plank of wood as back-support. We look at each other and then pick our way through the legs, feet, and packs to check out the seating arrangement at the back of the boat. Mats on the floor somehow seem more attractive, even though we do notice that we've passed the open diesel engine on the way. We spot a crude bunk, which must belong to one of the crew, and decide to be a bit cheeky and climb up into it. What have we got to lose? Our legs are fitted together somehow and we both recline back with our books, giggling. I look down at all the other passengers crowded together on the mats and ask, "How come none of you thought of this?"

We had thirty minutes of pleasure until the engine fired up and we realized we'd picked the worst place on the boat. The noise was deafening from the open diesel, and the room soon filled up with thick blue smoke. As we made a quick exit, hoping there were some seats left further forward, Linda commented on the dead rats floating in the bilge water. The rest of the passengers probably laughed at our situation, now the last people to find seats! We struggled forward, remembering to dip our heads at every crossbeam, but despite the caution, we still nearly knocked ourselves out on more than one occasion.

The front of the boat was more airy and away from the engine, so quieter. We all looked like cattle squeezed together on our little wooden benches, feeling the vibrations of the boat and wilting in the heat. Welcome to the Mekong River. Maybe it used to be peaceful, but not anymore.

These big, noisy, wooden boats ply up and down the river, dodging the fast boats that zoom along at 40 mph, swerving around rocks and shallows. The fast boats are so noisy they give their passengers crash helmets to quieten the noise a little, but also to give them a fighting chance should the boat slam into a rock at that speed. We have six hours in total on this boat before a night's rest, and then back on again for another six hours of torture the next day.

We spend the time chatting to the other passengers on the boat and we meet some other lone travellers who are heading for the same place. Lee is from Canada and she has met up with Jenny who is also from Canada; Julia is from Australia and her travelling companion is Mani (a guy) who is travelling from South Africa. Although we didn't plan it at the time, we all end up travelling together and celebrating Christmas and the New Year in each other's company.

The following day starts early again from Pak Beng, where

we stopped in a guesthouse with bamboo walls so thin, you could even hear the whispers in the room next to you. Last night, Tom (one of the other lone backpackers who has joined our group) read some graffiti on the walls of his room, warning guests to remove food from the room, or otherwise face the consequences of rats visiting in the night. You could hear the rustle of plastic bags as everyone retreated to the outside balcony with their bags of supplies, to hang them on a ceiling nail.

By 6:30 a.m., everyone is up and drinking Lao coffee mixed with thick sweet condensed milk. Some were brave enough to take turns with the cold shower on the chilly morning, while others departed early in the hope of getting the "best seats" on the boat. Some had opted to change for the "fast boat" and run the risks of the rapids and the danger. We'd been told it would be eight hours until we reach Luang Prabang, but yesterday was supposed to be six hours and turned out to be seven, so let's hope another hour isn't added to today's journey. The morning is cold and everyone is wrapped up in as many clothes as they possess or had the forethought to take out of their backpacks.

Diary Excerpt: December 3rd, 2002

We had a delay this morning while they loaded planks of wood onto the boat, slowly stealing more and more legroom from the passengers. Later, we discovered they had not stacked the wood evenly, so the boat heeled dangerously to one side every time we negotiated a rapid. The more seasoned travellers are dressed warmly, sporting earplugs or CD players to drown the sound of the loud diesel engine. The less seasoned ones look cold and miserable.

The scenery is magnificent but difficult to observe with the low windows. Every now and then, we spot a tiny settlement by the river with no obvious road access through the mountains; all their supplies arrive by boat. We stop at a couple of the bigger settlements and the passengers disembark to buy cold drinks served in plastic bags. You soon get used to this Asian way of serving cold drinks—first they put ice, if available, in the bag, and then pour the juice over the ice, pop in a straw, and secure the top of the bag with elastic, a bit like they do at the fair-grounds when they give a goldfish away! You can never be too sure what you are drinking. The usual sodas are sometimes available, but more often than not you will be drinking coconut milk, tang mix, or ice coffee, or something brightly coloured, which could be anything. All the passengers scan the makeshift market stalls for edible food (or food they recognize) while the crew offload supplies for the village from the top of the boat.

The journey in total took sixteen hours, broken by the night spent in Pak Beng. We heard lots of stories from other travellers about their boat experiences, and it seems we must have picked a particularly busy day and a particularly bad boat. Some travellers had the luxury of sitting on low windows with their legs dangling in the Mekong; others lounged with plenty of space, and so it sounds like we had bad luck. I still think the journey was worth it though, to be able to see Luang Prabang.

Luang Prabang—City of Temples

Luang Prabang had one road lined with restaurants and shops, which ran through the centre of the city; the rest of the city was more of a small town with dusty potholed lanes, scattered with stones, and surrounded by coconut palms and banana trees. Hiring a bicycle was a wonderful way to enjoy the atmosphere of the old city. A few of the group hired one for the day and observed young monks walking along in their orange robes and matching umbrellas. The schoolchildren shared bicycles; the passengers on the backs balanced umbrellas for shade and held their long silk skirts, which they wore as part of their uniforms.

Monks at Vat Thamphosi

Diary Excerpt: December 10th, 2002

Within five minutes, we felt like we had left the city as we rode on rough stone-strewn roads with breathtaking views of the lush green mountains. Nestled high on the hill was Pa Pao temple, an unusual Buddhist temple with murals on the walls depicting the atrocities carried out by humans, against humans, before Buddha brought love, peace, and respect. The Buddhist temple on the hill commands incredible views over Nam Khan River on one side and the Mekong on the other. In the distance of the Nam Khan, you can see the sparkling stupa of Wat Pa Pao we visited yesterday, nestled amongst the mountains. As the sun sets across the valley, the novice monks sound the large drums and cymbals adding to the atmosphere as we descended the 322 steps back to street level.

The incredible thing about Luang Prabang is the surrounding countryside and the insight into Lao culture within a ten-minute drive. Hiring a motorbike would be a wonderful way to see the sights, but in reality, the roads are so poor, and many of us travellers bear the scars of the falls we must expect to take. We are responsible for our own safety and in some places the road has slipped down the mountain, calling for some careful navigation.

Our group of seven hired a songthaew (a small open-cabin passenger vehicle with two rows of benches facing each other) and an experienced driver to take us on a thirty-five-kilometre ride through the outstanding countryside to a waterfall we'd read about in our travel guides. Within ten minutes, the road had turned into a dirt track and we were passing water buffalo walking in an orderly line, farmers carrying baskets balanced on poles across their shoulders, and children playing.

The mountains are incredibly enchanting and, as we climbed higher, we crossed small bridges across the river, indicating the waterfall was getting closer. None of us had expectations for the visual smorgasbord we were about to witness. How do you describe such beautiful waterfalls? We literally stopped in our tracks and our jaws dropped in unison at the incredible height of the tiered waterfall cascading through the rich rainforest. The water was crystal clear tumbling into turquoise pools before overflowing to the next pool as far as the eyes could see. We climbed to a vantage point until we could feel the water in the air and sat staring at the magnificent beauty of the water. Looking down into the valley, we could see the sparking green pools shimmering in the light. We clambered down, picking our way across mini-falls, sometimes above our knees in the little pools, sometimes navigating slippery rocks or balancing across fallen logs. The overwhelming beauty of the pools was too inviting to resist, despite the low sun and cold water.

Diary Excerpt: December 10th, 2002

We hung our clothes on a nearby tree and plunged into the first sparkling pool. We swam against the flow, close to the first mini-fall, where the water bubbled and sparkled like a Jacuzzi bath. Surrounded by giant vegetation and bamboo, the spectacle was quite overwhelming. Tom swam to the next overfall and peered over the edge to the larger deeper pool, and suddenly jumped off the edge with a whelp of delight. We all quickly followed, only Linda and I hesitating at the edge before taking the plunge. How exhilarating! We clambered over larger rocks to the next pool that was set in an oasis of smaller falls on each side. In this pool, you could swim toward one of the outer falls, which would then carry you back by the flow. If the sun had not been so low, I would have loved to continue our investigation of the lower pools until they eventually ceased to exist, but our bodies were beginning to shiver, and that told us it was time to exit.

Our songthaew awaited us to start the one-hour journey back. As the sun set, we watched the ever-changing colours as the bright red sky reflected off the mountains. As suddenly as the sun disappeared behind a mountain, the full moon rose spectacularly. We all took group photos of the giant white globe low in the sky and just stared at the incredible scene it painted. As the light faded, the potholed road ahead became a theatre of frogs leaping across the headlights.

Journey to Vang Vieng

Diary Excerpt: December 21st, 2002

As the minivan climbs up to the clear blue skies, the valley below is blanketed in soft white clouds. The tops of the mountains are bathed in morning light reflecting on the blankets below. Small settlements of bamboo huts are nestled on the hillsides and we pass children laughing and waving on the roadside. The minivan dodges chickens, goats, pigs, and puppies as it negotiates the sharp curves and potholes. The road snakes around the low cloud basin below and the intensity of the white glow strengthens. A herd of goats is around the next bend, a very pregnant mother and a flock of kids; they do not appear to be supervised by people.

Children walk along the side of the road, carrying bushels of grass, which we saw drying in the previous village, to repair roofs. The van slows for a section of the road that has mostly fallen away into the deep valley below. Small bamboo huts cling onto the sides of the hill with apparently no road or path to them. The people in these villages have not been touched by Western "advancement." They live a simple self-sufficient lifestyle, farming the land and raising cattle and chickens. They are always smiling and singing; they don't realize how beautiful the land is where they live. They probably yearn for Western luxuries like electricity or water on tap, while the luxury minivan full of white people secretly yearn for their simple life. The mist lifts from the valley revealing the sparkling river below. Despite the cramped uncomfortable conditions in the minivan, I never want this particular road journey to end.

One of the advantages of travelling in a group is that we were able to hire the minivan together to take us to our next destination. Often as a lone traveller, it is more difficult to find transport in these less-travelled places and you have to find other travellers who want to go to the same destination before you can hire someone. In this respect, our group of seven has given us all the benefits of booking "bulk" transport, although at times, we all wished to be alone and not part of the dynamics of a large group. The number seven was not that convenient when it came to sharing accommodation and someone always had to pay the price of a single room, which often caused dissent. The fact that there were two males in the group was quite insignificant—it didn't really matter who we shared with, although as time moved on "favourites" graduated together. I was a good ten years older than everyone else in the group, so I tended to step back when the dynamics started to cause problems.

My original travelling partner, Linda, started to behave more like a two-week tourist than a traveller, complaining about the road trip, and lack of rest stops with no facilities, and favouring some of the younger members of the group who had mp3 players and the latest music. It amazed me that some completely missed seeing the scenery, sleeping most of the way through, and that a couple of the girls preferred to read their travel guides to learn about their next road trip rather than enjoying the one they were on.

Our Christmas bungalow on the river at Vang Vieng

The Limestone Karst Mountains of Vang Vieng

Diary Excerpt: December 22nd, 2002

I don't know what time it is this evening; time has no significance here, but the moon is just rising and only two days after being a full moon, so I would estimate it's 8:00 p.m. I'm walking back alone to my riverside cottage; everyone I pass on the street respectively nods and greets me, "Sabaidee." I stumble a little on the stones in the dark and a group of travellers of European nationality stop to show me the way with their flashlights. I greet an Italian lady and her daughter as I pass through the gates to my guesthouse. She greets me, "Hello," and her daughter smiles and says, "Hi." It is completely impossible not to smile or greet strangers here if you're travelling alone.

This feels like the kind of place you would want to live out the rest of your years. It is so incredibly beautiful it defies the words to describe it. A unique blend of traditional Lao life with all the comforts of the Western world, no wonder everyone is smiling.

I ate a meal tonight equivalent to one in a five-star restaurant. A beautiful outside setting with good music at exactly the right volume, candles on the table, Christmas lights providing the only other light, and a festive spirit. Pepper steak cooked in cream and brandy, a fresh green salad with a delicious dressing; all washed down with (several) glasses of welcome red wine. The waitresses with those amazing smiling faces are dressed in traditional Lao skirts, eager to please. So attentive, they anticipate your needs before you beckon them for assistance. All this is available at prices that make you smile: two dollars for dinner, six dollars for a comfortable room, a good glass of wine for less than a dollar. Our riverside bungalow has three beds so I am sharing with Tom and Linda; it was the only accommodation left being so close to Christmas and although eighteen dollars seems pretty pricey for our own bungalow, we decided it was worth the treat. We have a large picture window that looks out directly onto the river and our own sunbathing balcony where we can watch the other travellers play on the river on their rubber tubes.

The other travellers in our group opted to share rooms in a cheaper hostel close to the town, but we ended up bumping into each other anyway since the town is so small. As soon as cheaper accommodation was available we moved into another shared room with three beds, but enjoyed the luxury of the riverside bungalow while we were there. We heard later that Kylie Minogue actually slept in that same bungalow with a boyfriend when she visited a few years ago.

Diary Excerpt: December 23rd, 2002

As I walked home, I glanced upwards to the evening sky and stopped in my tracks gazing at the incredible phenomenon of sparkling stars sitting on a gentle bed of soft white clouds aglow with the light of the rising moon.

I smiled at the memory of the giant rubber tube I'd hired for a dollar fifty. I'd floated down the river with a group of friends, consuming the beauty of the mountains and relaxing in the sunshine. What a day!

The giant limestone Karst Mountains had provided the perfect backdrop to the clean sparkling Nam Song River; tiny river islands turn into "Beer Lao" riverside bars and enough rapids to keep you on your toes after a drink or two. The smiling Lao women try to catch you with long bamboo poles as you speed past in your inner tube, and navigate your tube to ensure you don't miss their particular riverside bar. Several of the stops have signs pointing you to the caves, some of which you can take your tube into to explore the waterways inside.

We had such a giggle, the seven of us all forming a large circle as we drifted down the river together and held onto each other's inner tubes, passing beers and cigarettes between us.

We all complained of cold bums—they dangled in the cold water—and we fooled around trying to balance on our tubes holding them out of the water, some of us tipping up and ending up completely soaked. We spotted a Beer Lao bar on a sunny bank and all decided to head for it forming a line holding onto each other as we tried to steer our way toward the Lao ladies with the long bamboo poles. Once one of us had grabbed a pole we helped each other climb onto the sunny bank and dry out our wet pants! Sharing the last of our soggy cigarettes and enjoying a cold beer, we planned our return to the water, spotting a fast area ahead with some dangerous-looking boulders that would require some careful navigation.

As soon as you let the giant inner tube float, you take off quickly in the fast current, and most of us lost our grip on each other as we tumbled in the current. I recovered in time to notice I was heading straight for a large boulder sticking out of the water. I quickly decided I was going to collide with it and that the best course of action would be to "land" on it, which I successfully did. Much to the amusement of everyone else, I was suddenly stranded, high and dry, on a pinnacle boulder surrounded by fast flowing water, with no way off! The group knew about my back problems and Jennifer immediately rushed to my rescue, abandoning her inner tube to rescue me by fighting against the current to come to my aid! Once more, another example of the virtues of travelling in a group!

We quickly tired of water activities, and hired a bike for a dollar the following day, crossing the river to explore the paddy fields and two large caves we had heard about. We followed rough handwritten signs into the jungle where, under a grass hut, a Lao girl waiting for visitors greeted us. She requested a nominal fee and provided us with basic head lamps at which we giggled. The large head lamps were heavy on our heads and the battery packs were really cumbersome, like little mini car batteries with open wires connecting to the head lamp. They meant we could only walk with one hand free, and we had to keep untangling the wires so we didn't get them caught on anything! We were then left at the top of the rickety steps at the entrance to the dark cave to explore alone, and told to watch out for the spiders and the large deep crevices! Needless to say, we didn't stay long, our first sighting of the giant spiders was enough to make us turn back!

I've read critical articles about Vang Vieng and I cannot even begin to comprehend how anybody could think negatively about this incredibly wonderful place. Lao reminds me a little of Madagascar, which is probably my next favourite place in the world. I've now visited over thirty-seven countries and Lao simply sits on the top of that pile very comfortably.

Everyone searches for something when they're travelling, but deep down, you want to experience the true culture of the countries you visit without the discomfort of having to actually "live" their culture. We can all "rough it" for a few days to live with "the hill tribe people," eat their food, sleep on hard bamboo floors, and shiver in the cool night air. I wouldn't disparage these experiences. I've lived plenty of them as I've travelled around, and my heart has been warmed by the chance to experience that way of living. But the opportunity to experience life both ways? This morning I woke early and walked to the morning market and smiled at the Lao culture surviving strong and hard in this place that now caters to the Western tourist, and somehow, it all fits perfectly. I hope it stays that way forever; there is a good chance it will.

Dok Khoun Kham Island—Nam Ngum Lake

The last few days in Vang Vieng were overcast and dull with rain. It completely changed the appearance of the town—turning pretty sand roads into muddy puddles and shrouding the mountains in low cloud. Low tractor vehicles towed rough wooden trailers piled high with Lao girls clasping umbrellas. The overcast conditions and overflowing drains somehow allowed us to leave, and so the whole group headed for Nam Ngum Lake.

Travelling on a songthaew through the mountain villages was always a delightful way to observe village life. The locals filled their days with repairing their bamboo huts, tending their many chicken, pigs, and cattle, and looking after their many children. Our first sight of the lake from a vantage point on the road revealed green water dotted with islands and a backdrop of mountains shrouded in cloud. We were taken down to the boat dock for the short ride across Nam Ngum Lake to Dok Khoun Kham Island.

The island looked like a jungle, and we couldn't see any likely accommodation, but as we pulled into a small bay, a brick guesthouse was revealed. We clambered out of the boats and were shown to our respective rooms. Mine had dirty cream-painted walls, an old wooden floor, and a hard bed with a thin blanket. The bathroom was a broken Western toilet, a badly cracked sink, and a cold-water tap and bucket for a shower. We all prayed that the sun would rise the next day to brighten our spirits and provide nice weather to explore the island and the lake.

The dynamics of the large group came into play once again, and Linda suddenly decided to share a room with someone else. Up to that point, she had shared with me and Tom, and she had not mentioned to either of us that she did not want to share with us anymore. As soon as the rest of the group realized there was to be a change in room-sharing arrangements, there was a rush to the largest room with the best view and a balcony. Everyone started to argue about who was going to stay in that room and share with whom. I end up sharing with Tom, which I didn't mind, but we didn't have very much in common, and the small shared bathroom was difficult to negotiate when we were trying to maintain our privacy.

Kayaking Down the River

The sun obliged and we awoke to discover it teasing the shimmering green water. A lazy day of lounging in the hammocks and reading books was completed by a boat trip around the islands to watch the sunset. While planning our departure to Vientiane, we were asked if we would like to kayak there. We decided that would be a fantastic way to travel, and we arranged to have our bags meet us there. The group grew to nine, and we departed from the lake to start our journey down the River Ngum. Our first challenge as we launched ourselves into the river was to quickly paddle across stream to take advantage of the rapids. Shrieking with delight, some took a tumble and others delighted in watching their antics. The river quickly slowed to a muted flow and our Lao guide gently began to sing traditional songs as we silently paddled, consuming the incredible beauty surrounding us.

Diary Excerpt: December 27th, 2002

As we glided across the green water, we passed small farming communities, where locals were tending their vegetables in neat rows that lined the banks of the river. Groups of small naked children dashed from their bamboo huts as they spotted the colourful procession making its way down the river. They screeched with delight, waving and shouting, "Sabaidee." This Lao greeting translates as "Hello" and has a lovely sing-song quality about it. A little further downstream, it was bathing time and a group of children were jumping off a high bank and splashing into the river, while the women bathed in sarongs or did their laundry. Small wooden boats laden with vegetables occasionally passed us paddling upstream, powered by colourful Lao women dressed in traditional straw hats. They too greeted us, "Sabaidee" as they passed.

The sun beat down and we were all beginning to suffer from overexposure and tried to aim our kayaks into shady areas. Our legs were exposed directly to the sun, most of us having opted to wear shorts knowing we would get wet, but Julia and Jenny were both fair-skinned, and we all watched as their legs turned pink and then red in the sun. Nobody knew the journey was going to take so long and most of us were exhausted by the long trip and badly sunburnt. Luckily for me, I was wearing trousers and I had the Lao guide to take over my paddling when I tired, opting for a shared kayak rather than my own, like most had selected. Linda was particularly angry at the length of the journey and seemed to want to take it out on me. The journey ended at a riverside restaurant where a traditional Lao meal greeted us and prepared us for the further one-hour songthaew journey to Vientiane.

Vientiane—French Cosmopolitan Meets Traditional Lao

Vientiane was a curious mix of French cosmopolitan and traditional Lao, a city with a heavy French influence, thronging with Western tourist dining in five-star restaurants with high quality European food at inflated Lao prices. The atmosphere nearly tricked me into forgetting I was still in Lao, until I discovered there was no international ATM machine, no Western Union, unreliable and slow internet service, and city streets that turned into villages at the drop of a hat. I dined in a fine restaurant with well-trained staff and amazing food, then stepped out into the street, facing a random pile of garbage and drains that were covered with uneven stones or completely open, awaiting their next victim.

Although we had arrived as a group and booked into the same hostel, this marked the end of our travels together, and I witnessed little groups splitting off and deciding where to go next. I was sharing a room with Linda again, but she was expecting to meet up with another friend from England whom she would stay with. This immediately caused problems, because she didn't want to commit to sharing with me after her friend had arrived. Some room shuffling with other members of the group eventually meant I was sharing with Linda and her friend in a room with three beds.

Through Linda's friend, I met CJ, and we hit it off immediately, struggling to find any common ground with the other two girls who spent a good hour styling their hair and doing their make-up before going out to eat. CJ was an English teacher living on the River Mekong, and she quickly invited me to stay with her once she realized everyone else was moving on and I would have to pay triple for the room I had committed to.

I was very fortunate to have been invited to spend a few days staying by the Mekong in a traditional Lao wooden house in a small village community. I ended up staying with CJ for five days, and I quickly settled into her humble home, sleeping on the wooden floor on a thin mattress, and visiting the market each day to buy fresh vegetables to make dinner for her when she returned from school.

It was like being on *Khulula* again, truly integrating into the culture of the country, shopping with the locals, and fetching water for the neighbours. It was here in CJ's house that I started to work on the idea of writing a book, and I spent most days writing on her computer and copying what I'd written to disk.

The ninety-seven-year-old lady who shared the garden, outside cooking area, and communal sweeping brush, smiled when I helped her clean the cooking area outside; she mumbled constantly in Lao, grinning and showing her red mouth and her rotted teeth from years of chewing betel. CJ, who had been living there for three years, spoke fluent Lao, and so she understood her and joked with her all the time.

Diary Excerpt: January 17th, 2003

The community is close and welcoming, and CJ tells me tales of the times everyone helped her when she was bedridden by a motorcycle accident and when she had her appendix out.

Tonight, she has been invited to a wedding party and as the party waited for her, the old lady was giggling and pointing at CJ's outfit advising what she should wear with her traditional Lao skirt. Eventually, CJ shrugged her shoulders and the old lady rushed next door, returning with a peasant's blouse and insisting she put it on. CJ obeyed, but refused to change her motorbike boots or leather jacket that she always wears when riding her motorcycle.

I continue to pack by candlelight, ready for my flight tomorrow to Cambodia; I will be sad to leave this beautiful country and its warm, genuine, and friendly people.

✍ Reflections From 2015 ✍

To see "karma" in action, particularly at a time when I was feeling very unloved and alone, resulted in great learning and understanding for me. I guess if you feel abandoned and confused, surrounding yourself with kind, helpful people helps you see the best in people. Although I was really hurting, I was also beginning to see myself. Being alone, probably for the first time ever, taught me to trust my intuition and let my own heart lead me. Prior to this, I believe I was codependent on Graeme, so I easily let him make the decisions.

Trusting in myself actually freed me to trust other people, and everywhere I travelled, I only met kindness. There was no doubt in my mind that people only ever had the best intentions. I think this is also true for the travellers I met, so maybe travelling left everyone with that positive feeling. Reflecting back, Graeme was right: travelling was the best way I could ever heal. By finding myself, trusting in myself, and believing I was always making the right choices, I seemed to suddenly lose fears that had been attached to a codependent me. I put myself in several situations that tested this, seemingly not thinking twice about the consequences: choosing to be alone in a dark jungle, despite my fear of the dark, and becoming a snorkelling guide, despite being easily spooked by unknown creatures and not being a strong swimmer. I overcame fears without even really thinking about the process.

I did not like being alone, and at the time I saw my need to socialize with other backpackers as being "needy." I wanted to be more independent. I was relieved that I was not "alone" and that, in fact, everyone I was meeting felt "alone." People need people, and backpacking alone actually helped me to accept that community is all around us, if we are open to it.

Today, I embrace community and the importance of community. In fact, when I reflect back, I see this time was essential for my subsequent leadership of community through my business. No one needs to be alone; everyone needs support and love of other people in positive, loving ways. When I needed love and support, they were all around me; so today, I want to help create that for other people.

~

Cambodia and the Ancient Ruins of Angkor Wat

"If you want others to be happy, practice compassion; if you want to be happy, practice compassion."
Dalai Lama

I arrived in Cambodia alone, after taking the plane from Vientiane to the capital Phnom Penh and then stopping overnight in Phnom Penh to break up the journey to Siem Reap. I was looking for someone to share a taxi with, and spotted a backpacker just getting into one as I came out of the airport. There was no one else around and I had already been warned about taking taxis alone, putting myself at risk of being charged silly prices, or being dropped off at their choice of hotel. I started to run after the taxi waving my arms and shouting for it to stop, grabbing the back door handle just as it was about to accelerate away. This is where I met Katherine, another English girl travelling alone, who was also a little nervous of the taxi ride. She agreed to share the ride with me.

I asked her where she was staying and the taxi driver immediately answered saying he knew where to take us. I bet he did! It took some convincing to get him to drop us near a hostel I had already selected from my guidebook, which was located on the river. He had obviously decided where Katherine was going to stay and he was not happy about me changing the plans. He got his revenge on me by stopping the taxi about a mile from our destination, saying he would not drive on the rough road that led to the river and our chosen accommodation. We had no choice and had to bail out where he told us to, stranded on a rough road in the middle of nowhere with our backpacks at our feet.

At this point, I think Katherine regretted allowing me to get in her taxi and select our accommodation, and she looked at me for inspiration of where we should go next. At that moment, a friendly motorbike rider stopped at our feet and smiled at our situation, one he had obviously come across a few times; he offered to give us a lift to our accommodation on the river. It turned out that the taxis did not like to take people to these rooms, because they did not get paid commission to take guests there; the city hotels on the other hand paid the taxis commission to take people straight there from the airport. The motorbike boy gestured to join him on his seat and Katherine looked at me questioning if we could both fit on with our backpacks. Silly question really—it is not unusual to see whole families and the dog loaded onto these mopeds in the same way the Western world uses a family car. The experience was quite entertaining—two girls with large backpacks wobbling down the street on a small moped, laughing and giggling all the way.

He took us directly to our accommodation, which turned out to be in a lovely location right on the river, and happily headed back up the road to meet the next victims. I spent a lovely evening chatting with Katherine and we planned to take the boat together the next day to Siem Reap and maybe visit some of the sites together once we got there. It was always much more fun travelling with someone and it was always much cheaper to share a room rather than to take a room by myself. I was still living on the money Graeme and I had taken out of our joint bank account in Malaysia, and it wouldn't stretch too much further if I didn't stick to the ten-dollar-a-day rule.

The following day, we boarded the express boat from Phnom Penh to Siem Reap, a five-hour journey down the river, which I'd thought would take two days, but it took less than one. I don't think these boats had been offering this service for long, but they were old with no amenities. They had a very strange toilet, which I couldn't figure out how to use. It was an Asian standing toilet, but it was raised so high that you could not climb up to use it. I opened the door to find a raised porcelain bowl with two foot imprints, but at waist height. It was as though they'd designed a Western toilet, one that would take a seat, but still installed the standard Asian bowl. Well, it meant neither the Westerners nor the Asians could actually use it, which was one way of keeping it clean, but very inconvenient for a five-hour boat ride. It did provide some quite interesting entertainment, though. I watched many unsuspecting victims opening the door and scratching their heads at the sight.

Diary Excerpt: February 5th, 2003

The River Basacc and Tonlé Sap Lake seem to be a lifeline for the people here. The difference between Cambodia and Lao is the countryside, and this seems to add a certain sadness. The soil is rough and clay-like, the vegetable plots on the banks of the river haphazard and struggling to survive; there doesn't seem to be any mature vegetation and even the palm trees don't look healthy.

Still, the children wave and smile at the big, fast express boat that goes by with the white tourists; maybe the tourist has come to save them. The people here work the river, live in stilted bamboo houses balancing on the banks, and scull their rough wooden canoes across the wide river. Poverty is everywhere, and then suddenly there's a sight of a pile of modern red bricks and a flash of orange robes—money is being poured into another new temple. The floating houses—whole villages of them—look inhospitable.

The only flashes of colour are the hats and scarves of the fishermen. Everywhere is so flat and parched and desolate and brown; such a contrast to Lao. A beautiful bird skims across the water; it looks a little like a kingfisher but is white and grey. Large white geese flicker in the sunlight. A mountain is in the distance; although it has some vegetation it doesn't have the same lush green colour of Lao. Another enjoyable boat ride has given me an invaluable insight into the culture of the river people of Cambodia.

Less than ten years ago, Siem Reap was relatively unfrequented as a tourist destination. Now, it is a premier historical site in S.E. Asia and its rich cultural history is widely accessible. Many people think that Angkor Wat is the only monument, but Angkor actually with over forty accessible sites covers an area of over seventy-seven square miles in Northwest Cambodia. The name "Angkor" means "holy city"; it has a rich history dating back to the tenth century. The generally accepted dates for the Angkor period are 802 to 1432 AD, and are designated as the period in which the Khmer Empire reached its greatest territorial limits and its apogee in cultural and artistic achievements.

Katherine at Angkor Wat

The founder of Angkor was King Jayavarman II who established a new religious belief, the Devarajā god-king cult. Successive kings after Jayavarman II continued to unify and expand the Khmer Empire. Inscriptions give the names of thirty-nine kings from the Angkor period. Indravardhan set a precedent for future kings by building a temple mountain, which became a means for successive rulers to display their omnipotence. The last major king was Jayavarman VII (1181-1220 AD), who undertook a massive building program and is credited with constructing more monuments, roads, and bridges than all the other kings put together.

The Angkor site covers over 77 square miles of temples, many dating back to the tenth century, and tangled in jungle roots.

Angkor's proximity to its enemies—neighbouring Indonesia and Thailand—eventually caused it to move its capital. The kingdom shifted southeast to Phnom Penh in the fifteenth century as a more suitable base to develop interests in the maritime trade in S.E. Asia.

Although the ruins of Angkor were reported to the Western world as early as the sixteenth century, it wasn't until 1855 that the West took an interest, following a lively and interesting article written by Dr. A. House, an American missionary. Subsequent French expeditions in 1866 led by Ernest Doudart de Lagrée systematically publicized Angkor to the outside world and led to l'Ecole Francaise d'Extreme Orient (EFEO) studying the monuments of Angkor and disengaging the historical site from the jungle.

Today, many of the site ruins are still tangled in jungle roots and this is what makes these sites unique to visit. It seemed incredible to imagine that this now barren land was once the land of kings with splendour and riches beyond anything in Western history.

In a historical declaration during a visit to Angkor Wat in November 1991, Federico Mayor, Director General of UNESCO, declared Angkor, the City of the Khmer Kings; this led to international participation in saving Angkor. In 1992, it was included on the UNESCO World Heritage list of over four hundred sites, recognizing Angkor as one of mankind's most significant cultural heritage sites and the international symbol of Cambodia and its people. By 1993, the new Royal Government of Cambodia assumed the responsibility of protecting and maintaining historic monuments, realizing their potential as tourist attractions. I reminded myself that less than ten years earlier, I would not have been able to visit this country, and that independent travellers would not have been able to see these amazing historical and heritage sites. That must have been the best time to visit, before tourism began to destroy the unique culture of Cambodia.

Siem Reap has responded to this by building good tree-lined roads to the temples and a wide variety of restaurants, hotels, and guest houses. The infrastructure was still developing when I was there, so I saw tourists with large hard suitcases struggling off the express boat into a deluge of locals holding welcome signs on a rough muddy bank in the middle of a mangrove island. This was the nearest river port to Siem Reap.

At the time of writing, you could stay in a three-hundred-dollar room but you still had to arrive the same way as the backpacker, who could probably find accommodation for a few dollars.

You can now fly Thai Airways direct from Bangkok, and in January 2007 the first direct flights to Phnom Penh started from Vancouver, BC, Canada. However, judging by the number of digital cameras and videos monitoring the display on the mangrove island, this way of travelling obviously adds to the whole cultural experience and gives the higher-class tourists the rare opportunity to glimpse the real Cambodia. They probably pay a premium now to take the express boat rather than the direct flight!

Angkor Wat has introduced many more employment opportunities, but the greatest desire of many of the young boys I met was to be a tour guide. They know the standards are high so they practise their English, and try to learn and memorize the history of the temples. The backpackers provided the learning platform for them: they charged the same price it would cost to hire a motorcycle; they rented themselves to drive you as the passenger on the motorcycle, all so they could practise their knowledge. It was a great way for the traveller to gain an insight into these boys' culture, and I found it just as interesting talking to them as hearing about the ancient temples.

My guide was called Nat and he was twenty years old. He worked from my guesthouse and had been using the money he received as a motorbike guide to attend night school four and half hours a week to study English literature. He hoped this education would allow him to be a writer, a teacher, or a tour guide. When he lived at home on his family's farm, his job was to look after ten cows, his three brothers, and three sisters. The farm was not big enough to provide for everyone as he and his siblings grew older and more independent, so he chose to leave home to become a novice monk. This was a ten-year commitment, but he would learn basic English skills, which would then allow him to move to Siem Reap.

As an unofficial guide he earns around $200 a month and his school fees are $390 a year, leaving enough to help support his family. He was hoping to get work as a government teacher or as an official tour guide, which pays around $7,000 US a year. The tour guides are regulated by the tour companies, and they have to pay for their own insurance. However, Nat said that as long as his English is good, he will have lots of options open to him, even if he also has to work in a restaurant for free accommodation, but not food.

It sometimes makes me wonder whether, if we had to work so hard to pay for our education, we would appreciate it more. Even very young children aspire to the same goals as Nat, and hordes of young children hang around at the tourist bus stops to sell pineapple or bread for the opportunity to speak English with the tourists. As soon as the bus pulled up to the stop, young girls crowded us and asked "Where are you from?" "How old are you?" "What is your name?"

Then they eagerly told us about their school and the name of their teachers, and they asked politely if we had any pens or paper to spare.

The less fortunate families resort to begging, and a crowd of landmine victims were usually to be found at the bus stations and stops competing with the young girls who wanted to learn English. One family I watched from the bus had made a home on a rough piece of land near the bus stop. A mother and her young child lay in a hammock strung across two bare trees, while the husband slept on a mat under a mosquito net with three more little bundles close to him on a sack on the ground. The younger children were not old enough to beg and the husband still had all his limbs, but could not leave his family to learn English so that he could enter the tourist trade, so his only hope was that the passing bus passengers would take pity on him and give him some change.

Cambodian girls selling to tourists to learn English

It is families like these that can fall victim to some of the more unsavoury characters of Cambodia who are offering "tours" to the local orphanages to raise money in donations for the children kept there in very poor conditions. In reality, many of these children are not orphans, but have been bought for as little as twenty dollars from their poverty-struck parents who hope that they will have a better life in the orphanage. Once in the orphanage, some of the children are then sold into the sex slave market or exposed to pedophiles. The more tourists that visit the orphanages and donate large sums of money, the worse the situation becomes, so new awareness charities, such as Licadho.org, are trying to educate the tourists who want to donate to orphanages.

The tourist trade has improved employment opportunities with restoration workers on the temples, refuse collectors, gardeners, and security jobs now available for the non-English speakers. But unfortunately, the poor still end up being victims of the big developers who continually illegally grab prime land for more tourist hotels and facilities. Many of the traditional musicians and artists who survived the Khmer Rouge are now being moved on to rural areas with no amenities, to make room for new development. Indeed, it is commonplace to hear about the "government" sweeping up the beggars like refuse, so that the "tourist" does not have to deal with them, or look at their poor deformed bodies ravaged by landmines.

The most popular form of transport in Cambodia is the bicycle, and it is not uncommon to see five or six bicycles abreast across the road at rush hour. The farmers can now sell their produce outside the temples at a higher price to the tourists, and children learn young to produce local crafts to sell too. Cambodians have become some of the best entrepreneurs, with young children learning English quickly, together with cheekiness and some of the best sales skills I have ever experienced. They all compete, but they also all share and are humorously competitive. Indeed when faced with ten young girls all trying to sell their handmade scarves, I found it difficult to choose which ones I should buy. I ended up with ten scarves. They are never aggressive or rude; they always smile and are very polite. The lucky ones wear flip-flops, while most are barefoot wearing dirty, tatty clothes and unkempt hair.

I spent a week in Cambodia visiting the temples with Katherine, who then left me to visit the "killing fields." I didn't fancy seeing the famous pile of human skulls, so I decided to return to Thailand, following an email from my niece who was shortly arriving for a holiday.

This resourceful nation of people is never defeated by something as simple as an unreliable old bus, and on my return bus trip to Thailand, we were held up for several hours while our bus was pushed across a rickety bridge. Each time the bus changed gears, I could hear the screeching, especially shifting down gear, and finally the bus stalled on the bridge, blocking both ways of ever-increasing traffic, to anything other than a bicycle.

Diary Excerpt: February 15th, 2003

Everyone joins in to push the bus across the bridge and to one side of the road so that the men can scratch their heads together and work out what emergency repairs can be carried out. It only took twenty-five minutes and plenty of people helping to repair the gearbox, but meantime I noted some of the vehicles passing us. A motorcycle has four passengers, the father driving with his wife behind clutching her young daughter and her young son who are balancing on the rack over the back wheel. A truck is loaded with more than twenty workers, probably farmers because they are wearing many layers of clothes and hats and scarves to protect them from the sun (which will make them very hot, but they seem to prefer this to the damaging/darkening effects of the sun). Two bikes riding side by side balance the load of a giant ice block between them; they leave a trail of water as the ice melts in the sun. Another two motorbikes have two live pigs tied as pillion passengers, lying on their backs with their trotters in the air. One motorbike was piled high with coconuts, another with a stack of logs. These are just the local Cambodians getting on with everyday life, using whatever transport is available to ship their goods from one village to the next without the luxury of refrigerated trucks for ice or meat or a family car.

The road is dusty and rough, with lots of potholes and very uneven; it is not surprising they cannot keep their clothes clean! This reminds me of a joke that Nat had told me: "A man goes to a party wearing his old clothes. Everyone else is in new clothes, and so no one will talk to him or give him food or drink. He decides to go home and comes back wearing new clothes. Now, everyone talks to him and they ask him why he is putting food up the sleeves of his jacket. He replies, "You are not talking to me, but to my clothes, so I feed my clothes, not me."

Nat found this joke very funny, so I laughed along (a little sadly). His next joke was even better. "A cow and a pig cross a river infested with crocodiles. The pig swims across the river and is not eaten; the cow does not make it. Why? Because the crocodiles are Muslim."

It's a good job I knew that Muslims can't eat pork, otherwise I wouldn't have got that one.

The next time the bus stops, it is because the road ahead is blocked again, because the next bridge has collapsed. We may have to wait a few hours while the resourceful Cambodians rebuild the bridge. I use the opportunity to find a toilet and nip off into the dry barren landscape in search of somewhere to squat. Keeping an eye open for unexploded bombs, I find a clearing marked by human waste and a few wet patches and some discarded toilet paper. It is not entirely out of view of the bus, but I do not dare to go further off the path, so I make do. I am now beginning to look a little more like the locals, with muddy feet and dirty hands. As I join the waiting passengers, the Cambodians delight in joking with me—the tourist—and ask if I have brought my mat with me.

"You will have to sleep the night here if the bridge isn't mended."

Of course they may not have been joking, but fortunately for me, the bridge was eventually mended and we set off on our journey once again. I'm sure that if I had to stay the night, someone would have shared their mat with me.

Koh Samui and the Land of Consumerism

I had now completed my rough circle of Indochina and was back in Bangkok to decide what I should do with my future. My niece was visiting from England and staying on Koh Samui, an island to the south that I had not visited. I decided I should head down there to meet up with her. Koh Samui has attracted the masses through marketing, and undoubtedly its cultural ecology has suffered. The multinationals have moved in: McDonald's, Burger King, Pizza Hut, and even Starbucks have all recognized the consumer potential of this tourist haven and wasted no time in exploiting it. Money is a powerful demon and the bottom line is that Thai culture cannot absorb the effects of Western consumerism without losing something of its own uniqueness.

It was the beginning of the end of my love for Thailand and its people and the start of a series of events that led me to leave Southeast Asia altogether. All the things I had learned about Thailand, all the things I loved about Thailand, were suddenly compromised. It was as though I had travelled to a different country rather than a different island in the same country. I greeted the Thai ladies at the reception hall of my niece's hotel with the traditional "Wai" (hands are bought together in front of the chin) and they just looked at me strangely, without a smile. The usual respect for Buddha images and the Royal family were missing from the reception hall of the hotel, and many of the guests of the hotel were running around the grounds topless and openly flirting and kissing. All the traditional values usually associated with Thailand were completely missing from this island. I tried to explain the differences to my niece, but she wasn't interested in the culture; as with many two-week tourists, she was looking for "a home away from home."

Unfortunately, this is where I was involved in quite a serious back accident. If I had been in any other part of Thailand, I would have had plenty of "consideration" to help me recover, but I was in Koh Samui. My niece wanted to attend the full moon party that takes place every full moon on the beaches of Koh Phang Nga; this involved a speedboat ride across a short stretch of ocean. I was not that keen to go but felt obligated to my sister to keep an eye on my niece, since these parties did not have a great reputation. As I looked at the speedboat being overloaded with passengers and the rough sea conditions, I tried to talk my niece out of the trip, suspecting that this would be a very dangerous and uncomfortable boat ride. Against my better judgement and with my instincts screaming at me to turn the other way, I boarded the boat and squeezed into a standing space, since all the seats were already taken.

As soon as the boat gained speed, it would leap off the crest of a wave and slam down into the trough of the next. This made for an uncomfortable ride for everyone, but for me, with a weak back, it was really serious. I screamed in pain as the boat slammed into the waves sending shock waves down my spine and I begged for the boat to slow down. Everyone just stared at me, but no one would help. I grabbed a tall American tourist and held onto him in the hope his body would take some of the impact from me. Although he was really nice, he was a bit shocked by this woman who clung to him.

By the time the boat reached the beach, my back was in violent spasms and I was in extreme pain. I couldn't move but they wanted me off the boat so I was manhandled off by some travellers while others rushed to the first-aid station on the island for help. A makeshift stretcher carried me to the first-aid station, where a doctor prodded me and then gave me an injection for pain. They were too scared to move me and I tried to explain to them that I needed to rest to try and stop the spasm. I spent the night in the "hospital," and an ambulance was organized for the following day to ferry me back across to Koh Samui where they had a better hospital. This hospital fitted me with a back brace and gave me more painkillers; they didn't even take an x-ray. I had spoiled my niece's holiday and she wasn't about to spend the remainder of the holiday babysitting her aunty.

She found me a reasonably comfortable bungalow, not too near her luxury hotel, and left me there to fend for myself.

I spent the next two weeks in bed, forcing myself to walk across to the restaurant once a day to try and down a meal and buy water. No one helped, no one came to check on me or assist me, and no one wanted the nuisance of a disabled traveller to spoil their two-week holiday. One waiter took pity on me and helped me back to my bungalow one evening, only to be disciplined for leaving the restaurant while on duty. This was so unlike Thai people elsewhere in the country. Every day when I visited the restaurant, I called into the internet café opposite and emailed everyone I knew to come and help me.

I met an English woman called Jo who had a small business in Koh Samui, a gift shop with a yoga studio on the roof. She befriended me and helped with my recovery. If it hadn't been for her, it could have taken much longer, because I was in a downward spiral. I met up with Leanne and her mother whom I'd travelled with in Lao, and she arranged to meet me on Koh Phang Nga for some relaxation and recovery time, which really helped with the healing process. Thanks to these three women, I eventually healed enough to travel back to Bangkok and decide on my next move.

In Bangkok, I booked myself into the White Lodge Hotel for ten dollars a day, much more than my budget, but my travels were coming to an end and I needed the comfort of a nice bed, private shower, and fan. I spent many days in the room with a bottle of Mae Song Whiskey and a packet of cigarettes for company, contemplating my next move. The four years I spent with Graeme had chipped away at my confidence. Now, after travelling alone for six months, I had gained a lot of self-confidence, and so I was happy to travel on the skytrain alone, and go and see some of the sights I missed the last time I was in Bangkok.

The Grand Palace is an incredible sight, although I wished I had someone to share it with; oohing and aahing to myself doesn't have the same impact. The complex was established in 1782 and it houses the royal residence, throne halls, and a number of government offices, as well as the renowned Temple of the Emerald Buddha. The Emerald Buddha is in fact carved from a block of green jade and was first discovered in 1434 in a Stupa in Chiang Rai, in Northern Thailand. At that time, the image was covered with plaster and it was thought to be an ordinary Buddha image. Later, the abbot who had found the image noticed that the plaster on the nose had flaked off, revealing the green stone underneath.

The walls of the ordination hall of the Temple of the Emerald Buddha were decorated with mural paintings depicting several events of Lord Buddha's life, including scenes from his birth, childhood, and youth.

The Upper Terrace had four main monuments: a golden chedi (similar in shape to a stupa); the Mondop (meaning "pavilion"), a repository for Buddhist sacred scriptures inscribed on palm leaves, contained within a beautiful mother-of-pearl inlaid cabinet; a miniature Angkor Wat; and the Royal Pantheon in which statues of past sovereigns of the ruling Chakri Dynasty were enshrined. Scattered around the terrace were statues of elephants and mythical beings. All the other subsidiary buildings and galleries were equally splendid and extravagant with their decorated spires and golden roofs.

I was happy I had spent a good portion of my travelling budget on a new digital camera to capture the pure elegance and distinction of the palace. That is, until it was stolen.

I had enjoyed my trip to the Royal Palace and decided to visit the nearby marketplace for a barbecued chicken and a cool drink. While I was sitting down enjoying my meal, an old lady came and sat next to me and smiled. I had my bag next to my lap and didn't even consider it was at risk at all, so I didn't pay much attention to the old lady sitting next to me. I later went into my bag to get my camera to take a picture of the river boats and was confused when I couldn't find it.

I went to the information counter at the ferry terminal and asked them if anyone had handed in a camera; I couldn't imagine where I could have left it. The Thai gentleman at the counter laughed and said it was stolen. I was astounded and told him it couldn't be stolen—Thai people don't steal! He felt so sorry for me that he comforted me as I burst into tears defending his people, telling him stories of how Thai people returned things to careless farangs; they didn't steal! He sadly told me that theft was common near the Royal Palace, because of the number of tourists that visit the area. Everything I ever believed for two years about the Thai people was now in question. That kind Thai man escorted me back to my hotel room. I think he understood the significance of the event for me; it wasn't just the theft of the camera; it was my horror at such a change in the Thai culture influenced by Western consumerism.

I was seriously considering leaving Southeast Asia now, so all I had to do was decide where exactly in the world I was going to go. I spent the next few days around the hotel and met a group of Canadians who were travelling together from Vancouver Island. They invited me to join them on a trip to the floating market, which I readily accepted as I was glad of the company and had always wanted to visit the Klongs (canals).

Bangkok was once dubbed the Venice of the East, with hundreds of miles of klongs snaking through the city. These klongs ensure the continuation of a riverine tradition that dates back centuries—the bustling floating market of multi-coloured boats loaded with spices and fruits and vegetables is certainly a vibrant, awe-inspiring sight.

I was invited to dinner with the Canadians and I used the opportunity to question them about Vancouver Island where most of them lived. It occurred to me I had never visited that side of the world, and that might be an interesting place to visit. I had a Welsh friend who was living in Nanaimo on Vancouver Island, whom I had met through a cruising website, and she'd said I could stay with her for a few days if I was ever to visit, so that option was looking more attractive.

I spent the next few days emailing and doing a little research into Vancouver Island; I was expecting my share of *Khulula* soon, which would give me a start in a new country.

Tree roots at Angkor Wat

✒ Reflections From 2015 ✒

The last few weeks in Thailand had led me to question everything about the country I believed in and made me reflect again on what I should now be doing with my life. The time I spent in Bangkok was a time of great reflection and every time I was alone and started to ask "Now what?" I would end up coming back to this thought: I had had the perfect life living on *Khulula* providing new experiences to backpackers. Was my purpose to be the hostess and help other people see the world in a different way? I had a feeling of dread that if I had found my purpose, now what? Should I jump ship and start looking for another boat that did charters? Should I work on cruise ships or look for employment as crew on a boat? Should I be working with backpackers? I was beginning to see that community was important to me, and that my purpose would involve being a leader of a community, but which one?

Meeting CJ in Lao had left me feeling that she had found her purpose and calling in a less-developed country. I knew I felt disconnected from England, but where did I belong? Maybe in another country? Nowhere I had visited so far had felt right; it was not Asia and not Africa and not Europe. The only place I had never really spent any time was North America. I thought perhaps I needed to keep moving, and then I would find it.

The funny thing is, at that time, I was fascinated by the Canadians I met travelling and I turned away from the British I met—other than CJ who was more Lao than British. How come I was attracting all these British people as travelling companions? Was it because the British attract British? Even in Cambodia, it was Kat whom I travelled with, and she was British. It was Jo—also British—in Koh Samui who ran the yoga studio, and it was meeting my niece in Koh Samui that eventually sealed my fate of leaving Thailand.

My healing came through Leanne and her mother who were Canadian, as they nursed me on Koh Phang Nga, and spending that time with them ultimately led to my decision to come to Canada. The last group of backpackers I met in Bangkok served to stamp my destiny; they were all from Vancouver Island and Vancouver. Perhaps coming to Canada was fate, although I did not think that at the time. I just took it in my stride that I was visiting another country. I see now, reflecting back, this is why I never self-doubted that choice. Something deep inside me knew that this was where I would get to live out my true purpose.

~

The main temple at Angkor Wat

Lee and Jo nursing me on Koh Phang Nga

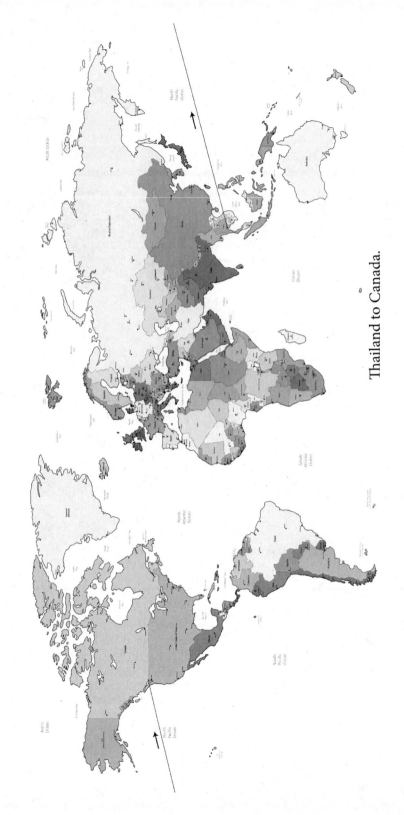

Thailand to Canada.

❊ Chapter Nine ❊

Back to the First World

"The world breaks everyone, and afterward many are strong in the broken places."
Ernest Hemingway

Now that I had completed my loop of Indochina, it was time to decide if I was going to continue travelling, return to England, or do something else. I had learned a lot about myself, most of which made me feel lucky and fortunate to be given the opportunities in life that many don't get because of their circumstances. The world really was my oyster with my education and background, so I decided I should make the most of my freedom and flexibility, and keep going. Opportunity knocks if you're open to hear it, so it didn't really matter which country I visited; I just decided I should follow my instincts and let life make its own choices.

I had already considered Canada, mostly due to the many Canadian backpackers I'd met who were always such nice friendly people. They helped me make the decision to go there, simply through their kindness to me. I'd spent ten days mostly locked in my hotel room in Bangkok, brooding over my future, and the intervention of Canadians guided my way. Once I had decided to fly to Vancouver, it was easy to go into the travel agent's office close to the hotel and book a flight.

My flight was via Singapore—where there's a smoking prohibition—so I decided this was also a great opportunity to give up smoking. I figured if I was going to start a new life in a new country, I should reinvent myself a little, and starting as a non-smoker seemed like a good beginning. Also the Canadians I'd met made it clear that smoking on their Western side of the continent was not a good thing to do.

When I arrived at Singapore International Airport, I had quite a few hours before my connecting flight to Vancouver, so I decided to visit the transit hotel and its wonderful swimming pool, Jacuzzi, and bar on the rooftop of the airport. I don't know why more international airports don't offer these kinds of facilities to make transit flights more enjoyable. The transit hotel can be booked by the hour and has all the facilities you need to relax, such as TV, baths, and comfortable beds. I decided to check out the leisure facilities but couldn't find my swimming costume. Not to be put off by a small problem, I grabbed my sarong and decided to wear that in the pool. It was really magnificent to be sitting in a Jacuzzi staring up at the evening stars on the roof of an airport.

I strolled to the pool bar and started to chat with a South African who was on his way to Dubai. "I'd decided to give up smoking, thinking this was a smoke-free airport and here I am sitting at a roof top bar watching everyone else smoke."

"I know how you feel," he replied. "I decided to do the same, so I'm suffering too."

"How about we split a packet of cigarettes and celebrate them as our last?"

"Can't think of a better way to give up smoking than to chain-smoke," he replied.

It was a great way to give up smoking; we chain-smoked so many cigarettes in a couple of hours that I didn't want to face another cigarette before I got on the plane. It was also a great way to kill a few hours swapping travel stories. He found it incredible that I was flying to Vancouver to start a new life in a country I'd never visited before and yet he was off to Dubai to work in a country he'd never visited either, so I didn't see the difference.

The twelve-hour flight was uneventful, after spending more than twelve hours in a day on buses and trains for the last six months, this journey seemed quite insignificant and quite comfortable in comparison. I kept trying to work out why I wasn't apprehensive or worried about my future, so I just figured I must be doing the right thing. I answered the usual questions at the airport, which you get when you have so many stamps in your passport, and then made my way to the ferry terminal for the ferry ride to Vancouver Island. I had already arranged for someone to meet me at the terminal at Duke Point in Nanaimo, and Roy recognized me by my backpack and suntan.

Arriving at Newcastle Marina in Nanaimo felt really good. I was overwhelmed by the scenery on the ferry with the snowcapped mountains and the rich green forest canopy. It felt really great to breathe in the fresh crisp air of the mountains and to feel cool for the first time in years. Everyone seemed to be smiling and very welcoming, considering they had only ever met me through the internet. Although it was February and I felt cold, the sky was a magnificent blue and the sun was shining; it was nice to feel the sun warming my skin instead of burning it. I had spent the last four years running from the sun and trying to avoid the heat and now I was contrasting the welcoming warmth of it on my skin against the cool air. It felt good to be back in the marina environment and the company of the extraordinary people who live on boats.

My first few days seemed to be a constant round of introductions and celebrations, including three boats that decided to go out to one of the nearby islands for a spontaneous picnic cruise in the February sunshine. I went as crew to Roy, who picked me up at the ferry terminal on his forty-five-foot sailboat. Greg Salisbury went on his sailboat *Seafire*, which was berthed next to Alexis, and Alexis took her West Coast motor boat, *Lois B*, which I was staying on. We rafted the boats together just off Newcastle Island and enjoyed the weekend together with several bottles of red wine.

I was immediately attracted to Greg, probably because he was so relaxed and comfortable with living on a sailboat in a marina, and he made a point to sit close to me the whole time. Greg invited me back to his boat for more red wine and we chatted at length about the cruising life and his dreams to set off in *Seafire*. We saw a kindred spirit in each other and we laughed until the small hours of the morning. Things started to heat up and before I knew it I was crawling into the v-berth and waking in the morning with a very large smile on my face.

Greg had to go to work the next day, so he left me with instructions to make myself at home and bring my bags across from next door if I wanted. I guess I never really left after that. I felt so comfortable in his presence and we fitted well together in the small confined space of his yacht. A whirlwind romance began and we started to make plans for our future together on *Seafire*. It just seemed like it was meant to be.

Greg was planning to take *Seafire* down to Mexico and invited me along. His plan was to work another two years to pay off the boat and cash in his pension, but I suggested we cut that to six months since that was as long as I could stay in Canada. I decided to invest my share of *Khulula* in *Seafire* and preparations began to get *Seafire* ready for the passage and tie up Greg's loose ends.

Seafire was a beautiful yacht, usually one of the prettiest in the anchorage. She was thirty-four feet long and slim with lots of wood detailing including wooden cabin hatches that let plenty of natural light into the accommodation below. Her deck was limited in space, barely enough room for two sunbeds since the cabin hatches took up a lot of deck space. There was nowhere to eat outside other than a small folding table we put in the cockpit area. She was beautiful below decks, lots of wooden trim, tongue-and-groove walls, wooden flooring and ceiling. She was a pretty home for two, but felt crowded even with one other couple onboard.

Vancouver Island is a paradise of glorious West Coast scenery with lush emerald forests, alpine peaks, freshwater lakes and rivers, rocky shorelines, and dazzling beaches. I wanted to see it all and balanced working on the boat with visiting as much of the island as possible. The rugged wilderness and old-growth forests provided plenty of vigorous hiking that I'd been missing out on in the hotter climates, and the City of Nanaimo was a delight of attractions with its many harbourside walks and farmers markets. Pristine wilderness and wide-open spaces, rolling green landscapes of hills and valleys, forests and farmland, sparkling lakes and crystal clear rivers were all so different from the landscapes I had been living in for the last four and a half years.

Greg and me at Newcastle Marina, Nanaimo, B.C.

Diary Excerpt: March 31st, 2003

Today, I stood under an 800-year-old Douglas fir that measured 250 feet tall and 30 feet in circumference. This old-growth forest was so arresting—Spanish moss drenched the branches and blanketed the ancient tree trunks, giving everything an eerie ambience. I was reminded of the rain forests of Malaysia, but the trees were so much more imposing and statuesque, and I was really enjoying hiking in a much cooler climate. I just adore hiking with Greg, because he is so engrossed in his environment and it's captivating to see such a beautiful rugged wilderness.

As we walk and inhale the smells and sounds of the forest, he constantly stops to take in another pleasure of nature, bending to smell the wild rose, crouching to look more closely at the mushrooms, and stopping suddenly to listen more carefully to the call of a bird.

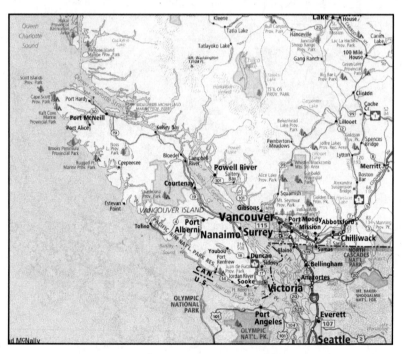

Vancouver Island, south west coast of B.C., Canada

My eyes opened even wider to the beauty of nature in his presence. It was as though my own awareness of nature was enhanced by his awareness, and before long I became more observant of our surroundings, pointing at the eagle soaring in the air, and the heron waiting patiently for his fish. I had never experienced this with any other hiking partner before and even travelling in Asia I'd struggled to find this quality in many other people. Greg was a rare bird, indeed.

Vancouver Island, B.C. is a paradise of glorious west coast scenery with lush emerald forests, alpine peaks, freshwater lakes, rocky shorelines, rivers and pristine beaches.

Greg's job as a technician meant he was on the road and he often surprised me by nipping back to the marina during the day to take me on a little trip.

"I have to go to Duncan, on call. I have to drive through some wonderful countryside to get there and pass through Chemainus on the way. Want to keep me company?"

"Now that's a silly question," I smiled, "or could I just stay here and paint the deck?"

Duncan is known as a hub for North American Indians and has several extraordinary galleries specializing in fine First Nations Art. Chemainus is world-renowned for its more-than-thirty colossal murals, making the town one massive outdoor art gallery. With Greg's nephew, Matthew, we visited a breathtaking river north of Duncan, called the

Cowichan River, and inhaled the pure majesty of this area. We stood on the bridge and looked down into the cobalt clear water that tumbled between mammoth boulders and we saw several people sunbathing on the rocks and cooling off in the water. We took a trail down to an area where we could walk down to a small beach with vast boulders and we slipped into the cool water. The day was so warm we stayed in the water for some time, letting the currents sweep us downstream and into little pools caused by the eddies.

Enjoying the dogwood flowers of spring on
Vancouver Island, B.C.

Diary Excerpt: April 22nd, 2003

I had one of the greatest birthdays ever—the sun shone and Greg took me to this astonishing site on the top of a rock bluff. Standing in the sun close to the rim of a sheer rock face, the view was magnificent. The blankets of tall fir trees were close enough to touch, or so it seemed; the backdrop was of snowcapped mountains. This country is so beautiful, and the spring is enchanting, that is, when it stops raining. I love to inhale the blossom trees, the magnolias in full bloom, and the diverse wild flowers that seem to grow everywhere. The woodlands are carpeted with tiny blue and pink flowers and look charming. The beaches are ideal for beachcombing, with their fascinating knurled driftwood and vibrant starfish that are washed ashore. I don't think I've ever seen such brilliant, stout starfish, a dramatic lilac and a subtle cerise, really delightful. The spring is contagious; everyone smiles and has a spring in their step.

Love is very much in the air, very much. I feel like I have a warm glow inside. I love the dogwoods, massive perfect flowers that layer the entire tree, and Frisbee golf, which I watched families play in the park. Instead of a hole in the ground, there is a pole surrounded by a basket that you are supposed to throw the Frisbee at and it should land in the basket. The parks are covered with magnolia and dogwood blossoms and have cool babbling rivers flowing through them. I love the call of the sea lions (I've never seen so many), and the Canada Geese that let me feed them by hand when they visit the marina. I love the fact that I've had fresh flowers to look at for the last two weeks, and I love the fact that I smile all the time again. If only I could be motivated to work harder toward cruising in September.

I was very happy with my life right then; I was putting on weight again after losing my appetite in Asia, and I was filling out in all the wrong places under the influence of the luxury food items Greg kept feeding me, like fillet steak, fresh salmon, and fresh cream cakes.

I had my very own pet goose who visited me daily so I could handfeed her from the dock, and everyone told me she was likely to bring me her babies once they were born. I was a very contented cheerful woman, the only problem being I was not allowed to stay in this seventh heaven longer than September. It had never really occurred to me that I wouldn't be able to stay in Canada longer than six months, because I had never made a plan as long as that in the last four years.

The contrast of the countryside compared to where I had been living before and the reminder of the beauty of the seasons (which I didn't think I had missed in Asia and Africa) gave me a fresh outlook about ever living in a hot climate country again.

Diary Excerpt: May 20th, 2003

I am so very happy and contented. There's been a wonderful long holiday weekend to commemorate Victoria Day in British Columbia and what better way to celebrate than to anchor out in the bay and watch the fantastic fireworks display from *Seafire*. The mood in town was magical with parades and bands and market stalls.

We also visited the City of Victoria, which is the provincial capital and called "the city of flowers," with its graceful, sophisticated heritage buildings and vibrant harbourside walks complete with artists and performers in the street to keep you entertained. The buildings reminded me of England and the gardens were all perfectly manicured, just like home. The imposing Empress Hotel is legendary for "English afternoon teas" and the striking architecture of the building is exceptionally impressive. The historical legislative building is especially appealing in the evening when it is lit by thousands of lights that reflect in the harbour waters. I really loved Victoria, and I commented at the time it would be a lovely place to live, with its warm climate all year round.

Vancouver Island, BC—a paradise of glorious West Coast scenery with lush emerald forests, alpine peaks, freshwater lakes and rivers, pristine beaches, and rocky shorelines.

Diary Excerpt: July 1st, 2003

We've visited the high alpine areas of Mount Washington and Forbidden Plateau, which have incredible scenery even though there was only a little snow at this time of year. The ski resort was shut down for the summer but there was a slight snow covering we could play in.

It would have been really pleasant to take the ski lift to the top to get the view, but of course it was not operating. We walked a little way, but it would have been a stiff hike to the top where I can only imagine that the 360° view would be spectacular.

My pet goose wasn't spooked by our absence and she was back this morning, honking for my attention so I would go and feed her and her babies; I'm getting quite attached to them all. She surprised me the other day by turning up with two families of babies just as we were motoring out of the berth, so Greg let *Seafire* drift while we fed the babies and took photos. I really look forward to the daily visit of the babies, which all take on their own individual personalities and let me feed them by hand. We joked that when we leave the marina maybe the geese would follow us in formation to Mexico.

Work is progressing on *Seafire* and we've managed to find a second-hand Aries wind vane, which we're going to pick up from a yacht sailing to the West Coast. This reputable wind vane will give us an autopilot when she's sailing, as it reacts to the wind's direction and works with an external rudder that is bolted to the rear of the boat. I've made it quite clear I won't be hand steering a sailing boat across a major ocean again.

We drove to Ucluelet across stunning country and headed for Long Beach, aptly named for its great length. The West Coast is open to the Pacific Ocean and tons of driftwood ends up on the perfect, sandy beach, from as far afield as Japan. The beach is piled high above the tide line with heaps of remarkably shaped driftwood, which the local children build into interesting hides and shelters. The local artists often pick through the piles to find inspiration for their art.

We took a trail that led us along the rocky shoreline and watched the Pacific Ocean crashing onto the rocks. The tide pools were crystal clear with intense emerald green sea anemones and vibrant starfish of amethyst and cerise, sitting in a perfect aquarium garden. We took countless photographs of the many vibrant coral gardens that have formed in the abundant rock pools. We laughed at the "beetle-head" seaweed that stood rigid in rows on the rocks and then bowed its head into the waves as the water crashed over it. As the water retreated the "pop stars" flicked back their hairdos and shook the water off. I had never seen seaweed with such shaggy hairdos, and I was fascinated by the way they danced with the movement of the water.

Time was moving on and we decided to use up Greg's holiday allowance to visit his family in Calgary to introduce me and say goodbye. The drive across to Calgary would take us through the Canadian Rockies and the National Parks of Jasper, Banff, Glacier, and Yoho, so we planned a circular return route and packed the camping gear.

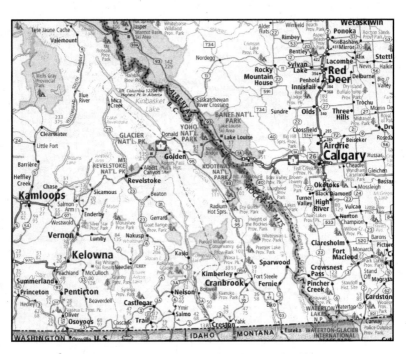

Southwestern British Columbia and Alberta

Diary Excerpt: July 15th, 2003

This is the first chance I've had since leaving Vancouver to take my eyes off the inconceivable panorama we've been driving through. The Canadian Rockies are so dramatic, they're almost a visual overload with my eyes feasting on glorious vistas in every direction.

Glacier National Park

Glacier National Park sports extravagant jagged peaks with frozen rivers slowly blanketing the slopes. Each park has its own distinctive splendour, and our first campground, nestled at the base of Mount Begbie, was the beginning of many impressive glaciers to come. The campsites provided all we needed for a comfortable night—a private area in the trees with our own picnic table, fire pit, and wood.

The following day, we took a leisurely drive through Glacier National Park, relentlessly oohing and exclaiming loud wows all the way at simply magnificent peaks topped with glaciers thousands of years old—substantial aged ice probably never touched. The exhibit at Rogers Pass information centre had a fascinating aerial photograph, giving us a three-dimensional view looking deep down into the valley and the road we had just travelled.

Yoho National Park

Yoho National Park is known as the land of rock walls and waterfalls. "Yoho" is a Cree expression of awe and wonder, which describes this whole area very well. We accessed Takakkawa Falls by the thirteen-kilometre Yoho Valley Road, which climbs precipitously and has tight, sharp switchbacks all the way up. The road had only been open for two weeks and we stopped on the way down for a snowball fight. Icy cold glacier snow had melted back from the road and cooled down our hot bodies that were cooking in 34° C temperatures.

The waterfalls were really glorious, tumbling from a vast height, and we could climb down to the base, or all the way up to the top if we wanted an icy cold shower from the spray. The river that flows from the falls is the colour of ice. It's the glacier melt from a glacier lake nestled behind the summit of the mountain. The outlook from the base of the waterfall truly is awe-inspiring, with glacier peaks, glacier rivers plummeting through pine forests and wildflowers, and a bright azure sky; it is quite perfect.

It made me feel so lucky to be able to appreciate such inconceivable, natural unspoilt splendour. I guess I was particularly impressed, because I had never seen a glacier before and I found them just fascinating. The price I've paid for living in hot countries for too long is a profound need for anything cool.

One of the many scenic campsites
in the Canadian Rockies

Our campsite that night had a splendid view of the glacier and we sat around our campfire watching the altered luminosity playing on the mountains and the glacier. Our two-person tent was cozy, and we cuddled together on our inflatable mattress warm and toasty under our comforter.

Fields of wild flowers and alpine peaks near the
Bow Valley Parkway

Bow Valley Parkway

The next day, we took the Bow Valley Parkway, stopping along the way to watch giant elk feeding on the wild grasses, and posturing for the camera in the tumbling mountain stream. We also spotted three black bears including a baby who still had his downy baby hair and was very content frolicking in the long grasses by the roadside, oblivious to the onlookers taking photographs.

Many mischievous ground squirrels sat on their hind legs amongst the smorgasbord of wildflowers and were very happy to be hand-fed by the passersby. It was a real novelty for me to see so many animals in the wild and it reminded me again of some of the things I had been missing. We camped at the base of Castle Mountain, beneath its remarkable rocky turrets, close to Johnston Canyon.

Johnston Canyon

Boardwalks clung to the side of the canyon following the natural contours of the rock face and giving inconceivable views right into the interior of the canyon. The arresting pristine aquamarine waters that plummet down from the lower and upper falls carve amazing shapes and colours into the rock walls of the canyon giving an ever-changing vision as they cascade around large water-gnarled rocks. We walked through the canyon on boardwalks and bridges until we reached the upper falls, which thundered down a sheer rock face, framed by a striking rainbow. We chilled ourselves in the cool spray before descending to see the canyon once again lit by the lowering sun.

Calgary

We spent two days in Calgary, a stark disparity of flat lands and city. We celebrated Canada Day alongside the river with Greg's mum and sister, and enjoyed the festive spirit of the fete.

The following day, we hired an inflatable boat with Greg's brother, Steve, to drift down the Bow River, which flows right through the city providing a unique view of the city skyline. As is usual for this part of the world, where the weather can change fast, what started out to be shorts-and-bikini weather soon turned to hail stones and an icy wind. We stood for some time watching the clouds move and darken, but decided to risk launching our inflatable boat anyway. Within five minutes of drifting down the river, the wind suddenly picked up and skewed the raft sideways and made it pick up speed. We rowed frantically toward an island and made landfall just as the icy rain began to fall. We made a campfire with twigs and fallen wood, and stood drinking bottled beer and warming ourselves on the small flames as hefty, icy hailstones bounced off the shoulders of our life jackets. The distraction of keeping the fire alive and drinking beer meant we could simply wait for the storm to pass before continuing our trip down the stream. It certainly was the nicest way to view the city and very pleasurable.

The following day we said our goodbyes to family and headed for Lake Louise. The weather had become quite overcast compared to the hot sunny days when we started this trip and the lake was not displaying its full glory of bright opaque colours without the sun. The odd slash of sunlight reflected off the water giving a breathtaking sneak at the famous colours of this lake, only making me long for more.

Johnston Canyon

Icefields Parkway

As we headed out along the Icefields Parkway, the weather seemed to get more overcast, and the tops of the Rocky Mountains were shrouded in cloud. Peeking out just to tease us were the edges of the ice fields that flow from the peaks. We looked down into Peyto Lake, which is probably one of the most photographed sites for holiday brochures. The turquoise lake was nestled in a perfect valley of alpine flowers and pine trees with a backcloth of the Rocky Mountains. Our next stop along this incredible Parkway was Mistaya Canyon—a breathtaking vista of the Bow River cascading through a constricted canyon, carving improbable shapes into the rocks as it gushed through the narrow gap. The alpine flowers and meadows alongside the river kept us occupied for over an hour and I couldn't resist the temptation to pocket some of the vibrantly painted, patterned pebbles that created a multicoloured border to the river. I was enthralled by these canyons. Perfectly smooth, rounded potholes peppered the top of the canyon walls. They were engraved into smooth curves and swirls from constantly being eroded by the cascading water. We still planned to walk the Columbia Icefield before it got dark, so we grudgingly left this little piece of dreamland.

Takakkawa Falls at Yoho National Park

We accessed the Athabasca Glacier from the road, hiked up a steep trial to where it started and walked on the ice. In some places, the ice was as thick as thirty stories high, but we hiked only a short distance against a sharp frosty breeze that was blowing off the top. We walked against the icy wind that took our breath away, despite being dressed up warmly. It stung any exposed parts of our skin, like our faces, which were not covered. We turned around, treading carefully so as not to slip on the ice, and put the freezing wind behind us.

Takakkawa falls in Yoho National Park

"I visited this same glacier fifteen years ago and it has receded so drastically since then that it's like visiting a different site," Greg said.

Indeed, as we walked up to the beginning of the icefield, we hiked past markers for the outside edge of the glacier. Greg pointed to one mark that was nearly a mile from the edge of the ice.

"This is where I walked to when I last visited. At this point of the mountain, it took a sheer drop and you could look into the ice, but you couldn't get onto the top to walk on it, so it was like looking through a frozen waterfall."

"I guess it looked more spectacular then than it does now," I replied.

"Yes, it was more impressive, because you were looking through the glacier rather than walking on top."

Cold and hungry, we headed to our campsite for the night and planned our last day.

Mount Edith Cavell

Our final visit was to Mount Edith Cavell, which we reached by a 14.5-kilometre precipitous, switchback road, which gave incredible views of the valley as we climbed through the clouds. At the peak, there was a beautiful trail that took us right to the base of the Cavell Glacier, where we touched the fifty-foot cliffs of ice, stood on the periphery of Glacier Lake, and watched the ice floes fall off and float in the lake. The solid ice cliffs are a dazzling, intense sapphire within and the lake is an icy, azure blue. My fascination with the glaciers made me promise to visit Alaska one day with Greg and see them in their real glory.

Our final night of camping marked a drastic change in the weather, and we woke to sodden bedding after a night of continuous rain. It was a reminder that we were lucky to experience such nice weather for most of this camping trip. We were forced to spend the last night in a motel with our wet gear stuffed into the back of the car. We were so glad this hadn't happened at the beginning of our trip. I guess that is the problem with camping in these areas—once it gets wet, it stays wet, unless you happen to be lucky enough to experience as much sunny weather as we got. We were glad to get back to the marina and the comfort of *Seafire*.

It was a timely reminder that winter would arrive soon and that we should start making progress down the Pacific Coast of Washington and Oregon before it set in. Greg had a few more weeks at work and then the preparatory work would really notch up for cruising. One of the biggest jobs we had still to do was the provisioning for the trip—we were taking several visits to Costco each weekend to stock up on the cans and bulk foods. We were not sure of our plans, but we were prepared to be at sea for several weeks if necessary and the weather was good enough. At this stage, we still planned to head directly for Mexico, perhaps making Isla San Martin our first landfall, but not checking into the country until we reached La Paz. We had purchased several cruising guides and large scale maps from another yacht that had cruised the area, and we spent some time with learning about the area and the various anchorages available.

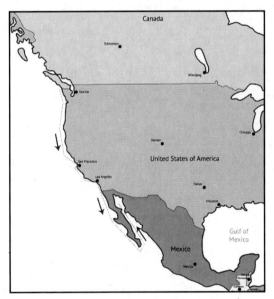

Sailing route down the West Coast
of North America

Heading to Mexico

Diary Excerpt: September 1st, 2003

We are anchored off Sidney Spit, Sidney, near Victoria; we're finally en route to Mexico. The first couple of days away from the marina have taught us both valuable lessons. Neither of us had actually sailed for over a year and I was astonished how nervous I was. Things soon settled down and yesterday we started to work well as a team as we tacked down the channel with the rail close to the water and reaching up to 5 knots. It was a good test for *Seafire* and for us.

Seafire

Diary Excerpt: September 2nd, 2003

We're at a really pretty anchorage here in Becher Bay. We motored up from Oak Bay with no wind on this charming sunny day, looking across Juan de Fuca Strait to the mountains of the USA. The wind is bitterly cold and the water is freezing; the closer we get to the Pacific, the cooler it seems, although the sun is still hot. We anchored behind three little rocky islands all by ourselves and went off exploring by dinghy the spectacular little coves in the almost tropical bay.

We keep seeing lots of curious seals. They're so cute the way they bob their heads out of the water and look at you as if to say, "What are you doing in my kitchen?" Yesterday as we left Oak Bay and visited the customs dock, a beautiful grey seal was begging for food and we could clearly see him playing in the transparent water.

As we passed Race Rocks before entering Becher Bay we spied and heard all the sea lions on the islands loudly barking their songs. We had to move to a different anchorage, because our paradise was getting a little choppy and the wind was due to pick up, so we headed for Murder Bay where there is some civilization and a couple of boats are anchored. That evening the wind died down again and we watched a family of sea otters playing rough and tumble and feasting on fish as the sun went down. We decided to stay the night and planned to depart for Port Renfrew as early as possible in the morning.

Diary Excerpt: September 7th, 2003

We've been socked in at Sooke Basin for three days now. We cleared Becher Bay by 7:00 a.m. with no wind and immediately hit a current going against us. Within an hour and still no wind, we were bashing into a southwesterly swell as high as six feet, achieving less than 2 knots over ground. As we spotted Sooke Bay from the water, the swell started to increase in size even more and we were climbing up the crest of the sharp waves, then splashing down, effectively stopping *Seafire* and achieving little more than a knot in speed overall.

We decided to take shelter in Sooke Basin, since this was the last available shelter on this coastline. The first evening the wind picked up as the forecast predicted 25 knots from the west (the direction we wanted to go, so no good for sailing). The following day, a fog bank moved in, bringing with it a bitter cold wind, so we decided to take a trip into the nearest town.

We followed the Galloping Goose trail, which a nice old

lady told us went straight downtown; not! We detoured out of our way two and half kilometres before getting a lift from a nice old gent who dropped us off right downtown and gave us instructions how to get the bus back. We exchanged money (now that we're talking about calling in at some US ports), did a little shopping for more fresh produce, and walked back out into the street into a thick fog bank. The icy fog shrouded the little town and it was quite a sight to see so much bare flesh dressed for summer suddenly assaulted by the cold fog. Back in the anchorage, *Seafire* sat underneath a sunny break in the fog bank giving us a window out of the wind and fog to work on the boat.

The weather seemed to have turned quite suddenly with gales up to 30 knots featured frequently in the weather forecast and lots of fog.

"I'm worried that this is a trend that will continue. Should we hang around for a window, or do you think it will get worse?" I asked Greg.

"The news from the Pacific is not good either with southeast winds blowing until Tuesday, which would put the wind on the nose. I was looking forward to some nice downwind sailing, but it's been like this ever since we started listening to the forecasts. I don't know if it's going to change," replied Greg worriedly.

Diary Excerpt: September 11th, 2003

We woke Tuesday morning to the wind blowing from a different direction across the basin and quickly turned to the weather forecast to hear about 10- to 15-knot winds coming from the east, just what we needed to get to the mouth of the strait. We made the decision to sail as soon as possible and quickly got *Seafire* ready to head for either Neah Bay (Washington State (WA), USA) or, the original plan, Port Renfrew (Vancouver Island), with little shelter. We weighed anchor at 12:45 p.m. and arrived in Port Renfrew at 10:30 p.m. We did a little sailing to start and then had to motor the rest of the way, entering the bay with a full moon, and using the radar to anchor off the beach.

It was a very uncomfortable night with the swell coming straight into the bay and hitting us beam-on, rocking the boat all night. The sound of the waves smashing on the nearby rocks didn't deter our imaginations from playing games. By the following morning, the fog had moved in to completely engulf us and we were socked in again, but this time in a relatively unsheltered anchorage. We had to spend another evening there but were quick to put an optimistic ear to the weather forecast the next day. We motored out of the bay and stayed optimistic for a wind change, eventually being forced to run off course to sail against the increasing swell to Neah Bay.

Our First Gale—Off Cape Flattery

The winds continued to gain strength from the west and the swells got higher. We didn't make the clearance of the rocks on our first tack and decided it was too risky to cross between the islands and rocks off Cape Flattery, so we tacked again. This area had appalling seas, confused steep waves, and currents that virtually boiled the water. Things started to go really wrong when we were forced to tack again, back toward the Canadian side, and the wind continued to pick up speed. The swell got bigger and steeper, and we were really over-canvassed, heeling right over with the rail in the water. Greg was physically sick after trying to reduce sail and suffering from the pitching of the bow, and I was desperately holding onto a sheet (the rope that controls the sail), waiting for things to calm down a bit so I could try and get the head sail down. Greg was hanging onto the helm, retching into the cockpit, and looking really ashen. My sheet started to get horribly tangled and thrashed around, held only by one stopper knot.

"We have to get that sail down and it will have to be you; I can't control this sickness every time I go on the bow, and you can't control the tiller with these waves; it's taking all my strength to stop *Seafire* from slewing," cried Greg as the boat pitched violently.

I crabbed across the deck, clipped on with my safety line, and collapsed onto my hands and knees on the bow of *Seafire*, timing my moves with her movement to reach up and pull the sail down. With my body as low as possible, I reached up with my arms and made several attempts to get all the sail down and tied off. I needed one hand to hold onto the boat as her bow nosed into the waves soaking me with green water and throwing me upwards as she slammed into the next wave. By the time I got back to the cockpit, I was violently shaking with fright and hyperventilating through sheer panic. Greg was fighting with the helm trying to keep *Seafire* from slewing sideways in the steep seas and we both heard a really loud bang indicating something was really wrong.

"I think we hit a large kelp bed. Remember the one we managed to avoid on the last tack?" I screamed. "It caught the rudder of the wind vane and it wouldn't let go, so it's sheared off instead."

We later found out that the fantastic design of the Aries wind vane had built in safety measures for such emergencies, and the bolts holding down the rig sheared off, releasing the rudder as it swung up and broke the wooden vane. Disabled, but still intact, it was time to run downwind back to the shelter of Neah Bay.

The timing was perfect.

"Look at the log barge. He seems to be having difficulty controlling his steerage. It's as well we're now heading away from him; you can't even see him when he goes into a trough of the waves," Greg said. "I wouldn't like to have been on a collision course with that."

We'd spotted him before the waves got so big, but didn't realize he was still around.

Neah Bay—Makah Indian Reservation, USA

It was approaching midnight by the time we made the entrance to Neah Bay, and the entrance proved to be difficult to navigate while we squinted into the confusing lights trying to read the pilot while feeling sick and tired. The wind was almost certainly a gale now—at least 35 knots and waves up to ten feet pushing us from behind.

The wind was gusting in the bay and we struggled to get the main sail down within the limited space of the bay and under limited vision. I was a physical and mental wreck, trying to keep *Seafire* pointing into the wind so Greg could get the sail down, but I was petrified of running out of space, convinced that the breakwater wall was much closer than it really was. My mind had closed down; I was overloaded with fright; I had an immense lack of energy, extreme back pain, and was worried sick. I just wanted it to stop.

We eventually anchored after the second attempt and crawled into bed after spending twelve hours tacking nowhere.

Diary Excerpt: September 18th, 2003

Our one week anniversary in Neah Bay was celebrated with gale-force winds almost identical to those we came in with. Last night, it blew and blew, and the wake from the swell came into our nice quiet bay we had got quite used to, rocking the boat and us. We now have the company of another four yachts we think are also heading south. We met Bob and Rita on the sailing yacht *Farewell* who are going to be harbour hopping down the US coast all the way to Mexico; we think we are going to take the same route, so we'll probably meet up again. A weather window of three days starts on Saturday and we're hoping we can get as far as Coos Bay, Oregon, before it changes again.

Neah Bay is populated by the Makah Tribe, and the people

are really friendly and smiley. They have one basic general store, which is expensive, but seems to stock about everything you'd need. They are quite cut off in this furthest northwest corner of the USA, so they are quite self-sufficient. They have an interesting museum with artifacts and information on the First Nations.

Diary Excerpt: September 20th, 2003

The area has prolific wildlife and two large sea lions are resident in the bay, splashing and feeding right off the dock. The water was so clear that we could see them diving for large halibut and then jumping out of the water with the big fish in their mouths and throwing them across the water to tear a piece off. The seagulls were going crazy scavenging off the fish before it sank and the sea lion surfaced again to feed and tear the fish apart once more. We could have watched it for hours, but the wind was bitterly cold on our faces. The bay was full of screaming seagulls following the seals around as they surfaced with fish in their mouths and threw them across the water.

We also spotted pelicans for the first time. Pelicans? Here? We got quite close before they all took off flying in formation, no doubt heading for California and warmer waters.

☙ Reflections From 2015 ❧

Meeting Greg when I arrived in Canada was a welcome distraction. I had arrived in Canada as a "new" me. I had given up smoking and I was in a different climate with people I really liked. I was in love: in love with Greg and in love with Canada. In fact, I felt overwhelmed by the beauty, almost as though the beauty was in technicolour. I think it was the fresh air, the cooler climate, and the bright, vivid green everywhere. It was almost as though my eyes were suddenly wide open and I was seeing everything for the first time.

I still feel like that today in 2015. I see everything in a different way. When I reflect back and recapture those heady feelings, I believe it was because I had never actually experienced this depth of feeling before. I struggled to remember if I ever felt this way about Graeme; yet didn't my journal notes describe being "in love" in the same way? Do we fall in love with the idea of being in love? Does our body just react in a different way on autopilot? I've never done drugs, but I often wonder if this euphoric feeling is the reason people take drugs. How long does the love affair last before it starts to change?

I often wonder if I would have stayed with Greg during those first cruising days, if I had a different choice. I had set off to sea with no way to "get off the boat." Our romantic, heady relationship turned into life and death, and then I was dealing with basic survival needs.

I quickly realized Greg had nowhere near the same experience as Graeme as a skipper. Suddenly, I had to be the hero. I was used to the man being the hero—talk about misunderstanding. Greg assumed that because I had spent the last four years crossing major oceans that I would make an experienced co-skipper. I assumed his ability as the hero skipper was the same as Graeme's.

Our first storm proved to be a very different experience from "danger at sea" on Khulula. So Greg was not the hero after all.

I realize now that the way I reacted was hard on Greg and our relationship. I blamed him and judged him for not protecting me and for putting my life in danger. I fell out of love with him quickly, and he went to a place of defence. I started to see a temper I had not experienced before. I had never dealt with anger before, and I didn't realize at the time that I was creating that situation. I'm quite sure that I made it apparent how I felt about Greg not living up to Graeme's hero image. I probably even said it aloud a few times, when I was feeling particularly vulnerable.

While I was at sea, the stress of not feeling safe was my priority and my relationship with Greg was often in conflict because of this. When we came ashore and explored the coastline, we were free of conflict and full of adventure and joy. Greg loved to hike and explore nature and take photographs, and I loved to go beachcombing and creating artistic pieces from shells; we were great travelling partners. Every time we arrived in a new port, we were both excited about exploring the new town or hiking the coastline. The stress and conflict only happened when we set back out to sea again, when my feelings dropped right back to basic survival levels. This certainly created high "highs" and low "lows," but somehow, I always kept going back out there knowing that once we reached our final destination, the relationship would be back on the roller coaster of high "highs."

I resolved myself that since we were living 24/7 in a very small space, we had to work at our relationship—there was no "leaving"— so we had to work on all our problems. This means today we are even closer, because we know each other so well and understand what makes the other tick. I know what triggers Greg and his anger, so I'm mindful and conscious of my words and actions. Greg knows I get impatient and I'm a bit of a perfectionist, so he allows for that. I'm messy and cluttered and I multitask all the time; Greg is a neat freak and can only do one task at a time. We both know these things, so my impatience works hard while Greg does one task at a time, and he has to be patient and understanding as he follows me around picking up after me! Patience, understanding, compassion and, above all, love and companionship make our differences all worthwhile!

USA Pacific Coast

"We all have the extraordinary coded within us, waiting to be released."

Jean Houston

We eventually left Neah Bay and rounded Cape Flattery to the west on September 20th. The weather forecast called for north to northeast winds at 5 to 15 knots, but we didn't get any wind at all and motored out into the Pacific until sight of land disappeared with calm seas, a clear blue sky, and lovely sunshine. By early morning, the temperatures had plummeted to 7° C, but the sun started to warm us as we sailed into our second day at sea. We were optimistic about reaching California, even if we had to motor the whole way, when the weather forecast suddenly warned of high winds building up to 30 knots in our area.

We decided not to risk it and headed back towards Grays Harbour, WA, rather than Coos Bay another thirty miles south. As we approached Grays Harbour, we called the Coast Guard to get the latest report. "This is the yacht *Seafire* approaching Grays Harbour; can you please give us a current bar report?" Greg called on the VHF.

"Conditions are good. Have you ever crossed a bar before?" asked the Coast Guard. We hadn't and we'd heard horror stories about the bars that cross nearly all the entrances to harbours on the West Coast. The bars are affected by the vast volume of water in the Pacific Ocean trying to force itself into the narrow entrance of the harbours. If you don't navigate the bars at the right tide, you can get swept into tidal rips and standing waves. In anything other than calm conditions and slack tide, it can be a very dangerous crossing and so yachts are always advised to check the bar conditions before entering.

"No, Sir, we have not. Do you have any advice?" Greg replied.

"Would you like the Coast Guard to give you an escort as a training exercise?" It seemed like a good idea to get an escort across our first bar while providing real training experience for the Coast Guard, so we readily accepted.

"Thank you. We will stand by for instructions."

It was interesting to watch the Coast Guard boat rush out of the bay to our "rescue" and escort us across the bar, giving us information along the way, which would be invaluable for the numerous bar crossings we would have to make down this coastline. Once inside the bay, we met up again with yacht *Farewell* and Bob and Rita, who came to take our lines as we came alongside the docks.

Diary Excerpt: September 24th, 2003

We're both still worried about the time clicking away, but don't want to be forced into weather that makes us nervous; we're determined to take our time and do day hops, next run twenty-seven hours at 5 knots, and after that we can do even shorter hops, which will be a lot easier for planning weather windows.

We're both very happy and beginning to enjoy exploring new territory, taking trips ashore at the harbour towns in Washington. We had a lovely trip yesterday into the sleepy little town of Aberdeen on the local bus. Temperatures went up to 25° C, which cheered us, proving summer was still around, although the fog is ever-present.

The Sleepy Harbour Town of Westport, Washington, USA

We both really liked Westport with its extensive beaches ideal for surfing and the affable people who are ever eager to help the cruisers. They really seemed genuinely interested in our voyage and eager to help out in any way. The harbour towns have a great respect for the sea and love to hear stories and plans. The ladies in the local souvenir store kept me talking for over an hour when I visited their store to see if I could buy a Mexican flag.

The town had a charming holiday ambience, and the wildlife was abundant with a troop of grey mottled seals in the bay, which amused us as we watched them fish and fool around. We also saw quite a number of pelicans, which we found enthralling to watch diving from incredible heights to fish. We really enjoyed walking the breakwater wall and watching the giant 360-foot paddle boat that was en route to San Francisco to be used as a museum. We could easily have stayed in this enchanting town for a longer period of time, but we were preparing to leave after a week's stay when the wind was forecast at 10 knots. We planned to go to Newport the next leg, and hoped to move on quickly to Coos Bay and onwards to California.

Diary Excerpt: September 30th, 2003

We arrived in Newport yesterday afternoon after a long day and night motoring into the wind and choppy seas. I actually felt quite seasick and was really relieved to arrive. Now, we're on our way again after a twenty-four-hour stopover. The sea is the flattest we've experienced so far, like a lake with virtually no swell and only a little wind. We sailed for the first couple of hours in a lovely downwind position in an eerie light caused by low thin fog close to the water. If you looked up, there was bright blue sky and we were trapped inside a moving halo of glassy seas and a fence of white cloud.

We're both feeling really good about our southerly progress; soon we'll be in California.

We only stayed for the night at Newport and left for Coos Bay the next day to catch a good weather window. At last, we will be leaving the State of Washington and entering Oregon with our next landfall. It was the best passage so far with completely flat seas and a little north wind that gave us a very comfortable passage, despite being back in a cold dense fog bank most of the way.

We had to slow down because we were going to arrive too early for the bar crossing, and suddenly we lost all forward transmission. The wind had died down and we were only fourteen miles off. We coasted at 2 to 3 knots, finally dropping our speed to as low as 1 knot, meaning it would take another fourteen hours to reach the bar at Coos Bay.

The timing for this bar was critical and so we called the Coast Guard to tell them of our intentions.

"We have lost all forward transmission and so we cannot use our engine. The wind has now dropped, meaning we can only make a speed of 1 knot. Our intention is to cross the bar at Coos Bay before the tide changes again and so we will sail slowly in that direction." For my non-sailing readers, this is approximately equivalent to one mile an hour; most people can actually walk a lot faster than this without even trying.

"Please keep in radio contact with the Coast Guard and report your GPS position and speed hourly," replied the Coast Guard. We kept this up for the next seven hours, but maintained the same speed, meaning we would not make the entrance in time for the change in tide. This meant the crossing would have been dangerous with no forward transmission from our engine.

The Coast Guard called us on the VHF to get our position and speed.

"We are still seven miles from the entrance to the harbour and we are currently making an average of 1 knot," reported Greg.

"Okay. We would like to come out and tow you into the harbour; otherwise, you will miss the slack tide and will be making a dangerous crossing against the tide with no engine."

"Okay. We will prepare for a tow," replied Greg.

And so, for the second time on the USA coast, the Coast Guard helped us out in our moment of need. We were very grateful for their assistance, which they again used as a training exercise. This service was provided free of charge since they preferred to take preventative safety measures rather than rescue a boat in danger. Across the bar, yacht *Farewell* and Bob and Rita were ready again to take our lines; they commented that the Coast Guard had once again assisted our arrival.

Waves as high as 27 feet at Coos Bay, Oregon, USA

Charleston, Coos Bay, Oregon, USA

The harbour of Charleston at the mouth of the inlet to Cook Bay is a popular fishing and crabbing port, and legendary for Dungeness crabs. Many weekenders visit the port to fish or crab in the bay. There was always an interesting crowd of people and the local RV Park provided good amenities including showers, internet access, and laundry. We knew we would have to stay more than two weeks there to sort out our transmission problem and so committed to a month's moorage, which was cheaper than the day rate as long as we stayed longer than fourteen days.

We enjoyed walking through the woodland up to the Coast Guard lookout, which has a superb view of the bar entrance. We could observe boats navigating the bar, and when there was a "rough bar" warning, we always headed up there to see if any crabbing boats attempted the entrance. We often saw the Coast Guard cutters training in the rip tides and we even saw Coast Guard helicopters on training exercises simulating sea rescues in some of the worse breaking waves. We would spend hours up there looking out at the violent sea, reminding ourselves why we were sitting safely in the marina.

Most of the RVs we met were also on the way down to Mexico, mostly Canadians escaping the cold winters—they're called "Snowbirds." We often joked they had a much easier journey than we were letting ourselves in for; their only concern being the cost of fuel. We marvelled at these "land yachts" that were mostly living the same self-sufficient lifestyle we were living on the sea, but without the inconvenience of the stormy weather and high winds to delay the journey. We often joked with the idea of trading in *Seafire* for a Winnebago.

We looked up Mike, who—when we'd met him in Grays Harbour—had invited us to visit him on his motor boat if we called in at Coos Bay. He and his wife lived on their boat in the marina, and happily took us on a tour of the area. We were very appreciative, since it gave us the opportunity to explore this craggy coastline and all it has to offer.

"We'll drive along the Cape Arago Highway that follows the coastline and head for Cape Arago lighthouse. We'll make a stop at Sunset Bay State Park for lunch and walk the sheltered beach and then head for the Oregon Coast Trail to Simpson Reef and Shell Island," said Mike, packing us into the back of his car.

"Both Simpson Reef and Shell Island have astounding rock formations where the sea crashes into the shoreline, and this is the breeding season for the seals and sea lions, so you'll be able to watch them from the lookout," he added.

We drove through spectacular scenery and arrived at the lookout for Shell Island, which is the northernmost breeding ground on the Pacific Coast for the Californian sea lion and Steller sea lions, as well as the gigantic elephant seal.

"It says here on the information board that the Steller sea lion weighs up to 2,000 pounds, can be as long as 10 feet, and the pups are 40 pounds at birth," I exclaimed.

"Well, the elephant seal is the largest member of the seal family and the deepest diving mammal, reaching depths of 4,000 feet; and it only comes to land to breed and to moult," replied Greg, who was also reading the information. "And they weigh as much as two and a half tons and are up to 13 feet long."

"Unfortunately, you see many dead pups though," said Mike. "The pups cannot survive alone in the water until eight to ten weeks after birth, and many of the winter storms wash waves over Shell Island, knocking them into the ocean, so the pups rarely survive."

We watched all the different kinds of seals and sea lions existing together on this island simply because it gave them the best shelter around from the storms. It looked like a carpet from a distance because every available space was taken by pups or adults. In the water nearby, the playful harbour seal pups, which can swim at birth and are independent within three weeks, frolicked in the water, teasing the elephant seal pups. The barking from the sea lions was thunderous and we had to shout to be heard above the racket.

Mike took us on a weekend trip to the Oregon Dunes north of Coos Bay, closer to the smaller bar crossing of Winchester Bay. This is a popular area for riding dune buggies on the massive sand dunes and the miles of continuous white sand beaches. It is a magnificent sight to see so much sand piled high with nothing else around for miles and miles. The sand is a fine chalky consistency and it reminded us of light snow. Indeed, from a distance the dunes could be mistaken for ski slopes. Our footprints made the only marks on the perfect sand and we clambered up the immense dunes, where there was nothing but sand as far as the eye could see. Some families bring their children to sledge on the sheer dunes, but we were happy to run up and down and make "snow angels" in the faultless sand. Nestled between the dunes is a small oasis of a little river made into a nature reserve; we had a picnic there while watching the birds.

Diary Excerpt: October 10th, 2003

While we were waiting to receive our new transmission, the seas really grew to incredible heights, caused by a storm off Alaska, way to the north.

Each day more fishing boats turned up at the docks and each day the surf got higher and higher, until on Saturday they were reporting swells of twenty-seven feet.

We visited Cape Arago with Mike who said there was a magnificent lookout on the top of the cliffs where you could watch the booming waves. The surf was crashing against the rock cliff face and the sheer capacity of water colliding with the land literally bubbled and foamed as it ran off the rocks, reminding me of whipped milk. The detonation of the waves was like a glorious fireworks display. Greg got some extraordinary photos and I could have spent all day there just watching the waves. The cliff trail took us right along the precipice and we watched the waves crashing all along the coastline, creating different rock formations. It seemed illusory that we were actually sailing this stormy coastline on our little thirty-four-foot boat and we reminded ourselves not to get caught in this kind of weather.

It turned into a lovely sunny day and we had a picnic in

Shore Acres State Park and enjoyed the botanical gardens there.

Diary Excerpt: November 2nd, 2003

By the time our transmission arrived, it had turned into November and we were still experiencing gales up to 45 knots.

Even though we were close to Northern California, the temperatures had plummeted to 4° C at night-time, and we were using our little electric heaters on the docks. We checked the weather daily and eventually a big high was predicted bringing calm weather and higher temperatures. We caught this great weather window that brought really warm temperatures for the time of year, and decided to make as far south as possible. We rounded Cape Mendocino in horrid seas with very light winds, but as we passed the cape at night, the wind suddenly accelerated and the autopilot alarm went off.

Cape Mendocino and Fifteen-Foot Seas

The autohelm could no longer cope with the increased wind and steep seas, so Greg jumped on the helm.

"We need to get down the sail. We are way overpowered and the GPS is showing a speed of 8.5 knots. We're going too fast down these steep waves and *Seafire* is slewing all over the place."

I remembered Cape Flattery in a flashback, and there was no way I was going to crawl out onto the bowsprit (the pole that sticks way out in front of the boat to which the sail is attached) in the pitch black and take down the sail. Unfortunately, there was no way I could take the helm with the heavy weather either, so something had to be done. The slewing of the boat meant that we were corkscrewing in the water; *Seafire* was being smashed from wave to wave in all directions; and we were being carried down the waves into a potentially dangerous wall of water.

"The seas are colossal. Those waves behind us must be fifteen feet tall; it looks like a wall of water bearing down on us. Maybe we should engage the wind vane, and see if that can handle the steering," I screamed.

"Okay, but you'll have to edge out on the boomkin at the stern while I try and keep her steady."

That was still a daunting thing to do—to crawl along two planks of wood extended out from the cockpit and beyond the external rudder, at the back of *Seafire*, and suspend myself over the water. This is what the wind vane is attached to, so I needed to scramble out over the water, gaze into the wall of water above my head, and try and release a tiny pin to engage the wind vane. This then meant the autopilot would take over while the vane reacted to the wind direction and steered the boat with the external rudder.

"I think I've engaged it," I shouted back to Greg in the cockpit, as I hung on for dear life while *Seafire* pitched ferociously in the water.

"Come back here and we'll look; it's too dangerous out there."

I had done it incorrectly and Greg explained the turning motion to engage the pin. It was a question of pulling it out and then turning it once clockwise. No mean feat on a pitching boat balanced on a plank of wood looking into fifteen-foot waves.

"Okay. I've definitely got it this time. Engage the vane."

That did the trick and the wind vane handled the seas well, keeping us on a good course and preventing the boat from slewing. Within two hours, the wind started to die down once we got away from the effects of the acceleration around the cape, and we were left with steep, confused seas and a light wind. We saw the entrance for Fort Bragg as the sun was rising, and considered the narrow bar entrance a cinch compared to what we had just experienced.

Fort Bragg, Northern California, USA

This was the only West Coast town where we did not receive a welcoming embrace. The boat basin was in bad repair with poor docks and facilities, and yet still charged a daily rate significantly higher than any other on the whole of the West Coast.

After four days of being on the wrong side of the river for town access, we decided to risk anchoring in the river now that the tidal range was less pronounced. At low tide, we only had enough depth to prevent grounding but the river was free and very peaceful, and the town was closer. The people with the local businesses would not allow us to tie our dinghy to their docks, so we had to motor downriver to the industrial area where we tied up behind a warehouse. From there we could walk up a steep hill into the delightful town and explore the whole area.

There was a wonderful trail that went the length of the coastline called the Ten Mile Trail, and the beaches off the path were craggy and striking. Glass Beach was an unusual beach with smoothly rounded multicoloured glass pebbles, remnants of a glass factory that used to be close by. I collected many unusually shaped and coloured glass trinkets from this beach and was not the only one doing so. In the meantime, we listened to the weather forecast. Winds were not such a problem but massive swells of eleven to twelve feet were reported with three- to five-foot waves. We didn't need eighteen-foot seas, and so we chose to wait for them to die down. It looked like the wind was switching to the south again, which was no good for us either, so we were stuck in Fort Bragg for at least another week. We heard from the yacht Farewell that they were stuck in Crescent City, further north than us, so their fate was worse than ours. The only good news was that the weather should start getting better the further south we progressed.

Diary Excerpt: November 7th, 2003

We decided to take off with a one-day weather window. The seas were really quite flat and got even better as we passed Point Arena. The wind was on the nose, which was not as forecast, and I was concerned this indicated the gales would reach us earlier than predicted, but we arrived in Bodega Bay with an uneventful passage.

Bodega Bay, California, USA

This beautiful sheltered bay is entered by a wide bar, which then turns into a narrow long channel leading into the main bay. The Bodega Head Trail goes high into the hills and up to incredible cliffs with multicoloured ice plants carpeting the ground.

Diary Excerpt: November 9th, 2003

Here at Bodega Bay, we seem to be anchored in a bird sanctuary. There are so many birds I've never seen before, neat little long-billed curlews with pretty, light-brown coats and a ridiculous outsized slender beak, and American coots that waddle along like little black chickens. In the trees sit big herons with red eyes and blue splashes on their wings—a type of heron that sometimes look like an owl and sometimes an eagle through the leaves of the trees.

We also saw many types of distinctive marsh birds that we couldn't identify and lots of pelicans diving from great heights. We had a wonderful few days in Bodega and walked the whole bay area. The Bodega Head Trail took us high up in the hills to incredible cliffs from where we could look down to the rocky coastline. We did a circular route that took us past some birdwatchers who were delighted by the sight of a group of large snowy white pelicans preening themselves. I was amazed by their size with a five-foot wingspan. It is a rare sight to see this type of pelican in the wild, so we felt really honoured that we could watch them for quite some time.

We also spotted ample osprey in elegant flight and plenty of turkey vultures with their distinctive bald red heads. We walked through hillsides of ice plants ranging in colour from jade and lime to ruby and crimson, and spotted many deer grazing. We also came pretty close to two giant skunks on the trails but were careful to not upset them so they wouldn't spray. As we headed back downhill, we walked through meadows of golden grasses and came across a cougar kill, and then crossed the sand dunes back to the marina, completing an eight-kilometre circle on a pleasant sunny day.

We really enjoyed ourselves and felt like we had eventually caught up with summer.

A walk along the beach in Bodega Bay, California, USA

One day, the wind really picked up and changed direction in the bay, and we were concerned that our anchor would drag, putting our boat too close to a rocky shoreline and shallower water.

"I think we should pull up anchor and head for shelter in the marina across the way," shouted Greg, as the wind speed increased and *Seafire* started to pitch in the swell.

"Yes, this wind is blowing from the south, so it leaves the anchorage exposed to a long fetch all the way down the channel," I agreed.

We radioed the marina to request a slip and the only option was a difficult manoeuvre for our boat. We entered the marina entrance with no problems, but as we turned the boat to head down one of the narrow slips, a sudden gust of wind overpowered the tiller, since we were going so slowly. *Seafire* was blown sideways and we were heading for the boats tied up to the opposite dock.

"I've lost all steerage against this wind," shouted Greg. "Get ready to fend off "

Luckily for us, some fellow yachties saw what was happening and threw us a long rope from the opposite dock.

"Okay, the line is secure," I yelled from the stern, and several strong men started to pull on the rope to get our stern straight so Greg could get some steerage back.

After a few attempts, we made it into the slip and sincerely thanked our rescuers.

As soon as *Seafire* was securely tied to the dock, we headed for the shower rooms and bumped into Joe who was on the way down to greet us.

"You've been providing a very pleasant view for me from my house while you've been anchored on the other side of the bay,"

"Well, thank you, and your house looks quite beautiful from the water too," we replied.

"I'd wanted to invite you to dinner but I had no way to come out to you on the water, so I rushed over here as soon as I saw you heading for the marina."

"That's really kind. When did you have in mind?"

"Well, I figured you guys might appreciate a lift into town to do some provisioning. There is no public transport from the bay and very few places in the way of groceries around here."

"That's really kind; we did wonder how close the nearest town was."

"Well, if you're free now, I'm just going to lunch in the little village nearby where Hitchcock's movie *The Birds* was filmed. I can show you the school house and church where it was shot and I'd like to treat you to lunch in a lovely little café nearby."

"Perfect. Give us thirty minutes to shower and change, and we'll be right with you."

This was so typical of so many people we met on the West Coast of the US. They were genuinely interested in our journey and our progress so far, and provided lifts to the local shops or tours of their area. This must be unique to travelling by boat; I can't imagine that a couple arriving by RV or car would get the same reception. I guess it just goes to show the kindness of people when they understand you don't have your own land transport.

We were invited into Joe's home; he bought us lunch, showed us his home town, took us to all the grocery stores in the main town, which was a good forty minutes away by car, and shared a bottle of very nice red wine with a home-cooked meal the following evening. We swapped stories and he gave us a WeatherFax demodulator so that we could download weather faxes onto our computer via the single sideband radio on our boat. His welcome, the yachties who helped us in the marina, and beautiful Bodega Bay would stay in our memories for a long time.

Diary Excerpt: November 14th, 2003

We're now underway again and crossing the San Francisco Bay right now. Point Reyes Lighthouse looks really remarkable, the way it is perched on a steep cliff and balanced on a small peak. It seems astonishing that we're so close to a big city when the coastline from the sea just looks like high craggy hills. Of course we can't see into the bay where the city is, but it still seems incredible that there is a big city behind those hills.

We had discussed at detail whether we should enter the bay or anchor off Drakes Bay or Half Moon Bay and do an excursion into the city. The tides and wind conditions under the famous San Francisco Bridge are notorious and we were eager to keep moving south, so we decided to head for Half Moon Bay on the south side of the city.

Diary Excerpt: November 21st, 2003

We spent the first few days exploring the local area and found the bus service into Half Moon Bay and beyond. We worked out the train services and decided to visit the city.

The Beautiful City of San Francisco, California, USA

The bus took a breathtaking journey across the striking hills and vineyard country of this area. It seemed unfeasible that a major city was somewhere amongst this rich green panorama, but we eventually saw the buildings that indicated we were getting closer. We crossed from the bus station to the rail station and took the short service downtown to the city.

Being tourists for the day, we rode the street trolley to Fisherman's Wharf, admiring all the handsome candy-coloured majestic buildings and the precipitous streets, just like you see in the movies. The old gent on the cable car held a microphone and told jokes, and explained the history of the buildings and pointed out the views down to the bay. It seemed impracticable that cars could park on such steep hills and many of the buildings had doors of different heights at street level.

We watched the old trams clattering down the street on the waterfront, and admired the view of the Golden Gate Bridge and Alcatraz Island from the historical piers. The weather was implausible for the time of year, hot and sunny, and all the tourists were wearing shorts and t-shirts, and merrily enjoying the famous San Francisco skyline view from the water. The city is striking and the architecture beautiful and very colourful.

Diary Excerpt: November 23rd, 2003

The weather is not being kind to us generally. One storm system after another, and we worry about safe anchorages or face very expensive marinas. At Half-Moon Bay, we had a safe anchorage and yet our anchor still dragged in 30-knot winds in the Bay. It means we are stuck on *Seafire* while the wind blows and when the wind dies down, either the swells are too high or the weather window isn't long enough to run to our next anchorage. We don't think Santa Cruz will be safe now, so we have to go the extra miles to Monterey Bay, where the anchorage looks iffy for protection.

That was the case, although we stayed one night off the pier at Santa Cruz and left the next day for Monterey. We tried to anchor outside the marina breakwater, but found the depth suddenly shelved and decided it was too dangerous. While we were sounding the area, a gentleman was shouting down at us from the pier to say the marina had winter rates available and lots of space. We decided it would be safer to go into the marina and found the same man waiting for us in the marina office with a big smile. We loved Monterey. It was well worth the $144 in marina fees that we had to pay, and we enjoyed the festive spirit of this historical tourist town.

We played the tourist again and visited many of the English pubs (we spotted four in one street) and drank Boddingtons Ale and ate lamb shank for Sunday lunch, and we shopped in the many nautical stores. We even bought matching Monterey jackets for twenty dollars in a sale, and laughed when we saw every other tourist wearing the same jacket that was for sale everywhere; the weather was a little cool by day and many of the tourists were not prepared.

We loved the fisherman's wharf with its many bars and

cafés and holiday mood, and enjoyed the sumptuous facilities of the marina that included internet, hot showers, and weather faxes. We had the usual mix of nice warm sunny weather and howling gales, although it was generally protected in the bay. As soon as we had the weather window, we set off for Morro Bay, leaving at 2:00 p.m. and arriving at 9:00 a.m. the following morning to catch the slack tide for the bar. As soon as we entered the bar, we were hailed on the VHF radio.

"Yacht *Seafire*. This is Mike from Morro Bay, I've been expecting you for months."

Mike had been following our progress on our website (nomadaroundtheworld.com), which Greg had been updating with photos and stories from each port.

"I've been following your trip and looking forward to meeting you. We're heading the same place."

"Great. Where are you? We'll come and meet you."

"I'm leaving today. I've been waiting for a good weather window to go around Point Conception, and today doesn't look too bad. You can use my marina slip while you're here if you want. I'll contact the marina and tell them I'm subletting it to you."

It was a nice offer, but without a car, it was too far away. We met Mike anyway and chatted for a short time before we helped him cast off.

"I think you'll be stuck here for a couple of weeks. I've waited for weeks before this window came along. Good luck, anyway."

"Thanks, but I'm looking forward to meeting up with my friend who lives here," I replied.

I had met Claire in the Cameron Highlands in Malaysia, and we'd spent a few days together hiking in the rain forest. We had kept in email contact and she said if I was ever in Morro Bay I should look her up. She was looking forward to us getting here too, so we had already planned on staying at least a week.

Morro Rock and Morro Bay, USA

Morro Bay is protected by Morro Rock, and we anchored in a relatively small area between the various mooring buoys in the estuary. Morro Rock is a dominant peak 580-foot high. It was once underground, until volcanic activity changed the shape of the land and created it as an island. Today, it forms one wall of the breakwater to the north; extensive sand dunes give shelter from the west and south, providing many hours of hiking entertainment. The estuary formed by the breakwater and Morro Rock is a protected park and attracts many birds to the wetlands.

This pretty tourist town had many sights to delight the eye. We spent two delightful weeks at Morro Bay and had plenty of side excursions, thanks to Claire. She took us on many trips around the area, and she loved hiking, so we got the chance to see some of the amazing countryside and farmland. We visited the nearby town of San Luis Obispo and its lovely historical district with quaint shops and cafés. The coastline of Morro Bay has many interesting rock formations and a hike provided many sights of unique caves and arches formed by the surf. We watched several surfers taking advantage of the high waves, and were quite surprised to see how close to the rocky shoreline they were.

Diary Excerpt: December 8th, 2003

The dunes form an eight-mile-long sand spit that protects the bay and gave us many enjoyable hours of hiking. We've seen many varieties of birds and enjoy watching the curlews bury their protracted beaks into the sand as they burrow for small worms and clams. We spend many afternoons sitting in the cockpit watching the white and brown pelicans as they dive for food, and the herons who stand perfectly still, balanced on one foot on the edge of the waterline.

The outlook from the estuary at low tide from one of the highest sand dunes gave us a charming view of the protected wetlands and the Salinas Valley in the background.

Greg stands on the sand dunes with Morro Rock
behind him at Morro Bay, USA.

Diary Excerpt: December 11th, 2003

Yep. After eleven hundred miles of awful swell and horrid seas and wind, there are just a few hundred miles left to go to San Diego and then Mexico. We've met another yacht here called *Scottish Mist* and we may be buddy boating with them on our first adventures into Mexico. Bob and Doreen have been stuck here with engine troubles and now they are also waiting for a weather window to go around Point Conception.

We had a great weekend with Claire and we invited some of her friends that we had met to celebrate the Christmas boat parade in the bay with us. Many boat owners made the effort to light up their boats with Christmas lights, some all the way up the masts and others creating sledges and reindeer models on their decks. It was a reminder that at least we had made it to California for Christmas, even though we had hoped to be in Mexico to celebrate.

That weekend, we had planned to hike up to the Pinnacles, but Greg had to stay with *Seafire* since our anchor had dragged when a squall hit us at 5:00 a.m. that morning. Claire had arranged to meet some friends at the Pinnacles, and it was a good two-hour drive through the Californian vineyards to get there. We arrived at 1:00 p.m. and by the time we met up with her friends and visited the centre to register, it was 3:00 p.m. before we started to hike. It was a really arduous hike to the summit of the Pinnacles, which stands at 2,714 feet, and I was always lagging behind, because of my back troubles. Several times, I wanted to stop or turn back, but I could see that it was going to get dark soon and I didn't fancy trying to find my own way back to the centre. It was unbelievable, seeing all the absurd rocky outcrops formed by earthquakes, these Pinnacles being right on the San Andreas Fault Line. The centre had warned of rock falls, and everywhere we could see evidence of recent falls, plus many vast boulders balanced, yet ready to fall.

Our aim was to reach the zenith for sunset and they all rushed ahead of me to try and make it in time. By the time I got there, it was dusk and we started to plan the long hike down, which would be dangerous in the dark. I wasn't that happy with this situation, usually being very cautious with my footing, because a fall would be very dangerous for my spine. Hazardous loose rocks and perilous paths meant this was going to be quite a difficult descent in the dark. Added to this, Claire warned of mountain lions (cougars), which were known to attack women and children, and bears that had the same taste. Further to that, with the howling of the coyotes and the possibility of snakes and spiders on our trail, I was pretty anxious.

We made it back down in one piece, mostly in the pitch-black dark, and immediately set off for Morro Bay. I said my farewells to Claire and promised to keep in touch.

One week later, I heard on the news that there had been a major quake in the Morro Bay area and that the Pinnacles had suffered more shifts in the rock formations and some major rockslides. By this time we were in San Diego, and I thanked my lucky stars it hadn't occurred a week earlier when I was climbing the Pinnacles.

Julie sunbathing on the sand dunes at Morro Bay

Diary Excerpt: December 19th, 2003

We agonized about which were the right conditions for rounding Point Conception, and decided to leave with *Scottish Mist*. It was well worth the wait with lovely calm weather, long swells, and a great passage. Once we got into Santa Barbara Channel, the swells were really knocked down and even the night passage became an enjoyable experience. The oil rigs were lit up like Christmas trees and provided plenty of visual entertainment; and then a giant pod of dolphins and great schools of fish provided even more entertainment. The phosphorescent fish covered large patches and we could clearly see each individual fish darting in different directions, and the dolphins left trails as they chased and dived and played in the bow wave—quite a show.

The sights along the coast have been amazing; right now I can see Malibu, film star mansions, and swimming pools high in the mountains. We're heading directly for San Diego and should arrive around noon tomorrow. Tonight is likely to be busy with shipping, so the night will go quickly again.

We arrived in San Diego a little later than expected, just in front of a storm as we entered the harbour. *Scottish Mist* was ahead and already tied up alongside the police dock, so we radioed for them to catch our lines as the wind had turned really gusty. Both boats secured moorage at the transient marina at the police dock for five days, and we immediately started to decorate the yachts with Christmas lights to get into the festive spirit. We planned to spend Christmas Day together, and took advantage of the plentiful provisions available to make it a special day.

We spent Christmas Day aboard *Scottish Mist*, with Bob and Doreen. We shared the cooking, bringing roast lamb, and roasted potatoes and parsnips from our barbecue, to join their roast chicken, green beans, and all the dressings. Doreen baked pumpkin pie and bread pudding and we sat at a fantastic table setting complete with a mini Christmas tree, fir cones, and festive napkins and rings.

The view from Shelter Island where we were docked looked across San Diego Bay, with the city in the distance. Shelter Island is a beautiful area with hotels and marinas and plenty of palm trees. We really enjoyed walking the promenade, which looked out to the Bay anchorage and gave a great view of the many yachts sailing on the weekend with their colourful spinnakers.

The *Star of India* sailboat was originally built in England in the early 1900s and is now a city museum exhibit that takes sailing trips around the Bay. With her many sails, she looks beautiful.

Shelter island is kept so clean that even the palm fronds are cleaned up as soon as they blow off the trees. The skyline of San Diego is really attractive and they visibly spend a lot of money on public art, judging by the display of "urban trees" along the whole of the sea front. These diverse sculptures were witty interpretations of trees, built from various materials and enthralling to look at.

The cruisers' anchorage was close to downtown and we loved to watch the sun go down on the city and see the orange sphere reflecting on the many mirrored buildings. As soon as it turned dusk, the city was ablaze with Christmas lights decorating all the skyscrapers and creating a glitter of reds, greens, and golds on the horizon.

Diary Excerpt: January 2nd, 2004

We explored downtown, taking the trolley bus on a circular tourist route and admired the stunning City of San Diego. We spent New Year's Eve at the first night celebrations on Shelter Island, and had an extraordinary night listening to the various bands and watching the many shows. Now, we're ready to go and tomorrow we plan on a final provisioning trip to Costco and then we're off to Mexico.

There is a local marina called Downwind that provides all kinds of information to boats taking off for Mexico. One of their perks was free use of their ancient truck to buy last-minute provisions. The weather forecast is good for Monday, Tuesday, and Wednesday, so with a three-day window, there is nothing to stop us from setting off, once we have the done the last shopping.

Unlike us, both Bob and Doreen on *Scottish Mist* and a family from Canada, both of whom had been planning to take off for Mexico at the same time as us, had major engine problems. The girls were in tears as we said our farewells and we hoped they could rejoin us further down the line, once they had sorted out their boat problems.

✒ Reflections From 2015 ✒

For the first time in my life, I started to experience panic attacks. Our life was ruled by the weather. I never wanted to leave our safe anchorages to go back out into the wide ocean. It was unpredictable, and even if the weatherman said there would be calm seas and gentle winds, I panicked as soon as the wind started to blow a bit harder. We had been through three major gales off three capes—each one life-threatening. The fact that we'd survived did not make me feel better. I started to think we wouldn't be so lucky the fourth time. I wanted off the boat. I wanted warm, tropical breezes and becalmed seas. I was holding on for Mexico when things would be better. The panic attacks would be short-lived and as soon as the weather settled, I would be calm again. The minute we arrived in port, I completely forgot I had ever had those feelings.

The panic attacks were my body's way of telling me that a life of constant travelling was not my destiny. Greg and I had originally planned to cross the Pacific and head to the South Pacific islands, but these experiences redirected our plans to the safe inland protected waters of the "Sea of Cortez." As long as we were travelling in safe waters rather than wide-open oceans, I no longer experienced any panic attacks.

I was still learning to live with conflict and anger. I was very curious that it seemed that "passion" bred the conflict and anger. This relationship was so different from my previous relationships with Graeme and John, which had no conflict, because there was no passion. Was it possible to have a passionate relationship and have no conflict? I always used to say that Graeme was so "laid back" I was surprised he didn't fall off his chair, but being that relaxed about life meant there were no moments of pure joy or excitement or enthusiasm. There was no passion so, because he did not "feel" enough about anything, there was no conflict, because nothing would "bother" him enough to create an emotion like anger.

Greg was the most passionate man I had ever met. We shared in the joy and excitement of new places, but this excitement often led to conflict because we were both so passionate about our feelings. It was time for me to face my feelings instead of brushing them off and hiding them, the way all good British were taught to do. Facing my emotions and feelings instead of suppressing them meant conflict was inevitable. I was now expressing my feelings for the first time in my life. Now, I was "alive," I was consciously aware of my feelings, curious about them, and willing to explore them, and eventually, even to start understanding that I could control them.

Sooke potholes

Sooke potholes

Baja California, Pacific West Coast, Mexico

"You must take your chance."
William Shakespeare

Diary Excerpt: January 5th, 2004

At last, sunshine, flat seas, and fantastic scenery. We've finally stopped at a place, just because we want to—not to wait for a weather window. We left San Diego on the 5th of January, in wonderful calm weather and some of the flattest seas we've experienced. We had a lovely sail for the first few hours, doing 4 to 5 knots with all three sails flying until the wind died down and we had to fire up the engine again. Still, I wouldn't have traded those flat seas and sunshine for anything. As the day warmed up, we stripped off our long johns and realized we were probably going to be storing them away, at last. We had a divine night sail with a full moon, and arrived at Isla San Martin the following afternoon.

Isla San Martin is an extinct twin-peaked volcano with a natural harbour formed by the lava flow—amazing stuff. The fishing post looked pretty run-down, and the beach was strewn with litter and bottles and a new-looking sailboat without a mast. We later found out that this boat had wrecked on Christmas Day when it dragged anchor in 30-knot winds. *Charlie's Charts*—popular cruising guides for this area—do warn that this can be a dangerous anchorage in northwest winds, so we were sorry to see that someone had been caught out here, especially on Christmas Day.

We understand that there were three boats all celebrating together when the wind started to pick up. The boat that was anchored closest to the rocks near the beach couldn't get its anchor up in time to escape to the safer anchorage on the other side of the island. The crews of the other boats were busy getting their own anchors up and saving themselves, and by the time they had re-anchored safely, the boat closest to the rocks had already been blown onto the rocks.

Julie reads a book on deck as *Seafire* approaches
Isla Cedros, Mexico.

Those on the re-anchored boats launched a rescue mission with their dinghies (a dangerous mission in itself with the rough seas) and got the crew to safety on one of the other boats. The older couple who had just started their cruise down to Mexico had to abandon their brand new yacht, losing their home as well as their retirement plan. Fortunately for them, they were insured, but their cruising plans came to an immediate halt and the items they could rescue from their sailboat home in the weeks to follow were distributed amongst the other boats that had helped in the rescue.

There is a safe anchorage on the other side of the island, but fortunately for us, we had very light winds anyway and are always mindful of the power of the weather.

We explored the Island of Saint Martin the next day, hoping to find a path to the top of the volcano, so I could look inside the crater. We found a trail that took us halfway around the island to the other side, and to the light-house, but no path to the top.

It was a hot day and the island was covered in different species of cactus. Without a path, navigating was impossible; we were already being spiked by the hitch-hiking plants. The day was breathtaking, the scenery inconceivable, the plants astounding, and the seals in the inland lagoon mischievous. We decided we didn't need to look inside a crater anyway.

Diary Excerpt: January 8th, 2004

We had difficulty finding paths amongst the curious ground scrub of diverse species of cactus, spiky bush, and large grey ice plants. The most remarkable thing was the lichen that was growing all over the cactus giving the lava-strewn landscape a really ghostly appearance. The lava was either jagged and razor-sharp away from the ocean or rounded near the shore where the water action had smoothed it off. One particular type of cactus attached itself with very sharp and protracted quills. If we got one on our trouser or shoe, it was impossible to pick off, since it embedded its spine into our clothing, even into leather.

Unfortunately, we still didn't find the top of the crater, since the scrub got too dense and the lava flow had formed sharp ridges that were impossible to walk along, so we satisfied ourselves by walking a good halfway around the island before heading back the same way. We visited the wreck on the beach, but didn't stick around for long once we spotted an armed guard who we assumed was supervising the salvage of the vessel.

Next, we are heading for Isla de Cedros, which is a night sail and a full day away. There we will stop for an overnight rest before a day hop to Turtle Bay. The weather is definitely

getting warmer and the scenery really different. The back
drop of the towering mountains is crimson and jagged—like
the pictures you see of Arizona—and a chain of volcanoes
lies along the coastline, in some of which you can clearly see
the craters. Sand dunes, porpoise, sea lions, and plenty of
whale-spotting make the day-sail a lot more appealing, especially now we can sit outside in the sun.

Isla Cedros was incredible. The north anchorage was alive with
wildlife. Colossal elephant seals were feeding their newborn
pups who squealed like chimps. Pelicans and different types
of seabirds swooped and fed from the little schools of fish,
and playful harbour seals jumped and played around *Seafire*.
We had sixty-foot visibility in crystal clear water and the
mountains towered over us, alight in the sunshine and looking
very majestic with their steep clefts and arroyos. I wish we
could have anchored there, but we were concerned that the
wind might kick up from the north, so moved further south to
a more protected anchorage.

Diary Excerpt: January 9th, 2004

Cedros Island is a completely marvellous island, just magnificent. Peaked mountains carved into yawning canyons with
colonies of gigantic elephant seals that have just birthed. You
can watch the babies suckling their massive mothers who
use their flippers to flap sand over the babies to keep them
cool. The baby elephant seals sound like chimpanzees and
the adults have a high-pitched bark. The young harbour
seals leap and bound around the boat in schools of twenty or
thirty, tumbling over each other, and then excitedly somersaulting and jumping high out of the water. These excitable
youngsters are really inquisitive and took delight in racing
Seafire as we were leaving the bay. The water visibility is crystal clear down to depths of sixty feet, so we could plainly see
their antics underwater from the deck.

The mountains looked desolate until we spied through the binoculars an enormous cactus growing abruptly up the hillside. The great grey ice cactus has a hefty flower head growing vivid lime green and yellow blossoms out of the top. At the right time of year, this mountainside must be a riot of colour with the entire cactus in bloom. This IS paradise—the amalgamation of dramatic mountains, crystal-blue waters, and nature so loud and prolific you hardly know where to look next. Against a blue azure sky and a bright sun, it really couldn't be any more perfect or beautiful; a truly spectacular place.

Turtle Bay was our next stop after pulling the anchor at 2:00 a.m. and heading out. The seas were a bit rolly, but we arrived at the anchorage early in the afternoon. This is a large sheltered bay with a fascinating—if a rather disheartened—town, but with basic supplies and an internet café. The internet is slow and expensive at five dollars an hour, and the @ key does not work, so the first time I tried to email it was unsuccessful. However, it was nice to be back in touch again with our friends and family, since this was our only means of communication.

The people were very gracious and we felt ignorant not being able to communicate very efficiently with them in Spanish. They were amused by our attempts though, and very smiley and accommodating. This town is quite cut off from the rest of Baja California Sur and has only one road out, which is in very bad repair, making supplies few and far between.

We had one very amusing episode when Greg was trying to find out if there were any washrooms nearby. He proudly read from his Spanish book.

"Dónde están los caballeros?"

The Mexican gent looked at Greg as though he was a little crazy, so Greg shouted it a bit louder and pointed to his zipper. This seemed to get an even crazier response until we tried another word, which he comprehended. We later found out that he was asking "Where are the men?" as he was pointing at his zipper, which was probably why they responded the way they did.

We decided to stay in Turtle Bay ("Bahia Tortuga" in Spanish), get a few jobs done, and explore. We climbed to the top of one of the mountains and were rewarded with an extraordinary view of an infinite, desolate desert landscape framed by sheer pointed mountains of diverse rusty red, orange, and sand, and again, different types of cactus. The mountain in the distance was about thirty miles away, so that gives some idea how good the visibility was that day. The desert road that leads to Morro Santo Domingo is the only road out of Turtle Bay and we could clearly see the rough scar across the desert. The outlook from the summit of the mountain on the other side showed the whole bay; the yachts at anchor looked like little black dots.

The weather was great, mostly in the 25° C to 30° C range and not dropping at night below 16° C, which was fantastic. The beach that led to the desert landscape was really striking, although the surf made it a bit tricky to navigate and land the dinghy. It was good to walk behind the beach through the desert landscape we had spotted from the peak of the mountain. We managed to land in the surf without mishap, but we weren't so lucky when we headed back to *Seafire*. As we timed the waves to push off the dinghy, a rogue wave broke over the bow, filling the dinghy with water, and giving us both a thorough soaking. We were saturated by the time we got back to *Seafire*, the cold wind causing us to shiver in our wet clothes, but it was well worth it.

The locals were really entrepreneurial and used their fishing boats—pangas—to come out to our boat and offer any services they could. Their wives offered a laundry service, of which most boats took advantage having a lack of fresh water, and the men organized diesel or gas delivery. We took advantage of the laundry and the diesel delivery, and even allowed them to dispose of our garbage. We did hear that their way of disposing the garbage was to sort through it in their boat to find anything useful and then throw the rest overboard. For many of the yachties, this was an appalling sight since we had been carrying around the garbage bags for proper disposal for days and sometimes weeks.

Many of the boats were very generous with their tips, giving much-needed clothes or school supplies for the children, and the locals always looked forward to the arrival of yachts for these reasons.

The Miniature "Village"

When we had sailed into Turtle Bay, we had spotted minuscule, multicoloured houses away from the main town, and we couldn't discern through the binoculars what they were; so we decided to investigate. We hiked for an hour into the mountains and valleys behind the main town, following a well-trodden path to a settlement of miniature houses painted in dazzling pinks, greens, pastel blues, and yellows, and decorated with many plastic flowers. Each petite house was complete with glass windows and a diminutive locked door, and we spotted small altars with photographs and memorabilia of their dead through the windows.

We couldn't help but notice that the dead were living better than some of the residents in the main town who didn't always have glass windows or doors on their homes. Looking close-up to one of the funeral homes demonstrated how neatly and tidily this area is kept, although they throw the garbage just over the fence that marks the area. We looked inside one of the funeral homes and saw all the toys and belongings of a child who had had an early death. It was so sad to see, but we felt awed by the level of respect they pay their dead, too. We gathered that some funeral houses had several family members and dated back as far as the 1960s, so these buildings were obviously maintained frequently; they looked so clean and neat. This is so contradictory to their homes—dust strewn with rubbish everywhere—that it seemed a travesty that they treated their dead better than their living.

Diary Excerpt: January 18th, 2004

After eight days in Turtle Bay, exploring the village and area, we set off south again. It turned out to be a wonderful passage, variable wind and a six to seven-foot swell from the northwest, which gave us a nice downwind sail. We spotted three whales sounding and diving, which we watched for about an hour; they came quite close at one point. As the wind picked up from the northwest, we approached Asuncion Island and our anchorage for the night.

We didn't go ashore that night, but made the best of a good weather window and headed for Punta Abreojos at first light. Greg tried to fish again and ended up losing the whole rig, weight, line, and sinker, so we needed to ask around about getting the right gear. We've spent so much on fishing licenses that it would be nice to recoup some of that cost on edible fish. We're both looking forward to getting to Magdalena Bay and having another rest.

The panorama on the coastline is really glorious: the mountains are diverse vibrant colours and the ranges are different heights and shapes giving us interesting views as we slowly sail past them.

Bahia Santa Maria

We stopped first at Bahia Santa Maria—the outside bay to Magdalena Bay—since we had been told it was really beautiful, and it was an incredibly stunning anchorage. We anchored first close to the mountains and off a small beach where we had access to a low valley across the mountains to the other side. We had a fantastic day walking through the valley, spotting many gorgeous wildflowers and different varieties of cacti; we are still fascinated by cacti—especially the flowering ones. The walk was absorbing with lots of different rock formations and types, many different plants, and even the occasional hare. We saw plenty of other animal tracks and heard coyotes.

The walk in the other direction was hot, but we were rewarded by a spectacular view across the Pacific Ocean and along to the lighthouse on the Cape. The following day, we moved *Seafire* to a different anchorage near the sand dunes, and were left quite alone when the other two boats keeping us company departed. We skinny-dipped in the water, which was cool, but refreshing in the hot sun. We then decided to walk the beach in search of sand dollars and shells, and to investigate the sand dunes.

Greg and I are standing on the pinnacle of the highest sand dune looking back over five miles of twenty-foot dunes we had walked through in Bahia Santa Maria, Mexico.

We started a leisurely walk along the beach and before we knew it, had started to meander into the dunes. We spotted a high dune in the distance and decided to scale to the top—then we realized that the two bays backed on to each other. We had an extraordinary day walking amongst twenty-foot sand dunes and were quite exhausted by the time we reached the highest dune. The view was unbelievable—looking over a five-mile range of twenty-foot dunes on one side and the mangrove estuary of Magdalena Bay on the other. By the time we got back to *Seafire*, we had clocked about ten miles and had healthy looking tans.

One of the many wild cacti that fascinated me

Magdalena Bay and Shops With No Produce

We moved to Magdalena Bay, which we had walked to the previous day across the sand dunes; by sail, it took us seven hours. In a way, I wish we had spent more time at Bahia Santa Maria; it had a much wilder, unspoiled beauty about it and we were quite alone. Magdalena Bay is also quite attractive, but not the same.

We anchored for the first week off the village, waiting for fresh supplies and dreaming of fresh barbecued chicken and cold beer. The supplies in the village were very limited with two or three tiendas (shops that are basically one room at the front of a family's home) selling a few tinned goods and fresh vegetables and meat only on delivery days. There was no ice or refrigeration, so nothing kept in the heat longer than a few days. Every day we visited to find out when the panga was due with supplies, and every day the fishing pangas buzzed us as they passed close to our boat. The curious fishermen got great satisfaction passing close to our boat; they particularly enjoyed doing this at 5:00 a.m. when they set off for their morning fishing expeditions.

We did have some very enjoyable walks across the mountains behind the village and our curious eyes had plenty to keep us busy as we drank our morning coffee watching the villagers. We decided to leave for the quieter anchorage off the sand dunes, and later found out that that was the day the delivery had arrived.

The port captain happily visited our boat with paperwork for port fees, climbing onboard in his cut-off white Wellingtons, and immediately inviting himself down below so that he could check out what we might have to give him. Of course, we had no beer and we'd depleted our supplies of other alcohol, so we could only offer coffee and biscuits. He gladly accepted, but kept asking for beer or whiskey, which I think other boats gladly gave him. The fact that we had limited communication with our poor Spanish and his basic English worked in our favour for a change. Paying port fees could have been avoided if we had just stayed in the paradise of Bahia Santa Maria. Oh well. That's hindsight for you.

The anchorage off the dunes was much quieter and much more picturesque. The dunes were pure white and quite striking. We spent many hours walking the beach and collecting many different types of shells. The sand spit that extended out from the west side of the sand dune anchorage was always inhabited by hundreds of pelicans, curlews, and other seabirds that let me walk pretty close to them before they decided to fly away. There was an eco-camp on shore set up for the tourists who came to whale watch, and their occupants always provided good entertainment through our binoculars. What voyeurs we were! But what a laugh. We walked across the sand dunes to Bahia Santa Maria and looked across the bay to where we had been anchored the previous week.

The Mangrove Forest

There is a mangrove forest that can be accessed at high tide and we can ride our dinghy right through the mangroves and spot many amazing birds. We spent a few hours exploring the inland waters of the mangroves in the company of another dinghy from the yacht *Exodus*, and took the waterways as far into the mangroves as we could get with our inflatable. It is a really scenic mangrove forest, clean and healthy, with a lot of new growth and plenty of wildlife. Since this was the first anchorage that had given us almost constant sunshine and beautiful surroundings, we were not in a rush to leave. Although other cruisers had spotted many whales in Magdalena Bay, it seemed that most of the sightings were in the entrance, and so, on our last day, we anchored for the evening off the small fishing camp, and saw many whales. We also heard another yachtie on the radio, anchored in the estuary at Soledad, at the north end of Magdalena Bay, where he was watching the whales nurse right next to his boat.

Passage to Cabo San Lucas

We set off for the last overnight passage to Cabo San Lucas and as we arrived off Cabo Falso, the sun rose and we were rewarded with magnificent sightings of whales doing full breaches close by. This was the largest sighting of whales we had seen and we took much delight in watching them even as we admired the architecture of the condos and hotels that lined the beachfront. There were many multimillion dollar buildings, brilliantly painted in coral, orange, yellow, and red, and balanced on the rock faces. They are nestled next to impressive hotels and provide a multicoloured splash of arches and windows facing out to sea. As we rounded Cabo, the magnificent and famous natural rock arches came into sight, gleaming white in the morning sunshine—very imposing. They framed an old square-rigger in the distance on a whale tour, which made for a very photogenic moment. This anchorage lived up to its rolly reputation, even in the very calm weather that we had, so we opted to stay on *Seafire* and just rest for the night before leaving for Los Frailes the following morning. We did visit the Cabo yacht club to take on fresh water and diesel, and learned that the mooring fees were over a hundred dollars per night.

Los Frailes

Our sail to Los Frailes started off pretty smoothly, motoring north through sharp three to four-foot waves, but with little wind. Within a few hours of reaching the anchorage, the wind had picked up to 15 to 20 knots on the nose, and the waves hitting us on the beam made things uncomfortable for a few hours, but otherwise it was an uneventful passage.

The anchorage had a really stunning setting: it can only be described as paradise, with perfect white sand beaches and aquamarine waters. We spent a week and a half in this paradise, hiking through the cactus landscape, exploring the mountains, scrambling to the top for the best views, and snorkelling in the clear chilly water. We followed the dusty road into the wilderness and really enjoyed clambering amongst the giant cacti. I commented that the rock formations were so clean and bright that they looked like a desert theme park made of Styrofoam. The dusty road that led to the beach made for interesting and easy hiking with only the odd recreational vehicle coming or going. I could see the sandy road cutting through the wilderness and if we wanted to, we could have walked all the way to Cabo Pulmo to the north, which was the nearest town for supplies. However, we found the cacti so interesting that every time we set off to do that, we lost track of time and grew hot and tired pretty quickly.

More cacti! Los Frailes, Baja California, Mexico

The RV community at Los Frailes was really friendly and invited us to join in their various activities and share their stories. We were really impressed by some of the gardens and clay ovens they had built for their winter retreat. This area was a secret paradise shared only with a few, so it was not the kind of place a casual traveller would even find. Many of the Snowbirds were Canadian and had all passed through many of the same ports that we had called in on down the USA coast. Some even remembered seeing us in Coos Bay.

The Provision Truck

Several times a week, various government supply trucks visited the area to provide much-needed provisions for the local fishing village, and that's when the RVs and yachts also took their turn to buy everything from chicken to fresh fruits and vegetables at subsidized prices. The local villagers lived side by side in harmony with the Snowbirds, selling fresh fish to them, developing close relationships with the women in the camp, and accepting help in the way of clothes and school supplies for their children. The atmosphere of the area was one of strong social bonding and mutual respect between the Americans, Canadians, and Mexicans.

Priority was always given to the Mexicans when the provision trucks arrived. The Snowbirds waited in line patiently while the Mexicans crowded around the truck to get first pick. The trucks would take special requests from the Snowbirds, so we could "order" anything special we wanted, and they didn't inflate the prices to "gringo prices" like some of the larger tourist towns are inclined to do. We were soon barbecuing that chicken we'd been waiting for since leaving San Diego. That was our first fresh meat since leaving there.

We could even hike to a small hotel at the opposite end of the beach that would sell us ice-cold beers at very reasonable prices. We really enjoyed the thirty-minute hike along the beach and a short distance through the mountains with the reward of an ice-cold beer at the end. Greg would pack the beers into his backpack and put in as much crushed ice as would fit around them to keep them cold. By the time we reached *Seafire*, his back would be frozen cold and soaking wet with the melted ice, but we still had ice-cold beers at the end.

Some days, the anchorage proved to be fairly windy. It was perfectly safe, but it was a wet dinghy ride and landing on the beach. As soon as the winds and waves died down, we set sail for our final leg to La Paz, anchoring overnight in Muertos to split up the bash north into the Sea of Cortez, also known as the Gulf of California.

The following morning we had a fantastically smooth sea and light winds with Isla Cerralvo in the east blocking the old North wind waves from the sea, and providing us with a flat passage to La Paz.

Diary Excerpt: February 19th, 2004

At last. Nearly six months and 2,263 nautical miles since leaving Nanaimo, we arrived in Bahia Lobos, just outside the Mexican city of La Paz, on February 19th, 2004. There, we spent a wonderful afternoon and evening, before approaching Marina Santa Cruz, "Virtual" Marina, the following morning.[1] Little did we know, Mardi Gras Carnival had just started, so we spent the first five days here, listening to live music, eating fabulous junk food, and watching the colourful parades. Since then we've been taking advantage of all the facilities a great city has to offer and sorting out paper work, etc. In the next few weeks, our adventure will continue as we cruise the twenty-nine islands of the Sea of Cortez.

The Marina Santa Cruz is an anchorage area with moorings for seventy-seven dollars a month, giving us the use of hot showers and a dinghy dock. We had to pay a small

---

[1] This La Paz marina is now known as "Marina Cortez."

daily fee for anchoring in La Paz harbour, so it wasn't that much more expensive to pay for the "Virtual" Marina. The view from the anchorage was of the "Malecón," which is a promenade along the waterfront; it always provided entertainment—watching the coming and goings of the locals. Despite La Paz having an airport and decent paved roads, it is not really a tourist destination, so the only travellers we tended to see were backpackers or independent travellers, and the Carnival was definitely a local affair.

Mardi Gras in La Paz

The streets got really busy for Carnival with 95 percent of the crowd being local Mexicans, plus a handful of yachties and tourists. Every evening, the parade floats would start their procession down the Malecon and the streets would fill with spectators, six or seven people deep. Each float was vibrant and extravagant, no expense was spared on the elaborate costumes of the princesses, and the music was loud and passionate. Various themes were adopted by various clubs and organizations. The local beer companies were the most popular with eye-catching Cerveza Tecate girls dressed in skimpy red and white corporate costumes, in competition with the Cerveza Pacifico girls in stretch Lycra electric blue skimpy shorts. The procession took place for five days and by the fifth day, February 24th, the princesses were sporting slightly dirty and torn gowns while the props had evidence of daily repairs. The beer was flowing and the bands were loud and entertaining. Street food was prolific and the special hamburguesa stands provided carnival entertainment when the Mexican cook danced with his various condiment bottles while dressing the burgers.

Mexicans love the opportunity to party and they are real night owls, dancing until 2:00 or 3:00 a.m. in the morning and shopping until they drop, buying the most unexpected items such as thick woolly blankets and plates. In fact, we found the stands selling blankets some of the most entertaining, with commentators shouting into cheap microphones to attract the customers, piling the blankets high and throwing in extras to give incentives to the customers. The kitchenware stalls did the same, piling plates and dinner services until the customers couldn't physically carry the bargains they had bought. But carry them they did. Everywhere in the crowds, we spotted Mexican fathers following their wives and children, balancing piles of blankets and kitchenware as they struggled through the crowds, not allowing the burden to spoil their fun or cut their night short.

There was never any sign of violence or drunken bad behaviour as I would see in North America or England at such a public event where beer was consumed in volume in the street. Everyone was there to have a good time and celebrate the Carnival, and that's exactly what they did. After Carnival finished, the streets were cleaned and the town looked as though all those people had never been there.

Life returned to normal and we took advantage of the many large stores just out of town, which we could get to on local buses. We visited the multiplex cinema to catch up on the latest movies and ate wonderful handmade ice cream, fish tacos, and burritos. Eventually, it was time to move on, once we caught up with Bob and Rita on the yacht *Farewell* and Bob and Doreen on the yacht *Scottish Mist*. Our reunion with Bob and Doreen meant we could keep our promise to cruise some of the islands together.

Isla Espiritu Santo and Isla Partida

By early April, we were ready to leave La Paz and move on to explore the islands of the Sea of Cortez. We took our time, slowly motoring up the whole west coast of Isla Espiritu Santo, the first island north of La Paz, nudging into each bay to check out the anchorages for future reference. The scenery was spectacular, with dramatic pink rock prevailing along the coastline. Some of the rock formations were inconceivable colours and shapes, the contours smooth and rounded by the waves and wind.

We arrived in Partida Cove on Isla Partida just north of Isla Espiritu Santo, and immediately started to explore the island, which proved to have some magnificent hikes to several great vistas. The two islands of Partida Cove have a beach that forms a sand spit joining the two islands. Access to this sand spit and the North Bay was dependent on the tides with shoal water giving limited access in the dinghy. We took care with the tides before approaching the beach, because it is very shallow and we could have ended up walking our dinghy in soft mud for quite a distance. We had to wade through the thick grey mud, sometimes up to our knees, being sucked into the sticky goo if we hesitated in our steps, a pretty horrid sensation. On one occasion, we came back from a hike to find our dinghy high and dry on the mud flats with the water dried out for what seemed like miles.

Bob and Doreen of *Scottish Mist* joined us on a strenuous hike and we all admired the view from a high point off the north beach. The hike took us through the arroyo and gave a fantastic view of the bay. We spotted many lizards of all sizes and admired the many giant cacti.

Unfortunately, we were blown out of this anchorage by a 30-knot westerly wind: the swell started to roll across the front of *Seafire*, rising the bow five feet into the air and then pitching us violently as it smashed down into the next swell. This became a very uncomfortable motion inside, so we decided to move to a calmer anchorage.

San Evaristo

We sailed north across to San Evaristo on the Baja side, a delightful fishing village and the first place where we could buy very basic supplies; we bought fish from the local fisherman. The road leading south to La Paz from San Evaristo is little more than a donkey trail, and indeed we saw plenty of donkeys on the road and captured some really special photos. Not only did the road lead to La Paz, it also led to remote villages in the mountains. The locals still used donkeys to transport water and other supplies from village to village, and it was quite rare to see a motorized vehicle on the road. We passed a Mexican on his donkey carrying water jugs while we walked on the road, and he greeted us with a friendly smile and wave.

This delightful fishing village had two bays—one to the south and one to the north—in both of which, boats could anchor to suit different winds. We walked from one side to the other across beautiful desert mountains giving fantastic views. The view of the north anchorage was backed by massive salt-drying flats; and this supplied a source of income for these villagers. There seemed to be a plentiful supply of fresh water and the houses were all nestled in the shade of palms. We followed the trails to La Paz for a few miles and came across a deep arroyo that led to another village, and a ranch. A herd of cows from the ranch was taking shade in the arroyo under a small oasis of trees, but we couldn't see how large the ranch would be, so we turned around and headed back to the beach to cool down.

Isla San Francisquito

Continuing our zigzag sail north through the Sea of Cortez, we crossed to the stunning island of San Francisquito. This incredibly breathtaking island had everything to offer with aquamarine water, a beautiful white sand beach, and fascinating hikes with stunning views. A trail led across the top of the mountains to a panorama of the Sea of Cortez in one direction and the perfect semicircular bay and beach in the other.

By the fourth day, the anchorage was beginning to get busy, so we had a beach party to meet everyone on the other yachts. Each boat brought a dish to share and one motor yacht arrived with a giant tub of ice cream. Who could wish for anything more perfect than ice cream in paradise? It goes without saying that all these remote islands have no stores. We really enjoyed this anchorage and would have certainly stayed longer if the wind had not switched to the southwest, which created a five-foot fetch into our northwest anchorage. Once again we woke at 5:00 a.m. as *Seafire* pitched in the swell, just as it had in Isla Partida. It appeared that the boats tucked into the hook were sheltered from the swell, so it was a shame there was no more room.

Julie is perched on the high trail looking down at the perfect beach at Isla San Francisquito, Baja California, Mexico. The small white dot far to the left is *Seafire*.

Los Gatos

As soon as the sun rose we pulled anchor and headed back to San Evaristo for a protected anchorage, leaving the next day for Los Gatos, a small bay on the mainland. This anchorage had the most unbelievable geology and we had an incredible week exploring the vibrant sandy pink mountains and rock, picking up many geodes.

Each day we hiked a different area, returning with arms full of extraordinary rocks and shells. The south anchorage was tucked between two reefs and gave easy access to the beach, which had a multicoloured rock face made up of many different shapes and colours of rocks, again with many geodes. Some of the rocks we collected had crystals at different stages and some were well-formed perfect crystals. Once we knew what to look for, we also found many on the beach that had been broken free by rock falls, and we spent many engaging hours breaking open the red rocks to reveal the geodes.

The north anchorage, which we moved to when the wind changed, gave access to smooth, coral-coloured rocks sitting on the pink sand beach. These were fun to explore; we found fascinating shapes formed by the wind and waves, such as women's legs and shapely bottoms. We could climb the undulating red domes, which created remarkable stepping stones and enthralling views.

Agua Verde

We had heard many good reports of Agua Verde on the Baja mainland, and found out they were all completely true. The south anchorage was a true paradise with clear aqua waters like a swimming pool and a really interesting village with a fantastic tienda that sold great fresh vegetables and meat. The villagers were farmers, and many goats and cows wandered the mountains alone leaving plenty of trails to follow. We also spent some time in the north anchorage, which also had clear waters, but was not as beautiful as the south anchorage.

We opted to stay a little longer so I could spend my birthday there, and I can honestly say that I can't think of a more wonderful place to celebrate. Very early on the day of my birthday, we heard drums and music right outside *Seafire* and rushed on deck to find Doreen and Bob all dressed up with Mardi Gras beads and headdresses, banging saucepans with wooden spoons and singing "Happy Birthday." The previous day, Doreen had asked me what I would like for my birthday, and I had joked, "A full English breakfast with sausage, eggs and bacon, and fresh baked bread."

The water was so clear that anchored boats seemed to float in mid-air. Agua Verde, Mexico

Doreen somehow pulled this off, and together with the music and costumes she delivered a full English breakfast for the four of us, kept warm in a large serving plate with a lid. They climbed aboard and we had a birthday breakfast complete with birthday cake and candles. It was one of the most memorable birthdays and one of the best presents I'd ever received. Their boat had a compact freezer and full fridge, whereas we had neither, so they were able to use their limited supplies to provide this treat. It is amazing how I missed the small luxuries in life.

Honeymoon Cove, Isla Danzante

Another favourite, the stunning island of Isla Danzante looked dramatic as we approached it, with its many peaks and arroyos giving the impression of large folds of silk reflected in the sun. The tiny north bight anchorage was just big enough for our boat, stern anchored. We could plainly see the reef on each side of the boat and the clear water allowed us to see the many multicoloured fish that swam around us. We could see how this anchorage had been christened "Honeymoon Cove," because it was so remote and private. The snorkelling there was great and we saw countless varieties of starfish with diverse colours and designs. They were some of the brightest starfish I'd ever seen, so we couldn't resist lifting them out the water for a quick photograph before we returned them to their watery homes.

Diary Excerpt: April 24th, 2004

We anchored forward and stern off the beach, and snuggled into the tiny north bight anchorage in crystal clear water surrounded by tropical fish; it was like being anchored in an aquarium. We had our own mini private beach, which was really picturesque with lots of trails leading off it, giving unbelievable views and photo opportunities. The water was warm and the snorkelling was great; lots of different kinds of tropical fish, big schools of damsel and zebra fish, which we fed bread to from *Seafire's* cockpit. We counted seven different kinds of fish just around the boat. This is the most stunning anchorage; definitely no need to get off *Seafire* here. We were entertained just sitting in the cockpit watching all the fish swim around.

Isla Carmen, Puerto Balandra

This was our favourite area for snorkelling; the rocks formed narrow canyons under the water and the fish sheltered from the sun. The snorkelling was really interesting here—great visibility, warm water, and plenty to see. Apart from the many different species of multicoloured fish, we spotted octopus and moray eels. The shoreline had interesting rock sculptures and arches, as well as nursery tide pools in which I could spot young fish fry.

As we walked along the shoreline exploring, we came across many seagulls nesting and almost stumbled across one seagull on a nest with a baby seagull that looked like it had not hatched much earlier. The nest was so accessible that we didn't realize we were walking through their nesting area and made a hasty retreat as soon as the seagulls started to squawk and dive-bomb us. A trail led to the other side of the island but we were prevented by the countless insects and the heat from investigating too far. It was very lush and had many green trees and flowering bushes. The golden grasses were simply beautiful, and the flowering yellow bushes were alive with the song of honey bees.

Bahia San Juanico

We had a bit of a bumpy ride getting to Bahia San Juanico, still on the mainland, and we were surprised how flat the anchorage was, giving protection from the southerly swell as well as from the old northwest swell that had given us the bumpy ride in.

It was a winsome anchorage with a miniature abrupt island connected to the beach by a sand spit and on top of the steep cliff grew impractical cactus. The beach on the other side of the island was too shallow to anchor in, but the near side gave good protection for two boats between the two reefs. We anchored here with *Scottish Mist* and, although it seemed like we had enough room, when the wind started to blow at least 25 knots, we both put out a second anchor for fear of dragging on the nearby reefs. It was this reef and its jagged rocks that gave the anchorage such good protection. The spiky pinnacles had giant bird-of-prey nests balanced right on the top and we watched them feeding young ones through the binoculars from our cockpit. A cheeky diving bird was really attracted to our boat and stayed with us the whole time we were anchored there. He was such a good swimmer and we watched him catching fish underwater.

A trail led behind the beach to a great vantage point where we took lots of photos. Sailing yachts that had visited this anchorage for as far back as twenty years had built a shrine in a sheltered area. The records were really interesting to read. Some were carved in stone and wood, some were written on shells, and one was even written on a shoe. We wrote our own names on a shell mobile for future visitors to see.

Bahia Concepcion

Bahia Concepcion was going to be our jumping off port to cross the Sea of Cortez to the mainland side and San Carlos. We only spent a few days here before heading across with a good weather window, so we didn't explore into the bay as much as we would have liked. This was the first time in the Sea of Cortez that we saw seaweed, and this was a very pretty but prolific hardy type that had the strength and appearance of plastic. I could just see it under the water and it was fun to row through, watching the little fish that live amongst it. We were in search of the hot water spring, but just found a shady cave instead where fishermen probably stop for a rest.

The architecture of the houses nestled in the hills was really interesting; their natural stone-clad walls allowed them to almost blend into the mountainside. We knew we were back in civilization as soon as we saw these houses near the highway that runs alongside with its noisy trucks, their air brakes blasting across the bay. Up until now, we had experienced nothing more than a few Mexican fishermen, a few Mexican farmers, basic tiendas, lots of unspoilt nature, and no roads or motor vehicles. It almost seemed like this road marked the end of our cruising. With the road came houses, tourists, loud trucks, buses, cars, bars, and hotels. We often commented how unique Baja California Sur is with its mountainous territory that restricts access to anything other than boats for much of the coastal area.

Bahia Concepcion is a very pretty village and the American-style homes were nestled together with open fronts facing out to the beach. There were more houses behind the beach, where there was also a natural hot spring bath in the village square. We enjoyed walking around the village and made our way to the far end of the beach where we spotted a camp and bar. Here we met Michael, someone who was looking for a yacht that needed crew across to San Carlos. Although, Greg and I had never taken on crew before, we decided an extra hand would make the night passage an easier one, and we invited him along.

At night, the bay was alive with catfish, and a giant heron decided to use our dinghy as a diving platform to catch them. We watched from the cockpit as he carefully waited for the right moment and then snagged a big fish for his dinner. The following day the weather forecast was perfect, the moon was full, and our extra crew member was ready to make the passage across the Sea of Cortez to San Carlos.

This marked the end of our current voyage and a time to

reflect on my travels of the last seven years. Not only had we run out of money several months early, we already owed a decent amount on the credit card. The credit card would buy our tickets to England so I could find work, introduce Greg to the family, and allow us to plan our next move.

Returning to England

Greg and I had been discussing our future and we had decided to extend our visit to the Sea of Cortez islands as long as possible before putting *Seafire* in storage and flying to England. I was ready to face my family and friends again, and I was looking forward to the challenge of work. I had not had a proper job for seven years, but I was confident my skills would enable me to start with senior office work as a temporary worker while I tried to get other employment. We didn't know how easy it would be to extend Greg's visa to stay there longer than the six months permitted, but we figured we would work that out when we got there. I knew the English pound was going to give us the best opportunity to quickly save enough money to continue our travels, and we knew the boat would be very safe in storage in San Carlos, Mexico. My parents were happy to give us accommodation in my family home for as long as we needed, so we knew we could keep our living expenses to a minimum.

We spent the next few weeks getting *Seafire* ready for storage and packing our bags ready to live the next part of our life in England. I didn't realize at the time, but this journey marked the final leg of my circumnavigation of the globe. I hadn't really planned it this way, but quite by accident I had been travelling easterly around the world continuously in one direction, crossing every meridian, over the last seven years. Flying to England completed another circle, this time, all the way around the world.

We both suspected we wouldn't end up staying there too long, and indeed six months later we were using our return tickets to fly back to Mexico and our beloved *Seafire*. I managed to secure a three-month marketing contract, which gave me a great income, but Greg could not get an extension on his visa to stay in the UK, so we decided to leave. I had spent enough years compromising my love and life for work, so I wasn't about to make the same mistake again. My bonus from a very successful marketing campaign for a land-investment company plus the salary I had made in six months were enough to pay off all our debts. I also negotiated a continued research project for the company while we lived on *Seafire* in Mexico. We had managed to find a way of life that cost only an average of eight hundred dollars a month, and this meant we could continue this lifestyle for at least another twelve months living off six months of my salary. When the money ran out, then we'd make a new plan.

So how can you travel around the world for seven years on virtually no income?

Not everyone can live this way of life. Most people require security, and cannot adapt to a different lifestyle where modern appliances barely exist and the support network of extended family and friends is virtually nonexistent. The ability to cope with the unknown, whether it is new places, languages, food, or customs, and the ability to overcome the fear of battling storms and being alone in a vast ocean are not skills you can learn in an institution. There is really no way before you try it to know if you can live with your partner in isolated and confined quarters virtually twenty-four hours a day, seven days a week. Many people think of this as an exotic lifestyle, but many are easily bored if their minds are not constantly challenged and active or distracted by television, radio, or newspapers. Perhaps the true definition of adventure is when the extraordinary becomes routine.

For me, the routine task of everyday life in the first world is a more difficult lifestyle. Carried back to a world where time is measured by something other than the sun, I didn't know how difficult it was going to be to become an ordinary citizen in the UK again. Dealing with the banks and immigration, insurance and household utilities seemed frustrating and complicated compared to the straightforward less-developed world where we were responsible for our own water, power, and refuse disposal.

Worrying about paying the rent and bills, owning the latest car or stereo equipment, and wearing the latest fashions to meet the expectations of a job are constant challenges. Seven years away from the mainstream of life, experiencing diverse cultures, scenery, and wildlife, made adjusting to a regular lifestyle and routine the real challenge. So much had changed in seven years and many things people just took for granted were still unfamiliar to me—cell phones no longer looked like large radio transmitters, people could do something called text messaging and could access the internet from the public phone booths in England. Technology had left me behind and I was faced with gadgets that scanned my card at the supermarket and in the gas station, and some cars that didn't even require gas. It made navigating the oceans, travelling alone across Lao and Cambodia, and being at sea for thirty-five days at a stretch seem easy by comparison.

I first thought I would not be able to fit back into the work environment, but as soon as I stopped looking for work as an "employee," I discovered that my unique creative talent in marketing was actually easier to sell. I was given the opportunity by Peter Sage, an entrepreneur, to really shine. I was so passionate about life he could see that my potential was limitless. He made me realize that if someone works with passion the results can be incredible. I can achieve anything in my life and the work environment that I choose too. I made lots of money as a consultant, for him and for me, and once again

I was playing the role of an executive in the UK, but this time, one with a purpose. At that time, it was to make enough money to sustain another year in Mexico.

Many people seem to admire my lifestyle and the things I have seen and done, but travelling around the world for seven years is not for everyone. Understanding what your passion in life really is and introducing that into your life is the first step toward finding your purpose. You can speed up this process with personal development workshops, retreats, and reading inspirational books. You can start to live a more authentic life based on following your intuition and your heart, and by only making integrity-based decisions. Do the things you love and that bring you joy, because these are the things you will be naturally the best at. Start to live life with more passion and purpose.

✐ Reflections From 2015 ✐

When something takes a lot of commitment, sacrifice, and personal perseverance, the rewards are rich. Would we have appreciated the magnificent beauty of the Sea of Cortez if we had just flown there? Was it enduring the six-month journey down there that made the reward so much richer? Did we make more effort than any other boater we met to visit each destination and savour the gifts each had to offer? Did I find more shells, see more wildlife and fish, and experience the whale shark pod because I deserved it? Or was it just that we appreciated each moment so much more?

I still do not know a single other cruising boat that savoured every bay and island of the Sea of Cortez in the way that we did. We found treasures no one else had discovered, like the only pelican rookery in North America. Our life was so rich every day, and we didn't want it to end. I had started to write my book, and although we had not yet decided where our future lay, we were living life to the full in the moment. I had forgotten why finding purpose was important, but I felt comfortable and even excited about the prospect of returning to England to make money and see my family again.

I did not discover until much later that flying to England from Mexico completed my circumnavigation around the world—full circle to find myself. Greg proposed to me in England and I accepted. We had spent so much time understanding each other and learning from one another that I was ready to embrace a relationship that added to my strengths and wanted to grow with me. When we made the decision to settle in Canada, Greg encouraged me to publish my book and start my business. It was the freedom of a relationship, rather than codependency, that gave me the courage to explore the question of purpose once more.

By letting go and living each day fully to show myself the clues, I discovered my unique talent to help other people write and publish their stories. It was through my own experiences that I realized writing your story allows you to examine the truth, to join the dots, and trace the clues of your life—to find your own unique purpose. The missing piece was community, and so I have created my own community of writers and authors. It is a myth that writers should be alone and that writing a book needs to be a solitary experience. I believe it takes a community to write and publish a book, and that is what I now lead. I do not question if I am living my purpose, because I know I am. It's too easy, I enjoy myself, and I have people tell me every day that they could not have written their story without the support of the Influence Publishing family.

In the last five years, Influence Publishing has gone from strength to strength, growing each year as I truly step into my purpose. I have now shared over sixty stories and there is a clear message in the universe that I am here to help share the stories that will change the world. Who knows what the future holds for Influence as we attract more authors who understand the importance of influencing how we all see the world. More fascinating stories that inspire healing, more knowledge on integrative health and how the mind and body are closely interlinked, and more inspiring stories of personal and spiritual development.

I realize now that leading a community of wisdom keepers comes with the responsibility to ensure these stories reach as wide an audience as possible on a global scale. This means my natural confidence and ability to speak from my heart enables me to take to the stage and to the TV and radio studios, to share the stories of my authors to a global audience of millions of people. This seems to be the direction my purpose is now leading me. I am stepping into my true purpose to help share these stories, not just assist with capturing and recording the knowledge, but distributing it to an audience of millions. It fills me with excitement and joy to know I am here to make sure these extraordinary stories reach millions. Whether it is sharing the personal journey of sexual abuse as a child that led to addiction and anger, or sharing the courage of a cancer survivor who healed themselves by facing their past, or following the determination and belief in a higher power as an author shares the will to walk again—these stories inspire and influence what we may have previously thought was possible.

More and more, higher profile authors are stepping up to the plate, with courage and vulnerability, to share their stories of trauma, to help heal other people suffering the same trauma. It often takes a celebrity who already has a strong following, to come forward as a spokesperson on controversial issues that are usually swept under the carpet because no one wants to face the consequences. It is people like Theo Fleury who have dedicated their lives to sharing the healing journey from childhood sexual abuse, that can have real influence on helping those who are using drugs and alcohol to mask the truth of their pain. When a sports hero has the courage to share his own battles with addiction and anger, it inspires those with little hope, that they too can get on the path to heal by sharing their stories. This story—Conversations with a Rattlesnake: Raw and Honest Reflections on Healing and Trauma, published in November 2014 by Theo Fleury and co-authored by Kim Barthel—has already reached tens of thousands of people who are being inspired to face their own challenges with addiction and trauma. As the book is featured on major TV, radio, and online channels, it is reaching out to millions to inspire them to read the story and start their own healing journey. This is just the beginning, and the universe is putting out a clear message that Influence Publishing is here to help bring these stories to the world.

Conclusion

How did travelling around the world change my outlook on life? How did it lead me to find my purpose and be open to love? I think I observed a lot without consciously being aware of how travelling was changing me.

I remember my first impressions of South Africa as a two-week tourist would see the country—wild animals, dark-skinned people, barbed-wire fencing around buildings, lush vegetation, hot sunshine, wild monkeys, cheap beer and wine, fresh abundant tasty fruit, and distant gunfire. After I'd lived there for six months, I saw wild animals kept in very large zoos; deep-seated racism from the white Afrikaans; cruel and hurtful aggression toward blacks (and vice-versa); warnings not to go outside after dark, because it was too dangerous; lock-down marinas after dark; black and white supermarkets, buses, restaurants and schools (many years post-apartheid); and hatred everywhere. Wild animals were for the tourists, monkeys were a nuisance, and cheap beer and wine kept us numbed from the real violence and death that were happening right next door to the locked-down marina.

I remember picking up a local newspaper at the black supermarket (we were the only white people shopping there), and flipping to the back pages that listed the deaths that had happened that week—Monday, twenty-three people shot at a bank robbery, four people knifed at a bread store, twelve people killed at gunpoint when a public bus was held up, six women raped outside a supermarket, four black children run over by a car outside a school. Each day, the newspaper listed the events like classified ads, each a page long listing the deaths. Suddenly, every white Afrikaner I met was spitting out his hatred of the black "kaffirs"; the lazy boat boy next door was beaten in front of my eyes, even though he had worked in the searing sunshine non-stop for eight hours without even breaking for lunch. The smiling black women in the car park were pointing at the white boy and black girl who were flirting, ignorant to the unacceptable nature of their mixed relationship. Black and white children held hands and played together but we were told by white Afrikaner friends that black children were still not encouraged as friends and not allowed to come to the white neighbourhoods.

Our white Afrikaner friend (whom we had paid over a thousand dollars to install on our boat a freezer that never worked) told us the sooner we left the better and it wouldn't be safe for us to make a fuss about trying to get a refund. I couldn't wait to leave South Africa, and for years after I considered myself a racist against white Afrikaners. I even saw myself labelling them all in this way, based on my isolated limited experience. No wonder such racial hatred exists in the world when I could turn against a race of people so easily in such a short period of time. It wasn't until I arrived in Canada and met many really nice white Afrikaners that I realized I had even done this.

I completely changed my views on religion when I observed Buddhism and the effect it had on people. As I observed the way Thai people live their lives trying to make merit, I saw a "religion" that promoted love instead of fear. I realized Christianity is fear-based, as are Muslim beliefs, and that a nation of people can be influenced by how their God controls them. "Be good or you will go to hell and burn."

I later realized that Buddhism was never meant to be a religion and that Buddha meant for it to be the middle way, but he was turned into a god and worshipped, to keep the people good. They were still manipulated by fear: "Be good and make merit in this life, or you will be reborn as a dog; make merit and be good in this life and you'll be reborn with a higher status in your next life until you reach nirvana."

I later realized it is always man who turns God into a religion to control the people, that God is within each of us, and certainly does not need to be feared or worshipped in a particular building on a particular day in a particular way. Religion is a way of exercising control over people and it is based on fear.

Women can lead Muslim men to sin, because the men cannot resist temptation; therefore, women must not be seen. I saw this many times during my travels—in Addu, Maldives, where the locals were banned from socializing with the bad white boat people, because we put temptation in their way; and in Malaysia, where I could not get a taxi ride unless I had my head covered, because otherwise the male taxi driver was giving in to temptation by picking up a white woman.

My whole attitude about health changed while I travelled. First, I was shocked to realize I was responsible for my own health while I was travelling. When you are a thousand miles from the nearest land, you have to be educated on your own health. I purchased the book *Where There Is No Doctor*, and that was the beginning of my education on health.[2] It was very empowering to educate myself on something for which I had previously given up my control to the all-knowing doctors in England. I was raised never to question the experts, especially those in authority like doctors and lawyers. I even researched my own back operation I'd had when I was eighteen, and was appalled to realize I gave the doctors permission to break my back to straighten it, without even asking any questions about the chronic pain this invasive surgery would cause me for the rest of my life. I really had given away my power with respect to my health.

I understood while travelling that preventative management was much better than seeking a "cure," and my experience of contracting malaria was a good example of that. I could have contracted malaria a lot earlier, if I had not taken such care

---

[2] The thirteenth revised printing of this book came out in May 2013, written by David Werner with Carol Thuman and Jane Maxwell. See hesperian.org/books-and-resources/

to avoid being bitten; but when I did get malaria, I knew the symptoms immediately and went for a test the same day. I started on medication that was actually on trial, but I had already read the reviews and write-ups, so I knew what was available, where, and when I should take it. It saved my life. Now, I make it my mission to stay informed and I jump at the chance to publish a book on alternative health solutions, because I learn so much in the process.

I was fascinated by the different values, beliefs, and customs of different cultures around the world. I realized we only know our version of beliefs and customs that we have learned from our parents, our peers, and the media. Often, this version is very insular, particularly so when you have lived most of your life on an island, insignificant in size, but housing sixty million people. The British Isles are steeped in deep beliefs about a class system and religion, both customs entwined by a king who created the Church of England so he could get divorced and have multiple wives.

I was raised as a Thatcher child; Margaret Thatcher was the first female prime minister of the UK and she was known as the "Iron Lady." Young, impressionable female teenagers were mesmerized by her strong leadership, by her voice that declared, "You only get what you deserve; work hard and be dedicated, and you will succeed in life."

I don't think I ever heard the benefits of love, art, culture, and nature from my peers when I grew up. Money, Success, Status—these three comprised my belief system. The middle class aspired to be upper class. The working class was just for lazy useless people. What you drove, where you lived and worked, and what you wore bore more importance than love, compassion, happiness, spirituality, and community. Yet I observed the opposite in all the less-developed countries I visited—genuine love and compassion, a sense of community and belonging, happy faces against all odds, and a lack of the material trappings of success—and I liked what I observed.

How can you experience these different values, beliefs, and customs unless you actually see them in action? You cannot really even experience this at a level that would make any difference as a two-week tourist visiting a different culture. You need to live with different values to understand them and then question your own values, because you have to wonder, Are these really my values?

How do you know what your values are if you have not witnessed other values to contrast yours with? Why would you question a religion that teaches blasphemy is punishable by death? If you have been told your whole life that to expose your head as a woman is a sin, why would you expose your head? If you have been told from birth there is only one God who lives in the clouds, why would you believe an Indian who told you there are hundreds of gods? Experiencing these different beliefs and values is the only way you can truly form your own opinions.

When I look back on my journals and when I wrote this book, I realized the person I am today is very different from the person who set off from the UK in 1998—no longer young and naive. When I visit the UK and witness the same values I had when I lived there, I know I could never fit into that society again. I could not wear the mask and pretend that class still mattered to me. I could not ignore the man on the street and scorn him because he was lazy. I could not pretend to worship a God in the clouds because I was afraid of going to hell if I didn't. In Canada, I fit in with a society that cares about neighbours, embraces multicultural differences, puts love before war, is compassionate and caring, and does not judge me by the car I drive, the house I live in, or the clothes I wear. I've found myself and I've found why I am here.

Afterword

It is now seven years later that I have re-visited this edition of my first book to publish it through my own publishing company. I would never have known then that the journey of writing this book would lead me to help others to become first-time authors. Now I realize this was always part of the divine plan: if I had not travelled around the world for seven years, I would never have written about my travels and what I learned through them, and I would never have discovered my passion for writing and helping other people to write and publish.

I wrote a song when I married Greg, and the chorus line was, "It took all the way round in order for me to see..." This must be one of the greatest challenges facing most of us: What is our passion and purpose in life, and how do we find it? I'm not saying you all need to take off travelling to find it, but it sure helps. Now I know this is my unique talent, passion, and purpose. I have my own publishing company called Influence Publishing, and my own author-coaching business called InspireABook. This developed as I realized how much I was helping other first-time authors. It came so naturally that it was quite effortless.

In the first year as a publisher, eight of my authors became first-time best-selling authors, and I received constant compliments on how effective my InspireABook Mastermind workshop is. I embraced the momentum and "went with the flow," modelling my business to react to the changing publishing industry and the increasingly confusing messages in the market about self-publishing. I realized how important my role is to carve a unique model of independent publishing that champions the author. My own experience of writing and self-publishing this book seven years ago has placed me in a unique position of really being able to identify with first-time authors and the enormous task ahead of them.

There is no way an author will know how much a book will change their life. It is an experience that allows a person to revisit their our own journey and make sense of what their unique purpose is; it is the opportunity for a person to "rewrite" their life.

With each author I work with, I experience another lesson from their own life. I help them "join the dots" and I become close to them as I use my gifts to assist them in picking up the breadcrumbs of clues they have left. Each memory, each story from their past, each breadcrumb is examined for the lesson. Patterns start to emerge and clues lead to clarity on how those experiences in their life have led to their own purpose and unique gift. Many authors embrace this knowledge and go on to create a business from the realization of their purpose. I am on their team, and not only do I want to help give birth to their book, I want to be there for its birth.

The journey is not complete until the ink is printed on the page, the book is bound, and it is launched to the world. That sense of accomplishment—understanding the purpose of all those life lessons and recreating a new life with purpose—is my constant inspiration.

It is not the journey that creates purpose, it is the retelling of the journey for the benefit of other people that creates the purpose.

Greg and I no longer have our beloved sailboat, *Seafire*. We sold her in Mexico when the heat of the summer became too much for us to sustain that lifestyle. We now operate our business together and I travel to mainland Vancouver every week to work in the office in North Vancouver with the amazing Influence team of staff and editors. I find wonderful balance in life, returning to the island every weekend, to enjoy life with Greg and Cortez our dog, in our sweet little float home in Cowichan Bay, Vancouver Island, BC. We couldn't stay away from the sea for long and we have found living on the water is our destiny. There is something quite unique about being at one with the wind and tides, sharing our home with the whales, otters, sea lions, seals, eagles, and swans that come daily for their bread. Some days, the 650 square feet starts to feel small, despite it being four times the size of the boat I lived on for seven years! We live a simple life, with very little "stuff" but it is a life full of love, joy, and purpose!

Julie Salisbury—Cowichan Bay, January 4th, 2015

Order More Books

Around the World in Seven Years is available at all good bookstores and online at Amazon, Chapters, and Barnes and Noble, as well as the Influence Publishing bookstore on our website, InfluencePublishing.com. If you would like to order bulk copies of this book please contact us: contact@InfluencePublishing.com

By telephone: Influence Publishing 604-980-5700

See our website for more stories and photographs on NomadAroundTheWorld.com/adventure

Also available at 30,000 bookstores across the world and online. If you are in Canada, ask your bookstore to order via Red Tuque Books or Jaguar Books or Midpoint Books in the USA and the UK, and anywhere else in the world via Ingram Book Group.

Price before postage and packaging: $17.95 US Dollars; $19.95 CA Dollars; £12.95 UK Pounds.

About the Author

Julie Salisbury is the founder of Influence Publishing and InspireABook coaching. She specializes in helping authors to write and publish their books as a strategy to live out their purpose to the full. Influence Publishing publishes stories that influence the way we see the world and attracts celebrities and high profile authors who want to reach a global market, as well as Entrepreneurs and Visionaries, who want to be of service to other people and inspire change.

Julie is more than a publisher—her company focuses on strategic business and marketing goals to reach a global market via traditional and online media and publicity, and through strong global distribution and sales. Since publishing the first edition of her book in 2008, she has been featured as a guest on many radio talk shows, Shaw TV (three times including one that became a "best of the year") and in the press. In the UK, she was interviewed on prime time regional TV and was the subject of a four-page feature article in the *Daily Mail* "Femail" edition.

She is a professional speaker and won the 62nd Golden Gavel Speech Competition in 2008 as well as many other Regional and National Toastmaster speaking awards. She is a sought-after speaker and has been the keynote at many conferences including "FlightCentre" National Conference in Las Vegas. Julie was honoured with the Woman of Worth Award in 2013 in the category of "Spirit, Success & Soul" and was awarded "Women of Creativity" 2013 by Unlimited.

If you want to get on the path to be a published author with Influence Publishing and you have a story that will influence the way we all see the world, please email admin@ influencepublishing.com with your proposal.

For more information on our other titles, to sign up for our newsletter, to be invited to our events, plus read about our authors in the media, and listen to the interviews:

www.InfluencePublishing.com

Keep in touch with us at:
Facebook @influencepub
Twitter @influencepub
LinkedIn Julie Salisbury

Professional Speaker

Available for keynote and break-out seminars

Burning Your Bridges—Around the World in Seven Years

This inspiring keynote teaches us all the valuable lesson that if you don't live your dreams while you can, it may be too late. Julie encourages you to "burn those bridges—you can always rebuild them!"

Be the Author of Your Dreams

This inspiring keynote will help the audience look for the book inside them. Julie believes we each have a story to share and it is our willingness to be vulnerable and come from a place of helping other people to learn from our mistakes and triumphs, that leads to the inspiration to take on this challenge. The side effect of delving into your story, often leads to uncovering your own purpose in life. "Be the Author of Your Dreams" will change your life forever and probably inspire you to start thinking about sharing your story.

The Changing Publishing Industry

First time authors beware. The self-publishing industry has turned into a money-grabbing monopoly that preys on dreams! In this keynote, Julie gives you fascinating facts about the industry and why the buyer needs to beware as they make the choice between traditional publishing, hybrid publishing, and self-publishing.

Influence Publishing

Inspiring Books That Influence Change

First-Time Authors

InspireABook is a coaching program that takes the writer with ideas to a published author. The two-day publishing mastermind workshop is an intensive process with up to eight authors and the publisher. Once you have gone through the workshop, you qualify for publishing with Influence Publishing, subject to your book proposal.

Email admin@influenepublishing.com for more information.

Seasoned Authors

If you are looking for a publisher to help you reach a global market and your book will influence the way other people see the world, we would like to hear from you.

Email admin@influencepublishing.com with your book proposal.

If you want to get on the path to becoming a published author with Influence Publishing please go to www.InfluencePublishing.com

Inspiring books that influence change

More information on our other titles and how to submit your own proposal can be found at www.InfluencePublishing.com